MW00574960

GUIDE TO THE GALAXY

ITS

L CREATION

enage

G AND DESIGN

enage and Matt Forbeck

R ILLUSTRATIONS

Brase, Mark Brill, Ron Brown, Darren
, Mitch Cotie, David Griffith, Dave Lynch,
Myles, Jim Pavelec, Philip Renne, Brian
burg, Chris Stevens, Tyler Walpole, Kevin
n

DESIGN

chomburg

ESIGN

chomburg

AND LAYOUT

enage

ECTION

Vood

ER

PRINTING

Bang Printing

PLAYTESTING AND FEEDBACK

Chad Boyer, Andrew Christian, Mike Coleman,
Jacob Driscoll, Claus Emmer, Greg Frantsen, Tod
Gelle, Jason Kemp, Tracy McCormick, Ragin
Miller, Brian Schomburg, Erik Tyrrell, Chris White
Brian Wood, and everyone on the Dragonstar mail-
ing list

GREG'S DEDICATION

To Ryan Dancey, for pioneering the open gaming
initiative and making this possible.

MATT'S DEDICATION

To my wife, Ann, the mother of all mothers.

CONTENTS

INTRODUCTION

Fantasy Flight Games is pleased to present **Dragonstar**, a unique space fantasy campaign setting for use with the d20 System. This book, the *Guide to the Galaxy*, is the second of two volumes that together define the core rules and setting of **Dragonstar**.

The *Starfarer's Handbook* provides all the rules you need to play in the **Dragonstar** universe, including new character classes, skills and feats, rules for firearms combat, new equipment and spells, and much more. The *Guide to the Galaxy* presents a wealth of setting information and background material to help DM's bring **Dragonstar** to life in the players' imaginations.

HOW TO USE THIS BOOK

The *Guide to the Galaxy* is designed primarily as a tool for DMs. It provides detailed information on the **Dragonstar** universe, offers extensive tips and guidelines on running **Dragonstar** adventures and campaigns, and presents additional rules such as spellware and magic items, monsters, vacuum and gravity effects, world-building, and much more.

THE OPEN GAME LICENSE

The **Dragonstar** *Guide to the Galaxy* is published under the terms of the Open Game License and the d20 System Trademark License. The OGL allows us to use the d20 System core rules and to publish game products derived from and compatible with those rules.

In fact, all rules-related material is designated as Open Game Content. You can use this material in your own works, as long as you follow the conditions of the Open Game License. You can copy the material to your website or even put it in a book that you publish and sell.

Not everything in this book is open, however. The following text is designated as Open Game Content: The complete text of Chapters 6 and 7, all NPC stat blocks, and all game rules and statistics derived from the d20 System SRD.

The following are designated as Product Identity pursuant to section 1(e) of the Open Game License, included in full at the end of this book: the **Dragonstar** name, logo, and trademark, the graphic design and trade dress of this book and all other products in the **Dragonstar** line, all graphics, illustrations, and diagrams in this book, and the names Mezzenbone, Khelorn, Lazalius, Shul, Bazzrit, Asamet, and Qesemet.

Dragonstar offers characters the opportunity to travel across light years of space, discovering uncharted star systems and exploring new worlds. The setting for these adventures is a spiral galaxy known in the Empire as the Serpent's Eye. It is believed the galaxy was so named because to early astronomers the galactic plane in the night sky looked like the slit pupil of a great celestial snake. At 150,000 light years in diameter, the galaxy is the largest in the Near Star Cluster. The spiral arms—including the one in which the Dragon Empire is located—are about 2,000 light years thick. The galaxy's globular core is 2,000 light years in diameter and more than 5,000 light years thick, and it is incredibly dense with ancient red stars.

The Serpent's Eye galaxy is just one of literally trillions of galaxies that fill the universe with light and matter. Imperial cosmologists estimate that the universe is about 20 billion years old. Scientists and clerics of the Unification Church agree that it was created by the gods in a titanic explosion of energy both magical and mundane. Evidence of this explosion can be observed today in the microwave radiation that pervades the universe and the arcane energy that flows through this ocean of space like invisible currents.

The scientists and clergy also agree that the gods created the universe such that it would obey certain immutable physical laws. As a result, the universe is a very ordered place—even the entropy that draws it inevitably toward destruction is an axiomatic principle to which everything in the universe is subservient. This order allows scientists to study and understand the universe; it allows engineers to harness that understanding in the crafting of ever more sophisticated tools; and it even allows wizards and sorcerers to learn and cast spells that channel arcane energy with astonishing accuracy and predictability.

Gravity is the dominant force at work in the universe, the glue the universe uses to bind matter together in a discernible structure. Gravity causes the gaseous matter that fills the universe to coalesce first into great clouds and then into stars. It causes planets to form and draws them into orbit around the stars. It pulls the stars together to create galaxies, and the galaxies together to create clusters and superclusters. To clerics of the Unification Church, gravity is the hand of the gods, the divine touch that draws the universe together and binds it.

Entropy is always at work in the universe, but it works in ordered and predictable ways. The universe is expanding, the galaxies and superclusters moving away from each other at dizzying speeds. Eventually, the universe will expand sufficiently that it freezes itself out, or it will collapse in on itself in a second fiery explosion. Dualist clerics believe that when this happens, a new universe will be born from the old in the eternal cycle of destruction and renewal guided by the Creator and the Adversary.

While there are billions of stars in the galaxy and uncounted trillions in the universe, the people of the Dragon Empire and their predecessors have explored only a relative handful. The Empire is a rough sphere of space about 1,000 light years in diameter straddling the galactic plane about 50,000 light years from the core. This volume of space encompasses some 1.5 million stars, and imperial explorers have visited perhaps a third of them. Of these 500,000 star systems, the most recent estimates indicate that only about a thousand have been colonized by the Empire.

The reasons for this are many. First, most of the stars in the Empire—and indeed the entirety of the known galaxy—are of little interest to explorers and colonists. Only about half of them have planetary systems, and of those, only a fraction support life or offer rare resources. Astronomers identify and catalog these stars, and explorers typically pass them by in favor of stars more likely to reward their efforts. Second, interstellar exploration is expensive. Starships must be built, crews must be trained, starcasters must be crafted, and the ships must be equipped and provisioned for lengthy voyages. Even the Empire has limits on the number of expeditions it can finance each year, and it therefore focuses on those likely to provide a healthy return on investment. Third, sustaining lines of communication, supply, and trade with a far-flung colony can be even more expensive and challenging. For the royal houses, it's much more efficient to develop those systems in relatively close proximity to their domains. And finally, with every expedition along the frontier, the Outlands grow and new worlds are discovered. As the borders of the Empire continue to expand, new stars are added to the charts so quickly that explorers can't keep up with them.

THE ANCIENTS

Clerics believe that the gods have seeded the universe with life throughout its long history. In the oldest galaxies, millions of light years from the Empire, uncounted civilizations may have blossomed and died billions of years before the stars and planets of imperial space coalesced from interstellar matter. Most stars in imperial space are no more than 10 billion years old, and life appeared in this region of the galaxy only 5 billion years ago. Once the gods had seeded these worlds with life, they waited patiently across eons for it to grow and develop, always guided by their divine hands.

Once the gods had created fertile homes for their children, they created them in their own images and popu-

lated these nascent worlds with the offspring of their imaginations. The sentient races were scattered among the stars and the living worlds spinning in orbit around them, each destined to know their gods and discover their fate in their own ways.

Throughout the galaxy, the children of the gods shared common forms. The same races—elves, dwarves, gnomes, halflings, humans, orcs, and many others—were born to countless worlds. These races also shared common gifts of language and culture that allowed them to experience their worlds and express that experience in the same voices. Throughout the galaxy, these races offered the same prayers to the gods, sang the same songs in celebration of life, and told the same stories. Details of dialect and culture were different from nation to nation and world to world, but at their roots they were the same. The gods knew that their children would eventually reach for the stars and find each other across the vast gulf of space. When they did, they would know each other by their kindred forms and common tongues.

The first civilization to achieve interstellar spaceflight was the Forongorn Confederation, a global union of nation-states on the planet Aranal in the Gulinar system. Gnomes were the only major sentient race indigenous to Aranal—there had once been a sizable dwarf popula-

tion, but it had completely died out long millennia before the rise of the confederation. Because they were the dominant race of their world, the gnomes of Aranal had little competition and were left to develop their science and technology in relative peace.

A few previous civilizations had succeeded at visiting or even colonizing nearby planets using magic or technology alone, but the gnomes of Aranal were the first to build machines that could take them to the stars. Had they been entirely dependent on either magic or technology, they likely would never have escaped the bounds of the Gulinar system. However, the scientists and arcanists of Aranal learned to meld magic and technology, and eventually, this led them to the discovery of starcasters.

In these early days when the explorers of the Forongorn Confederation visited the nearby stars, most believed that they were alone in the universe. They had Aranal all to themselves—why not all of creation? It didn't take long, of course, before they were proved wrong, and they discovered that the galaxy, while vast, was a more crowded place than they could possibly have imagined.

THE DRAGON EMPIRE

SCALE

100 Light Years

10 Light Years

You can use this map of the Dragon Empire to calculate the distance between star systems. However, because this is merely a two-dimensional representation, you need some method of showing the relations between systems in the third dimension. That's what the arrows and numbers alongside many of the system names represent. A ▼ indicates that the system is located the listed number of light years below the galactic plane. A ▲ indicates that the system is located the listed number of light years above the galactic plane. For example, Arador is 10 light years below the galactic plane, and Turasir is 3 light years above it.

To find the distance between two systems, first count the number of grid squares between them; we'll call this the horizontal distance between the planets. If both planets are located on the galactic plane, this gives you an approximate distance within about 10 light years—sufficient for the purposes of resolving most starcaster teleports. If the planets are not on the galactic plane, you need to account for the vertical distance between them. If both planets are above or below the galactic plane, take the difference between the two and add the horizontal distance. If one planet is above and one below the galactic plane, add these distances together and then add the horizontal distance between them.

Once you have the above totals, you can get an approximate measure of the distance between the planets by multiplying by 2/3 (0.66). If you need to determine the precise distance, use the Pythagorean Theorem.

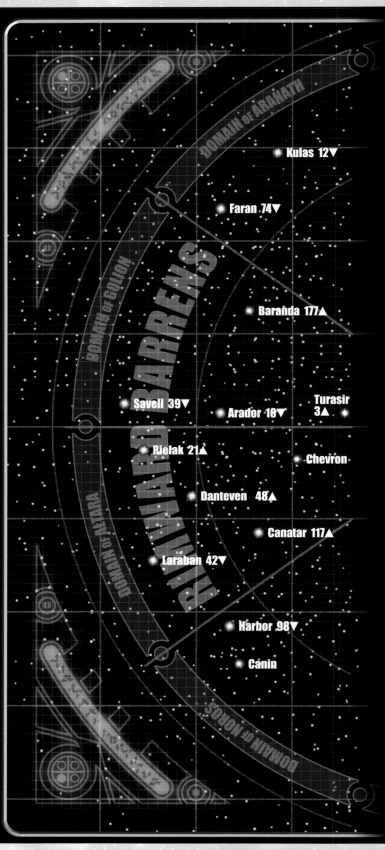

DOMAIN of HANDOR

DOMAIN of SARAVA

DOMAIN of DESERNE

CORENARD REACH

Labanin 63▲

Taran 66▲

Buliban 95▲

Fargul

Zinas 15▲

Rinur 211▼

Tunin 10▼

Cadis

dran 138▼

Farathorn 252▲

Irdal

Galdarast 11▲

Aumbry

Echo 30▲

Kalban 47▲

Perlant 107▼

Tangorn 181▲

Idradon

Rovan 42▼

pic 21▲

Magrant 4▲

Serenity 281▲

Andragus

Casenore 273▼

Raza 15▼

Arlant 84▼

Harbor 162▲

Draconis

Endragar 9▲

Eloine 39▼

Heridor

Birinas 3▲

Kalain

Gulinar 185▼

nacle 295▲

Irindul 254▲

Savain

Penbigan 103▼

Parvan 102▼

stion

Holdfast 2▲

Tinas 79▲

DOMAIN of OSORUS

Banshee 13▲

Gorogond 130▲

iana 16▲

Scepter 10▲

rth 6▲

Amaril 5▲

Inferno 49▼

DOMAIN of MAZORGRIM

da

Beacon 45▼

DOMAIN of ESMER

FIRST CONTACT

The first contact between people of different worlds occurred on Irindul III, a lush planet circling a star hundreds of light years distant from Aranal. The people of Irindul III—who had many of their own names for their world—had developed an industrial civilization, but they hadn't yet managed to pierce the atmosphere of their homeworld. The gnomes of the Forongorn Confederation were the first to accomplish that feat.

The gnomes of Aranal greeted their newfound kin with even greater awe than the people of Irindul III had for them. For while there were gnomes on Irindul, there were many other races besides: dwarves, who the visitors recognized from the ruins of the lost civilization on their world, as well as elves, halflings, humans, orcs, and a dizzying variety of other races. With so many quarrelsome species all competing with one another, the gnomes of Aranal were astonished that the people of Irindul had managed to survive, let alone build a civilization only slightly less advanced than theirs.

The Forongorn Confederation readily shared its advanced technology with these newfound neighbors. Unsurprisingly, their closest relations were with the gnome nations of Irindul III: While they attempted to develop close ties with all of the races of this new world, they remained most comfortable with and trusting of their own kind. Unfortunately, the generosity of Forongorn proved to be the undoing of Irindul. The gnomes of Aranal had acquired their high technology through centuries of painstaking experimentation and development in relative isolation. In the process, they developed the social and political maturity to use it responsibly. The people of Irindul never had that opportunity, and many of them were unwilling to serve a lengthy apprenticeship to their benefactors in the Forongorn Confederation. Their new technology gave them an undreamed of freedom to explore the galaxy, and they wanted to test their wings immediately.

The dark nebula that would eventually become known as the Dark Zone spread across the sky like the black, slit pupil of the Serpent's Eye. Long before the discovery of spaceflight, it had drawn the attention of mystics and astronomers and spawned countless stories, superstitions, and speculative theories. The Forongorn Confederation had steadfastly avoided it, but to the people of Irindul, it seemed the ultimate symbol of the unknown and they dedicated their newborn spacefaring civilization to conquering its mysteries. For decades, they mounted countless expeditions into the Dark Zone, and every starship they sent into the dark nebula was lost.

Finally, a spacecraft did emerge from the Dark Zone—but it hadn't been launched from Irindul. The strange ship was crewed by alien, evil creatures that used the powers of their minds to prey upon and enslave the other races. The ship was responsible for much destruction before it was finally defeated. In the aftermath, scientists from the Forongorn Confederation confirmed that the alien creatures were mind flayers. They theorized that the creatures were not indigenous to this part of the galaxy, and that their homeworld must lie somewhere in the interior of the Dark Zone. They argued that the rare mind flayers encountered on the worlds visited by the confederation must be the remnants of ancient colonies or enclaves.

Once the mind flayer threat had been dealt with—at least temporarily—diplomats from the Forongorn Confederation met with the leaders of Irindul and forged a treaty covering spaceflight, exploration, and colonization. This treaty banned travel to or exploration of the Dark Zone. Every time this restriction has been lifted or ignored, it has proven costly. To this day, no imperial ships have explored the depths of the Dark Zone and returned.

THE STAR LEAGUE

Over the centuries, the peoples of Aranal and Irindul III carefully explored the star systems closest to them, gradually expanding their reach farther into the void. Inevitably, they encountered other inhabited worlds and slowly inducted them into their growing community. When this community had grown large enough, they formed an umbrella government to peacefully administrate the many competing nations and worlds. This interstellar organization was called the Star League, and it was based in large part on the institutional and legal structure of the now-venerable Forongorn Confederation. Each world was allowed a great deal of autonomy, as long as it respected the rights and interests of the other member planets.

Usually, contact and assimilation of new worlds occurred without incident, but on occasion, weapons were fired in anger and blood was shed. While the children of the gods had left the worlds of their birth behind, they'd inevitably brought aggression, greed, and preju-

The imperials use a standard calendar in which time is reckoned from the founding of the Empire. Years prior to the founding of the Empire are denoted "Ancient Era" (AE) and years after the founding as "Imperial Era" (IE). Thus, the current year is 5040 IE.

dice along with them. Fortunately, these conflicts were always contained to relatively small regions and were never allowed to engulf the whole Star League.

As a general rule, the people of newly contacted planets were pleased with the development. There was often a necessary period of adjustment, but the benefits of advanced technological civilization were a powerful incentive to peaceful integration. Within a few centuries, the Star League encompassed dozens of inhabited worlds and stretched hundreds of light years from its historical center in the Gulinar system. This was the Star League's golden age, and like all such eras, it was destined to come to an end.

DRAGONS ASCENDANT

On most of the planets the Star League contacted, dragons were encountered. By nature, these creatures were few in number and rather reclusive. As planetary civilizations were globalized through technological development, however, the dragons found it more and more difficult to maintain their privacy. Inevitably, the dragons were faced with a choice: either integrate with this new civilization or be overcome by it. As the centuries passed, more and more dragons chose integration. Harnessing their native power, intellect, and hoarded wealth, they became industrial and commercial giants, political and military leaders. Some rose to positions of power in established national, planetary, and interstellar states, while others built their own pocket empires through conquest or subversion.

With access to star travel, the dragons were able overcome the primary obstacle to their influence in the known galaxy: their rarity. As they traveled throughout the stars, they encountered others of their kind and forged alliances, whether social, economic, political, or military. Before long, these dragon networks controlled—often secretly—the most powerful corporations, governments, political and military institutions, and social organizations in the Star League.

As the dragons grew more powerful and influential, jealousy and prejudice toward them became more common. Few races in the Star League could match the dragons' powerful bodies, immeasurable life spans, innate magic, seemingly limitless wealth, and countless other gifts. Inevitably, resentment toward the dragons grew. They were characterized as greedy, aggressive, arrogant, and self-absorbed. Even the good dragons gained reputations in some quarters as megalomaniacal, self-styled gods who would squeeze every last drop of power and wealth from the galaxy for their own benefit. On some worlds, hate groups formed and dragons began to be targeted by acts of covert violence and terrorism. On others, local governments passed laws restricting the

rights and activities of dragons, including corporations and other organizations they were involved in.

The dragons responded to these developments in very different ways. Many of the chromatic dragons lashed out with violence and retaliation, launching military campaigns, trade wars, and covert operations against their rivals and enemies. These actions created an era of great instability in the known galaxy, and it looked like the Star League's delicate political structure might tear itself apart from within.

The metallic dragons decided they could win a secure future for themselves only through unity. At a great council on the planet Scion III, the metallic dragons founded Qesemet, which means "golden kingdom" in the Draconic language. The great gold wyrm Khelorn was crowned the first king of Qesemet, having received the unanimous support of the attending delegates. The territories of Qesemet were spread across dozens of worlds, but it offered membership and security to all of dragonkind. The dragons organized into individual clans based on subspecies, but all the clans were ultimately answerable to King Khelorn. The king's homeworld, Galador, was established as the capital of Qesemet.

Of course, the chromatic dragons refused to send delegates to Scion III and scoffed at the idea of serving King Khelorn. Led by the blue wyrm Lazalius, the chromatics founded a rival dominion called Asamet, the "iron kingdom." Fearing the unified power of Qesemet, the evil clans flocked to King Lazalius and began to spread the influence of Asamet throughout known space.

Led by the great dragons, the wealth and might of Qesemet and Asamet grew quickly. The twin kingdoms—one light and one dark—soon became the dominant powers in the galaxy. The old Star League faded away, becoming little more than a treaty and advisory organization. As their influence grew, the relations between Qesemet and Asamet grew colder: Their worldviews, values, and beliefs were diametrically opposed and could never be reconciled. Inevitably, the two kingdoms made war on each other.

While the buildup to war lasted decades, the first incident between forces of the two kingdoms occurred in 242 AE. A battleship group of House Mazorgrim, the red dragons of Asamet, was interdicted by a small patrol of destroyers in the service of House Golion, the copper dragons of Qesemet. The Meniach system, where the incident occurred, was the main staging point in a contested zone between the two houses. While it officially remained neutral and open to traffic from both houses, the quick-tempered commander of the patrol force interpreted the appearance of the powerful battleship group as an act of war. The commander hailed the Asamet flagship, "denying" the fleet access to the inner system.

The battleship responded by vaporizing the commander's destroyer with its ion and plasma cannons. The rest of the patrol attempted to withdraw to the Qesemet space station in orbit around Meniach IV, but it was pursued and utterly destroyed by the Asamet fleet.

The great war that followed this incident was the most destructive catastrophe the galaxy had ever known—or has known since. Great fleets of warships clashed above forgotten planets, whole continents were riven by powerful magics, and billions died as worlds were crushed under the clawed feet of the great dragon armies. Most other races, nations, and worlds became engulfed in the conflict, allying themselves with either Qesemet or Asamet, usually along lines of alignment. Before long, the terrible war had spread throughout the galaxy.

In the year 12 AE, the consequences of war became so terrible that the tides of history were finally turned. The planet Krellis, a haven for the minor clan of rare yellow dragons, was invaded by forces of House Handor and House Aranath, the brass and bronze clans. The yellows had never been major players in dragon politics, and they tried to remain neutral in the war despite their formal allegiance to Asamet. During the battle, a weapon of mass destruction was unleashed that completely destroyed the planet, reducing it to a chaotic field of tumbling, superheated rocks in a matter of seconds.

Some have suggested that antimatter weapons were responsible for the destruction. Others believe that a planar bomb was detonated on the surface of Krellis: an arcane artifact that channeled and combined energy from the positive and negative energy planes to create a titanic explosion orders of magnitude more powerful than anything mere technology could achieve. This theory is supported by the scar that now revolves in the orbit once occupied by Krellis: a space-time rift. This tear in the fabric of reality emits lethal quantities of hard radiation, and its mass seems to constantly be in flux. One second it appears to have negligible mass and gravitational pull, and the next second its mass is greater than a colossal black hole's. The system has been rendered completely uninhabitable by the rift, and scientists believe that its unstable orbit will eventually cause it to collide with the primary star, to uncertain but no doubt devastating effect.

FROM THE ASHES

In the aftermath of the destruction of Krellis, it became clear to King Khelorn that the war would never end, that the dragons would exterminate themselves and most of the population of the galaxy along with them. Their artifacts and machines of war were simply too powerful and their hatred for each other too deep. The king realized that if he didn't do something drastic, all

would be lost.

In a moment of sublime humility and wisdom, Khelorn admitted that the war was ultimately his fault. When he founded Qesemet, he'd known the chromatics would not participate, that they would be excluded and would inevitably feel resentment because of it. Despite their differences, dragonkind could only enjoy a lasting peace if a new kingdom were formed in which all were included: gold and red, silver and blue, good and evil. Khelorn also knew that the evil clans would only agree if they were allowed to share rulership of the new realm.

Khelorn called a new council on Scion III, the historic site of the founding of Qesemet. This time, the leaders of all the clans—good and evil—attended. All were wise enough to recognize that they faced extinction if they were not able to forge a permanent truce.

Khelorn proposed the creation of an empire that would span the known galaxy. This empire would be ruled in a line of succession by each of the dragon clans. The elder of one clan would rule for a thousand years and then pass the crown to the successor clan, who would in turn rule for a millennium. While the debates and political battles over the line of succession lasted for years, the leaders of all the dragon clans eventually accepted the proposal. The five clans of Qesemet would rule first, beginning with Khelorn himself. After 5,000 years, the elder wyrm of the red dragons would assume the imperial throne. Blessed with practically immeasurable lifespans, the chromatics were willing to wait and prepare for the day when they would rise to ascendancy over the galaxy.

Many of the leaders of the other races, nations, and world powers were not entirely pleased with the prospect of subservience to a dragon emperor. Through a combination of political pressure, rewards, and outright threats, all but a few isolated frontier worlds eventually submitted. The benefits of citizenship in the new empire—peace, security, and prosperity—were simply too enticing to ignore…and the price of defiance simply too high. Scion III was renamed Draconis Prime and the Dragon Empire was born.

THE EMPIRE TODAY

The Dragon Empire has endured and prospered for more than five millennia. The Imperial Council is wracked by political infighting and intrigue, armed skirmishes often flare up along the borders of opposed royal houses, emperors have been deposed—and if the rumors are true—even assassinated. Despite these continuing problems, though, the Empire has to date succeeded at its primary objective: preventing a new outbreak of the total war that almost destroyed the known galaxy.

Forty years ago, the copper wyrm Emperor Kupric surrendered the Golden Throne to Mezzenbone, and even this dreaded event was not the catastrophe that many had feared it would be. With near-absolute rule invested in an evil dragon for the first time, the Empire held its collective breath and waited for disaster to strike on that fateful day. Upon assuming the throne, however, Mezzenbone failed to satisfy the predictions and prophesies of the doomsayers. He did not declare himself emperor for life, dissolve the Imperial Council, suspend all civil liberties accorded to imperial citizens, or impose martial law.

The dawn of the Red Dragon's reign has brought changes to the Empire, but they have been of a more subtle nature. Mezzenbone appointed a drow to the Elven Nation's advisory position in the Imperial Council and filled the ranks of his new Imperial Special Police Directorate with the dark elves. The Emperor has channeled trillions of credits into the Imperial Legions and launched a widespread campaign in the Outlands to bring dozens of new worlds under imperial rule. For the first time in history, Mezzenbone is using conscriptions to expand the size of the Legions—many of them displaced citizens of the Outlands worlds that have already been conquered.

While the Empire under Mezzenbone has a nasty edge it never had before, most imperial citizens have experienced little or no disruption of their everyday lives. Even under the rule of the Red Dragon, the Empire is still wealthy, prosperous, and powerful, and the average citizen leads a comfortable, untroubled life. The tone of the newscasts is darker than before, with reports of wartime atrocities in the Outlands and political dissidents kidnapped from their homes by ISPD agents, but these incidents have very little impact on most people's lives.

A Tour of the Empire

The known galaxy is divided into two broad sections: the Dragon Empire and the Outlands. The Empire, in turn, is subdivided into 10 imperial domains, each of which is controlled by one of the royal houses. Thus, the region of space controlled by the gold dragons is the Domain of Deserene, while the red dragons' holdings are known as the Domain of Mazorgrim. When viewed from a vantage point well above the galactic plane, these political borders would look like regular wedge shapes and the whole of the Empire something like a wagon wheel. The three-dimensional topography would look rather like an orange, with each of the sections representing one of the imperial domains.

THE ROYAL HOUSES

House Name	Dragon Subspecies
Deserene	Gold
Sarava	Silver
Handor	Bronze
Aranath	Brass
Golion	Copper
Mazorgrim	Red
Osorus	Blue
Noros	Black
Esmer	Green
Altara	White

The borders of the imperial domains were drawn during the decade of negotiation and compromise between the ceasefire and the founding of the Empire. As a product of compromise, these borders are completely satisfactory to none of the parties involved. The holdings of the various dragon clans, of course, were not so neat and tidy prior to the war. In this era, a system controlled by House Sarava might be only a few light years from one ruled by House Noros. The often-ambiguous borders and the conflicts they led to played no small role in the events that ignited the war. By the terms of the Imperial Charter, all of the royal houses lost some systems they had once controlled and gained some new ones. As with many aspects of the current political order, these compromises were eventually accepted simply because the alternative was unthinkable.

The borders of the imperial domains, in principle, extend into the Outlands to infinity. This, of course, creates a political geography in which some domains are more strategically placed for long-term advancement than others. Specifically, the domains facing coreward have much more room for expansion than those facing rimward. The dragons' solution to this problem was fairly typical: The most powerful clans got the most favorable locations and applied pressure to the other clans to accept the arrangement. Thus, Houses Deserene, Sarava, Mazorgrim, and Osorus control the so-called "coreward domains."

Over the last 5,000 years, the houses have developed complicated structures of alliance and vassalage within the individual kingdoms of Asamet and Qesemet that have alleviated these political inequities in one sense and entrenched them in another. The lords of the powerful houses often grant territory within their domains to dragons of other houses, and these fiefs are often in

K·WASDEN

strategically advantageous coreward sectors. The overlords may further grant these vassals the right to expand their holdings into neighboring systems in the Outlands. The overlords gain the gratitude of other houses and the service of new vassals, as well as an increased capability to expand the holdings of their houses. The vassal lords gain valuable alliances with more powerful houses and new holdings with possibilities for expansion that are, in theory, unlimited. The end result is that a given royal house may have at least limited authority over systems in several different domains.

DRACONIS PRIME

With the founding of the Empire, the Scion system was renamed Draconis. Scion III, the system's only habitable planet, was named Draconis Prime and became the imperial capital. The Imperial Palace and offices of the Imperial Council are both located on the verdant world. Draconis Prime is the administrative and political seat of the Empire, but in some ways, it is rather isolated and underdeveloped. Unlike the throneworlds, it is not connected to the Long Road. It is also completely lacking in any kind of industrial or commercial development. Its sole purpose is to provide a central location for the imperial government and bureaucracy.

The "Imperial Palace" is actually something of a misnomer, for it is not a single building as most races would use the term. It is instead a sprawling network of structures that winds throughout the Imperial Range—a great mountain chain on Draconis Prime's largest landmass. This network includes massive, vaulted chambers, open-air terraces, sprawling parks and gardens, several state-of-the-art spaceports, and innumerable underground bunkers, command centers, supply caches, and ship hangars. It is designed to provide comfort and efficiency for the imperial government in peacetime and impenetrable security in time of crisis or war.

While it is not connected to the Long Road, rumors suggest that the Imperial Palace may actually exist on—or be accessible to—each of the throneworlds. Rumors have surfaced that permanent teleportation circles at secret locations in the palace network link to corresponding structures on the capital planets of each of the royal houses. A visitor might be walking down a corridor in one of the great vaults on Draconis Prime only to discover that, at some point, he crossed into a seemingly identical structure on Galador, the throneworld of House Deserene. The existence, location, and linkages of these gateways are a closely guarded secret, though it is believed that the Emperor has access to a complete map of the teleportation network.

THE LONG ROAD

The Long Road is an interstellar superhighway that links each of the 10 throneworlds by means of a series of teleportation portals. This highway serves as the main commercial artery for the whole Empire. The Long Road is 20 lanes wide and runs for about 10 miles on each of the throneworlds. Massive commercial, industrial, and distribution facilities crowd both sides of the highway all along its length. Using the Long Road to transport both cargo and passengers is vastly more efficient than starships, so the throneworlds serve as the commercial and distribution hubs of the Empire. Rather than transport a shipment of darkwood across the Empire from the Canatar system to the Harbor system, a merchant or corporation can instead send the shipment by starship to Andragus, down the Long Road to the throneworld of the Casenore system by hovercraft or maglev train, and from Casenore to Harbor by starship. In many cases, the Long Road cuts millions of credits off the price tag of cargo and passenger transport. This immense increase in efficiency makes interstellar trade in the Dragon Empire financially viable.

The Long Road links the throneworlds in order of the line of succession. For example, House Deserene is linked to House Sarava, House Sarava is linked to House Handor, and so on. It does present some security concerns, especially on the border worlds—the planets where a throneworld of Qesemet is linked to a throneworld of Asamet. The checkpoints controlling the portals between the planets Meneer and Arangorn and between Rilion and Galador are among the most heavily policed and secure locations in the known galaxy.

THE THRONEWORLDS

The Dragon Empire is ruled at the highest level from Draconis Prime. But the greatest concentration of political, military, and economic power is found on the throneworlds of the royal houses of Qesemet and Asamet.

These planets have truly ancient histories, and the various dragon clans rose to dominance over most of them centuries or millennia before the discovery of star travel. As a result, they have been bastions of strength and security for the dragons for thousands and thousands of years. Nevertheless, while the dragons are preeminent on their throneworlds, these are cosmopolitan planets and systems, and their populations are filled with representatives of many different races.

The imperial domains, systems, and throneworlds are

listed below. For further information on the throneworlds, see Chapter 2: The Dragon Empire.

Imperial Domain	Star System	Throneworld
Deserene	Arlant	Galador
Sarava	Casenore	Aelding
Handor	Idradon	Endagar
Aranath	Magrant	Ambrant
Golion	Savain	Meneer
Mazorgrim	Andragus	Arangorn
Osorus	Heridor	Thormorath
Noros	Kalain	Morngond
Esmer	Parvan	Malaval
Altara	Eloine	Rilion

THE OUTLANDS

Beyond the settled star systems of the imperial domains are the Outlands. Technically, any region of the galaxy not settled and developed by the Empire is classified as part of the Outlands. In practice, the term refers to the frontier region surrounding the Empire. The borders of this frontier are constantly being pushed outward, and many formerly Outlands worlds are colonized and brought within the imperial fold. As a result, this indistinct region is constantly in flux.

The Outlands are divided into two hemispherical sections: the Coreward Reach and the Rimward Barrens. As their names suggest, they each account for two halves of the outer shell that surrounds the Empire. In general, the Coreward Reach has been more thoroughly explored and colonized than the Rimward Barrens, because the royal houses that control the coreward domains typically have more resources at their disposal to do so. Isolated colonies and outposts in the Rimward Barrens are some of the loneliest places in the known galaxy.

Despite the commonalities of life throughout the known galaxy, the planets of the Outlands are as varied as the stars. Some of these worlds are home to civilizations that predate the Star League. Others are teeming with plant and animal life but not a single sentient race. Some are incredibly rich in magic, dominated by wizards and sorcerers of astonishing power. Others are dominated by theocracies in which arcane magic is punishable by death. Some know little of the arcane arts or divine magic, but have built thriving civilizations based on science and technology. On at least one occasion, a slower-than-light starship launched from such a world made first contact with the Empire—rather than the other way around—at a remote outpost in the Coreward Reach.

Most of the Outlands worlds, of course, are not as unified as the above might suggest. These worlds support many races, cultures, and civilizations, each with different characteristics and different levels of development. The greatest civilization on the planet Nenlach in the Kalban system is an elven empire many thousands of years old. This realm is steeped in magic—some of it more advanced than the imperial standard. The rest of Nenlach's population, however, is remarkably primitive: Dwarves dig shallow holes in the mountains with flint tools, and human nomads hunt on the savannas with sharpened sticks. The characteristics of these worlds are often generalized and simplified in imperial records, but visitors soon learn that the reality is always much more complicated.

The experience of Outlands worlds that have made contact with the Dragon Empire varies greatly. Predictably, the royal houses of Qesemet are usually more delicate in their dealings with Outlands cultures than are their counterparts in the Kingdom of Asamet. The Royal Exploratory Service is responsible for most of the first-contact operations in regions controlled by Qesemet. This prestigious organization has strict rules and procedures governing when, why, and how a new world is contacted. In most cases, extended periods of covert and non-intrusive observation are required before any contact is made. Full contact follows only after it has been determined that it would benefit both Qesemet and the Outlands world.

First contact with Asamet is usually a more difficult and disruptive event for the Outlands worlds within its zones of influence. Most dragons—even the good-aligned subspecies—have an innate biologically, magically, and spiritually driven greed often referred to as the "hoarding instinct." Just as most species are driven by instincts of survival and reproduction, dragons are driven to acquire wealth, possessions, and power. The hoarding instinct is, unsurprisingly, strongest in the dragons who rise to positions of leadership and dominance. And in most evil dragons, this instinct is often satiated through violence. Simply put, if they see something they want, they take it. If someone else already claims it, they are merely an enemy to be defeated in pursuit of the prize.

As a result, the royal houses of Asamet have a long history of annexing Outlands worlds using all manner of violent means. Their most common tool is straightforward military conquest, and the viceroys assigned to rule these worlds in the aftermath are typically ruthless in the measures they use to keep the native populace in line.

In some cases, though, a planet is too powerful or a house's resources too limited for the military option to be viable. On these worlds, the royal houses of Asamet often conduct extended campaigns of covert destabilization to break or corrupt their enemies from within. These campaigns may last decades or even centuries, but the near-immortal great wyrms who direct these actions can afford to be patient.

Under Mezzenbone's rule, the Imperial Special Police Directorate is a sinister shadow of Qesemet's Royal Exploratory Service. While their activities are never proven publicly, ISPD agents operating covertly on Outlands worlds have assassinated kings, wizards, and clerics and touched off devastating wars between rival nations to soften them up for eventual conquest. On Primogen II, the ISPD secretly funnels high-tech weapons to both the good- and evil-aligned factions, simply to perpetuate the age-old conflict that prevents them from threatening the imperial presence on the planet (see Chapter 4: The Primogen System).

When an Outlands world is formally colonized by the Empire, a viceroy is assigned as the imperial representative on the planet. In the domains controlled by the royal houses of Qesemet, the viceroy may be little more than an advisor, working with existing, traditional governments to facilitate the planet's transition from fully autonomous Outlands world to imperial colony. The viceroy maintains the authority to step in and take control if necessary, but otherwise interferes in the day-to-day government of the planet as little as possible. On planets annexed by Asamet, the viceroys typically rule with a tighter fist. On some worlds, the governments of the major nations have been wiped out entirely to paralyze any opposition to the viceroy and his rule.

The viceroys are, in principle, nominated by the leader of the royal house in whose domain a planet is located. For example, Khelorn, the Grand Duke of Deserene, is ultimately responsible for naming the viceroy of a new Outlands colony founded within the Domain of Deserene. In reality, the royal houses have whole semi-feudal bureaucracies to which the Grand Dukes delegate these responsibilities. Usually, these assignments are made for purely political reasons: to forge stronger alliances with powerful families, to reward service, or to appease an influential lord's displeasure with some matter of policy or anger at some perceived slight. The result is an intricate feudal game of obligation and privilege, service and reward, of which the valuable Outlands are the ultimate prize.

THE DARK ZONE

A dark nebula shrouds the Deep Outlands far above the galactic plane. The Dark Zone cuts across the top of the Empire, a black and seemingly impenetrable cloud hanging over each of the imperial domains. The nebula is formed of thick gas and dust that absorb nearly all the visible light emitted from the stars within the nebula's embrace. The dark nebula is less than 100 light years wide where it intersects the Empire, but imperial astronomers believe it is many thousands of light years deep. The borders of the nebula are somewhat indistinct, as it twists and turns in on itself in almost serpentine fashion.

Explorers have been testing the Dark Zone since the first days of star travel. Few of these expeditions have returned. The crews of those rare ships that have entered the dark nebula and returned describe it as a terrifying place of eternal blackness, a place where barren planets are dimly lit by the baleful light of ancient and bloated red stars, planets where alien and terrifying things rule the perpetual night.

Scientists believe the mind flayers originated in the Dark Zone, and that their subterranean lairs throughout the Empire and the Outlands are remnants of ancient and long-lost colonies and enclaves. Based on the accounts of survivors and rare encounters, it is thought that the mind flayers have an advanced technological civilization of their own. All of the evidence points to a technology that is very different from the standard of the Empire, emphasizing biotechnology and strange devices powered and controlled by psionics.

The Royal Exploratory Service has declared the Dark Zone off limits, and no official expedition has been launched into the dark nebula in more than a thousand years. There are rumors of ISPD teams charged with penetrating the Dark Zone and gathering intelligence on the starfaring mind flayer civilization it conceals.

A GALAXY OF ADVENTURE

Beyond the Deep Outlands and the black curtain of the Dark Zone lies a galaxy of inscrutable mystery and limitless possibilities. Within the borders of the Dragon Empire, the royal houses scheme and intrigue, explorers discover new worlds, and fortunes are made and lost in starships and corporate boardrooms. The arch-wizards of the Imperial Society of Arcane Magic use powerful technology to advance their art. And throughout the Empire, invisible pockets and cells of dissidents and insurgents organize and prepare, unified in their opposition to Mezzenbone's harsh regime. This regime, however, is only one part of a delicate political framework that has kept a catastrophic war at bay for more than 5,000 years. If, despite all the odds, the insurgents are successful, what price will be paid for victory?

CHAPTER TWO

THE DRAGON EMPIRE

The Dragon Empire is a semi-feudal state that unifies two politically distinct kingdoms under a single sovereign authority: the emperor. While the grand dukes of each dragon clan are ultimately answerable to the emperor, they nevertheless retain a great deal of autonomy simply as a matter of necessity. The dragon lords were willing to sacrifice some of their individual sovereignty in exchange for a permanent end to the great war, but they were not willing to give up any more of their power than absolutely necessary.

The Empire therefore has an established political hierarchy; this structure can be viewed as a pyramid, with the common people at the base and the emperor at the top. Immediately below the emperor in the feudal hierarchy are the kings and queens of Qesemet and Asamet. Khelorn, the gold wyrm who founded the Kingdom of Qesemet more than 5,000 years ago, still rules his people.

Asamet was originally founded by the blue wyrm Lazalius, but he was killed and his spirit lost beyond recovery in the late stages of the great war. Lazalius was succeeded as king of Asamet by Mezzenbone, who is also the current emperor. Rumors have persisted ever since that Mezzenbone was involved in Lazalius's death, but no evidence of this has ever been brought forward. The legendary rivalry between Lazalius and Mezzenbone highlights a fundamental problem with which the Kingdom of Asamet has always struggled. House Mazorgrim, the red dragon clan, is generally recognized as the strongest and most powerful of the chromatics. However, House Osorus, the blue dragon clan, is very nearly as strong, and it has a much better track record when it comes to effective and orderly rule. Therefore, while House Deserene has remained unchallenged in its rule of Qesemet, Houses Mazorgrim and Osorus are always at odds and their rivalry has sometimes undermined Asamet's political position.

Immediately below the kings of Qesemet and Asamet in the imperial hierarchy are the grand dukes and duchesses, the leaders of the royal houses. These leaders are drawn from the most powerful families within each house. By tradition, the grand dukes are responsible for electing their king from among their number when the position becomes vacant. A dragon can hold the titles of both grand duke and king at the same time, so Khelorn is both Grand Duke of House Deserene and King of Qesemet. When it is a house's turn to ascend to the Golden Throne, the grand duke of that house is traditionally named emperor. Thus, Mezzenbone is Grand Duke of House Mazorgrim, King of Asamet, and Dragon Emperor.

House Name	Grand Duke
Deserene	Khelorn
Sarava	Daernatha
Handor	Adenil
Aranath	Perlion
Golion	Kupric
Mazorgrim	Mezzenbone
Osorus	Doraith
Noros	Ivaldor
Esmer	Lemradon
Altara	Nimgroth

Within each of the royal houses, the grand dukes are in turn served by nobles of lesser rank, called dukes and duchesses, counts and countesses, viscounts and viscountesses, barons and baronesses, lords and ladies. The nobles of each house are responsible for governing their lands for the benefit of their betters. A noble's power is typically related to the extent of his lands or position and the prestige of his family. Some nobles—especially half-dragons—have gained their titles by virtue of their birth, but have no lands of their own. These landless lords are considered the lowest rung on the aristocratic ladder. Most houses have additional ranks and titles that refer to specific positions or responsibilities. For example, the heir to a grand duke may be referred to as prince, and a noble who governs a planet for his grand duke, king, and emperor is called a viceroy.

Only true dragons can ever become grand dukes. A person's chances of attaining any noble title are largely proportional to his draconic blood. Half-dragons who are recognized by their draconic parents are given the title of lord, while sorcerers of non-dragon races very rarely gain a noble title, and then only as a reward for long and exemplary service.

THE IMPERIAL COUNCIL

The Dragon Emperor wields a tremendous amount of power, but this power is somewhat mediated by the Imperial Council. The council is comprised of one representative from each of the royal houses. Nonvoting representatives of other groups are named by the emperor to fill advisory seats on the council.

While the emperor is responsible for making all laws, a simple majority in the Imperial Council must approve them. In principle, this sounds like a powerful limitation on the emperor's power. However, the emperor himself gets to cast a vote. Since the imperial councilors almost always vote in accord with their houses and kingdoms, the emperor can almost always cast the deciding vote in his favor to pass a law over which the council is divided. Nevertheless, the Imperial Council places some restraint on the power of the emperor: At the very least, the emperor must gain the support of the grand dukes of his kingdom if his measures are to receive the necessary support.

IMPERIAL LAW

The Imperial Charter, a document drafted and signed by the grand dukes when the Empire was founded, sets forth the laws governing the relations of the royal houses and the administration of the Empire. It codifies the rights and obligations of the emperor, the imperial councilors, the grand dukes, the rest of the nobility, and the ways they can and cannot interact with one another. The

Imperial Charter says very little about the rights of the common folk or laws governing everyday life and activities in the Empire. Instead, these are considered *sovereign laws*, or those that each royal house is expected to establish and enforce within its domain.

The few exceptions to this rule are *imperial laws* designed primarily to keep the peace—the Empire's whole reason for being. The principle of active morality (SHB 13), for example, was first outlined in the Imperial Charter, and it therefore trumps any sovereign laws a royal house attempts to pass and enforce. Whether in the Domain of Deserene or the Domain of Mazorgrim, indiscriminate killing based solely on alignment is illegal. Likewise, imperial law prohibits such crimes as murder, assault, and theft. However, these terms have very specific, technical meanings. For example, "murder" is defined as the unjustified and intentional killing of another sentient. So, while such acts are illegal everywhere in the Empire, the individual houses—and even individual nobles—can define "justification," "intent," and even "sentient" with a great deal of autonomy. In general, it is much easier to be convicted of murder in the Domain of Deserene, where the laws are very tight, than it is in the Domain of Noros, where they are exceedingly lax.

As a result, issues such as gun control, fair trade practices, tax codes, property, and countless others are treated very differently from one imperial domain to another, and within limits, from one star system to another. The latter is especially true on the frontier: In most domains, laws on the colonized Outlands worlds are much more lax than in the Empire proper. Frequent travelers, especially those whose livelihoods depend on their ability to operate effectively in many different domains, must often be well educated in local laws.

THE ROYAL HOUSES

The Royal Houses of Qesemet and Asamet are the most powerful institutions in the Empire. Even the emperor himself could not challenge the might of a royal house without at least enjoying the backing of his own. Each house represents thousands of families and millions of dragons, half-dragons, and non-dragon nobility. Their wealth and assets are literally immeasurable, and their holdings extend across hundreds of light years of space. Their political and military supremacy has remained unchallenged for thousands of years.

Most dragons mate very rarely. However, their life spans are incredibly long and they do not marry, so a prominent great wyrm may have dozens, scores, or hundreds of offspring by many different partners. Family groups are generally organized around lines of relation to powerful patriarchs and matriarchs. In reality, of course, most of the families within a royal house are related to each other, though sometimes only distantly. An amazingly complex system of social status and prestige governs the dragons' relations with one another—even among the chaotic clans—but non-dragon observers have never been able to fully untangle it. The result is that, to outsiders, social rank among the dragons often seems completely arbitrary: A lord might enjoy great status and prestige within a family, while his older brother has very little, for no discernible reason.

Despite these quirks, the royal houses have endured as the social and political foundation of the Empire for 5,000 years and of the kingdoms of Qesemet and Asamet for much longer.

HOUSE DESERENE

Home System: Arlant
Throneworld: Galador

The royal house of the gold dragons is perhaps the most powerful in the Empire. Many thousands of years before the birth of King Khelorn and the founding of Qesemet, the gold wyrm Galador Aradan ("the Great") unified his homeworld and led it to prominence and prosperity in the Star League. His homeworld was renamed in his honor shortly after his death. Khelorn is the sixth-generation descendant of Galador, and he was born in the capital city of Betherian in 1143 AE—more than 6,000 years ago.

Under Khelorn's leadership, House Deserene has played a crucial role in imperial and pre-imperial history. It was responsible for establishing and building the Kingdom of Qesemet, and no other house served as well or paid as dearly during the great war with Asamet. Today, the Domain of Deserene boasts the largest number of colonized worlds in the Empire, and it is by far the wealthiest and most economically prosperous of the royal houses.

The throneworld of House Deserene is the third planet in the Arlant system. Galador is one of the most technically advanced planets in the known galaxy. Betherian, a vast, sprawling metropolis that spans more than a million square miles, dominates its central continent. The silver spires of steel, mithral, and glass at its heart reach several miles into the sky. The political center of the Kingdom of Qesemet is located in the Royal District of Betherian. From a great palace in this exclusive sector of the city, King Khelorn still rules his realm. The district is nestled in a wide mountain valley, and a 500-foot-tall statue of Galador the Great watches over the city from the rock above.

The Arlant system is the largest single producer of

manufactured goods in the known galaxy. Most of its industry is located in the orbital stations that ring Galador, and nearly inexhaustible raw materials are mined in the system's extensive asteroid belt. While local law prohibits polluting industries from operating on the planet's surface, the commercial districts of Betherian are leading centers for many vital services, including banking, insurance, and medicine.

HOUSE SARAVA

Home System: Casenore
Throneworld: Aelding

The silver dragons of House Sarava are justifiably proud of their long and illustrious history. House Sarava was the second to inherit the Golden Throne, and its first emperor, Alarion, is nearly as legendary as Khelorn. Most historians agree that it was Alarion who proved that the Dragon Empire was not just a desperate experiment—that it could truly work. When the silver dragon took the throne, many feared that only Khelorn's charisma and leadership had held the Empire together. With less capable hands at the helm, this fragile ship might quickly founder and sink. Alarion's just and efficient rule put those fears soundly to rest. Ironically, he abdicated the throne less than halfway through his reign under clouds of a scandal that was never publicly disclosed. It was both his triumph and tragedy that his reign proved that even an imperfect sovereign could rule the Empire. Grand Duchess Daernatha, Alarion's mother, now rules as House Sarava's matriarch.

The secluded mountain eyries of Aelding offer some of the most breathtaking vistas in the Empire, though few common folk ever see them. The cloud city of Vespar, the capital of Aelding, is suspended in the atmosphere by massive antigravity generators. Vespar is one of the greatest achievements of arcane technology in the Empire, and the dragon lords of House Sarava built it at monumental expense for the simple joy of living in the sky.

House Sarava has major interests in countless industries, but the Casenore system is most renowned for its aerospace manufacturers. Factories on Aelding produce state-of-the-art aircraft and starship components, and these are transported by space elevator to the massive shipyards in orbit. This space elevator, or skyhook, stretches from Mount Rimidil on the equator to an asteroid counterweight in a stationary orbit around Aelding. The skyhook is a 100-foot-thick cable constructed of carbon fiber and reinforced with magic. It runs from Mount Rimidil, through the center of Vespar, to Andrin Station. The skyhook allows cargo to be transported between the planet and orbit at very low cost, and it has made the Aelding shipyards the most profitable producers of spacecraft and starships in the Empire.

HOUSE HANDOR

Home System: Idradon
Throneworld: Endagar

Grand Duke Adenil rules House Handor from the pristine waterworld of Endagar. More than 90% of the planet is covered with clean, blue-green oceans—a literal paradise for the bronze dragons. Othilian, who would later become Dragon Emperor in 2001 IE, established Endagar as the throneworld of his house shortly after the founding of Qesemet. In the years leading up to the great war, Othilian transformed the planet into the economic powerhouse it is today. Endagar's vast kelp fields and fish farms provide fresh food and delicacies for all of the worlds connected by the Long Road, and many more beyond it. Endagar Pearls are among the most sought-after precious stones in the Empire, prized by jewelers for their luster and treasured by alchemists and wizards for their reputed mystical properties.

Endagar's stretch of the Long Road is anchored on one of the planet's larger islands, but more than half of its length is constructed along a series of rafts and causeways that connect several floating cities. Many of these cities extend as far below the waves as above them, and several are linked by umbilical lines to vast habitats and industrial complexes built on the seafloor. Endagar boasts the most advanced deep-sea engineering and industry in the Empire.

A small power-generation facility near the Ambrant Gate was attacked by a kraken more than a hundred years ago. The damage was so extensive that the Long Road was actually closed for repairs for several weeks. Scientists claim that the creature was attracted to electrical emissions from the plant, and the Long Road is now equipped with deterrence systems to prevent attacks by marine predators.

Today, Endagar is best known for its aquaculture, marine industry, and exclusive island resorts. Less public but perhaps even more influential, however, is the Endagar Royal War College. At an isolated island and seafloor complex on Endagar, the bronze dragons' passion and respect for warfare has led to the creation of the leading military academy in the Empire. Admission is typically granted only to the aristocracy of Qesemet, and most of the highest-ranking officers in the kingdom's military forces are alumni of the War College. These experienced officers filled the ranks of the Imperial Legions and Imperial Navy until Mezzenbone ascended the Golden Throne.

HOUSE ARANATH

Home System: Magrant

Throneworld: Ambrant

The brass dragons of House Aranath have a legendary reputation as the information brokers, diplomats, and spies of the Kingdom of Qesemet. Grand Duchess Perlion, the daughter of a former emperor, has continued the work of her ancestors, accumulating the favors and secrets of other powerful dragon lords, building House Aranath into a political force to be reckoned with.

The throneworld of House Aranath, Ambrant, is the mirror image of Endagar. It is a hot, dry world with very little industry or developed economic base. The one notable exception is information technology: House Aranath is an imperial leader in the design and manufacture of computers and information networks, and Ambrant is home to many of its largest research labs and production facilities.

Many of these facilities are clustered along the Ambrant stretch of the Long Road. The city of Arakel in the Helras Desert is both the capital of Ambrant and the most active hub of the InfoNet. The basic structure of this worlds-spanning information network was designed and developed by House Aranath engineers. While the InfoNet does not allow faster-than-light communication over interstellar distances, it does connect the 10 throneworlds via fiber-optic lines running under the Long Road.

The dragons of House Aranath are not the great warriors of their kingdom, but they excel at politics, diplomacy, and intrigue. More brass dragons can be found among the courts and backrooms of Draconis Prime than those of any other clan. Relations between House Aranath and allied houses are sometimes a bit strained, because the brass dragons do not always limit their intrigues to the houses of Asamet. Indeed, Grand Duchess Perlion is thought to have voluminous records on the families and activities of all the houses of Qesemet—even her own. Rumor suggests that these records are more extensive than those on the houses of Asamet, and some of Perlion's allies find this troubling. Still, the grand dukes rarely complain because every one of them wants access to the information: They can't very well protest the brass dragons' spying while at the same time requesting intelligence reports on their rivals.

HOUSE GOLION

Home System: Savain
Throneworld: Meneer

The copper dragons are still riding the wave of prestige they enjoyed during the imperial reign of House Golion. Always considered the least powerful of the houses of Qesemet, House Golion was, for one brief millennium, the most influential in the Empire. All five of the emperors who ruled during this term used their position and power to reform imperial law, expand the rights and liberties of citizens, and support the flowering of art and magic in the Empire. Some observers and scholars have pointed to the fact that there were five different emperors during House Golion's rule as evidence that the coppers are not psychologically suited to rule. It is true that most dragons of House Golion are little interested in politics and that they often seem to let their own domain run itself. On the other hand, planets within the Domain of Golion always rank at the top of independent quality of life surveys.

The copper dragons are renowned architects and builders, and the towers, temples, and vaults of the Irunath Mountains on Meneer are some of the most awe-inspiring structures in the Empire. The grand duke's palace winds over and through the majestic peaks, a beautiful stronghold carved of native stone that is more than 10,000 years old. House Golion has forged professional alliances with several other races to pursue long-term projects. The copper dragons work with elven biologists and ecologists on terraforming science, and with dwarven engineers on materials and construction technology. While it is little more than a figurehead organization, the government-in-exile of the Dwarven Commonwealth has its offices on Meneer.

Unsurprisingly, professional expertise is Meneer's chief export. While House Golion—like all the royal houses—has extensive commercial interests in countless industries, the throneworld is dedicated to the advancement of art, science, and craft. The various branches of the University of Meneer support a student population of more than 1,000,000, and its College of Architecture is widely regarded as the best in the Empire. The Royal Exploratory Service's training academy is also located in the wilds of Meneer, where it takes advantage of the planet's varied terrains and climates to prepare its students for survival on unfamiliar worlds.

While he willingly and peacefully surrendered the Golden Throne to Mezzenbone 40 years ago, Grand Duke Kupric feels a great deal of personal responsibility for the fate of the Empire during the Red Age. He believes that if the Empire spirals into darkness as some fear, it will mean that he should have broken the pact and denied Mezzenbone the throne. Kupric has little love for war, but he does not want to be remembered by history as the dragon who gave the known galaxy over to evil. As a result, the Grand Duke pours an enormous amount of House Golion's resources into the temples of the good-aligned deities of the Unification Church, into charities and relief agencies, and into education programs and other projects. These efforts are designed to spread light throughout the Empire and the lives of its citizens and keep the darkness at bay.

HOUSE MAZORGRIM

Home System: Andragus
Throneworld: Arangorn

The throneworld of House Mazorgrim is the second planet in the Andragus system. Arangorn is an infernally hot, rugged world orbiting just on the inside edge of its bright yellow star's habitability zone. Wasted badlands and barren mountain ranges dominate most of the planet, and few living creatures can survive for long on the surface without protection. Arangorn is tectonically very active, and major earthquakes and volcanic eruptions frequently ravage the planet's crust. The planet is also extraordinarily rich in precious metals and minerals, however, and the surface is dotted with mining, refining, and industrial facilities. The red dragons typically live in vast underground complexes, where bio-engineered algae provide an abundant supply of clean air. There are also a few fully enclosed habitats scattered about the surface and the length of the Long Road.

Visitors to Arangorn often wonder why the red dragons, with all their wealth and a vast number of planets to choose from, would make the inhospitable world their capital. The simple answer is that red dragons don't share the aesthetic values of other races. The truth is, they admire the hellish vistas of the surface and feel at home in the tangled subterranean vaults and warrens of the planet's sprawling undercities. The planet's infernal temperatures and barren landscapes also ensure that visitors won't often bother the dragons of House Mazorgrim.

With Mezzenbone on the Golden Throne, House Mazorgrim is unquestionably the most powerful of the royal houses. It is well known that the red dragons care for little beyond accumulating wealth and power, and they have been extraordinarily successful at fulfilling this lust for millennia. They are treacherous, deceitful, and ruthless, in the boardroom as on the battlefield. But they are also cunning, resourceful, and patient. No one in the Empire trusts them, but the benefits of political and economic alliances with the red dragons are so great that they never have a shortage of partners and pawns.

House Mazorgrim is the largest manufacturer and distributor of defense industry products and services in the Empire. The red dragons supply everything from personal weapons to dreadnoughts to the militaristic houses of Asamet.

HOUSE OSORUS

Home System: Heridor
Throneworld: Thormorath

Throughout much of Asamet's history, House Osorus has been even more powerful and influential than rival House Mazorgrim. The blue dragons are certainly the most politically savvy of the chromatic clans, and it was the blue wyrm Lazalius who originally founded the Kingdom of Asamet. Many believe that the red dragons are too selfish to ever concern themselves with the other houses or the overall welfare of the kingdom. House Osorus has always been ready to step in and fill that void.

The blue dragons are natural leaders and faction builders, and many consider them the hardline traditionalist conservatives of Asamet. They value their house, kingdom, and race over individuals, though they reverse this order in their political rhetoric. They favor strong centralized rule—with House Osorus, of course, in the position of power. They desire a rigid system of economic and social stratification in which everyone—from the grand dukes to the lowest non-dragon commoner—knows his place. They are outspoken opponents of awarding titles to non-dragons. Grand Duchess Doraith, the half-sister of Lazalius, strives to impose these "standards" and "disciplines" on the other houses of Asamet, and indeed, on the Empire as a whole.

The warm, arid world of Thormorath offers little in the way of natural resources, and few regions receive enough rainfall to support large-scale agriculture. Instead, the planet is reserved for the vast, sprawling estates of the dragon lords of House Osorus. The capital city, Kazar, is rooted at the base of a great mountain range in the Abzaman Desert. Its lush gardens and gilded palaces set the standard for ostentatious indulgence of aristocratic excess. It is said that hidden teleportation circles are scattered throughout Kazar, and that a blue dragon lord can slip into the shadows and arrive on Draconis Prime or the other throneworlds of Asamet from anywhere in the great city.

The Long Road does not approach within thousands of miles of Kazar. It runs through a sort of "border town" called Azalkar. This city serves as the "foreign quarter" of Thormorath, and few non-dragons are permitted to venture beyond its boundaries. It is in Azalkar that representatives of other races and political groups must seek audience with the bureaucrats and low-rank-ing lords of House Osorus. Azalkar is also one of the primary commercial hubs of the Empire. House Osorus has built its own economic empire on financial and legal services, and Azalkar is the central battleground for the dealing and double-dealing that greases the wheels of commerce in the Dragon Empire.

HOUSE NOROS

Home System: Kalain
Throneworld: Morngond

The throneworld of the Domain of Noros is the hot, humid planet Morngond. Perpetually shrouded in thick cloud cover, Morngond's single major landmass is dominated by dense jungle and marsh. House Noros has historically been loosely allied with House Mazorgrim, but this alliance is always circumstantial and temporary. Both houses are political opponents of House Osorus: The blue dragon lords are both powerful and all too willing to restrict the activities of the other houses.

These differences have created a long-standing division within the Kingdom of Asamet. On one side are House Mazorgrim and House Noros, whose lords favor maximum autonomy and sovereignty for the individual houses and domains. On the other side are House Osorus and House Esmer, whose lords support a centralized, semi-feudal dictatorship with the power to guide and restrict the policies of the individual houses. House Altara often finds itself in the middle, shifting allegiances between these two blocs as best suits its interests.

While their allies in House Mazorgrim wield brute military strength and political power, House Noros is dedicated to intrigue, intelligence, and covert warfare. In many respects, it is the counterpart of House Aranath of Qesemet, but House Noros's activities have a meaner, sinister edge. The Adamantine Order is the house's legendary but secretive intelligence apparatus. Formed during the great war, it is notorious for its reputed acts of assassination, abduction, sabotage, and destabilization against rival houses and political groups. The ranks of the Adamantine Order are filled with the lesser nobility of House Noros, including a great number of half-dragons. It is believed that the Adamantine Order coordinates closely with, and perhaps even trains, the drow officers of the ISPD.

Grand Duchess Ivaldor, the Black Mother, is the cunning and ruthless matriarch of House Noros. Her massive, almost bloated body is testament to her appetites, and the priceless gems and jewels she adorns herself with are testament to her greed and vanity. Ivaldor claims to have spawned more than a thousand offspring in her long life and never more than one clutch to the same mate. The Black Mother dwells in an ancient stone fortress sunk in the muck of a marshy river basin deep in the jungle. She occasionally visits the courts of the other throneworlds of Asamet in humanoid form, but otherwise rarely leaves her lair.

The only truly developed region of Morngond is the narrow corridor clustered around the Long Road. The superhighway runs along a flat coastal plain, and a huge, state-of-the-art spaceport adjoins it. House Noros's principle economic activities center on the transport and transfer of cargo and information. Despite its torrid climate and dangerous jungles, Morngond is one of the leading distribution hubs in the Empire. Most of the largest shipping companies are backed by House Noros, and it is widely known—though unproven—that the black dragons sponsor several different smuggling and piracy operations within the domains of Qesemet. Rumors have circulated for centuries that the black dragons are the secret masters of the Black Hole Syndicate (see Chapter 3: Organizations, page 40).

HOUSE ESMER

Home System: Parvan
Throneworld: Malaval

The throneworld of House Esmer is the beautiful forest world of Malaval. A young planet by cosmological standards, most of Malaval's landmasses are covered in primeval forest. From the dense jungles of the tropical climes to the vast deciduous forests of the temperate latitudes, the endless woods of Malaval are a natural paradise for the green dragon lords.

There are stories of a large, indigenous fey population on Malaval that the green dragons hunted down and systematically exterminated when they arrived on the forest world. Similar atrocities reportedly occurred during the great war, and the lords of House Esmer are legendary enemies of fey folk and elves throughout the Empire. The Elven Nation sponsors an ongoing program intended to relocate elves and fey from planets within the Domain of Esmer. The green dragons are rarely cooperative, however: Perhaps they wish to use their elven and fey populations as political bargaining chips, or maybe they simply like to keep them around as objects of their spite. Regardless, life in the Domain of Esmer is difficult for the elves and fey, and the Elven Nation has turned to more covert means to liberate them.

While House Esmer's wealth and power are no match for House Mazorgrim's, the green dragons are perhaps even more militaristic and aggressive. They have been staunch allies of House Osorus ever since Lazalius established the Kingdom of Asamet. House Esmer is the

primary military arm of the kingdom's traditionalist faction, leaving most of the political dealings and policy making to their allies in House Osorus. The standing army of House Mazorgrim is the largest in the Empire aside from the Imperial Legions, but House Esmer's is widely regarded as the most highly trained. The green dragon lords have been characterized as xenophobic with some justification, and they defend the borders of their domain with jealous zeal.

Grand Duke Lemradon and his court live and work in Nashak, the capital city of Malaval and the heart of the Domain of Esmer. This small, exclusive city is located deep in a continent-spanning temperate forest clustered around the Rilion Gate of the Long Road. A sister city, Marak, is located at the Noros Gate. Marak is a much larger metropolis and is much more open to non-dragons. While Nashak is the political center of Malaval, Marak is its commercial center. House Esmer's extensive defense industries are headquartered in Marak.

HOUSE ALTARA

Home System: Eloine
Throneworld: Rilion

Rilion, the throneworld of the Domain of Altara, has been locked in the frigid grip of an ice age since it was colonized by the white dragons before the great war. The vast glaciers extend well into the temperate latitudes, and even the tropics suffer long, frozen winters. Like many of the throneworlds, there is almost no industrial development on Rilion. The white dragons of House Altara are widely considered the least sophisticated of the dragons, and they have preserved the cold wilderness of Rilion as a planet-wide preserve for the huge populations of dire animals that roam the frozen wastes. Hunting these animals is the Altara aristocracy's favored pastime.

Grand Duke Nimgroth is shrewd enough to recognize that he and the other lords of his clan are positioned solidly at the bottom of the imperial hierarchy. Compared to any political group, race, or faction but the other dragon clans, of course, House Altara enjoys great power and influence. The fact is, though, that while the gods provided dragonkind with many gifts, they did not bestow those gifts equally. They are magnificent creatures in their own right, but the white dragons are unquestionably the least gifted of their kind—mentally, physically, and magically—and the resources of their house likewise suffer in comparison.

Nimgroth recognizes these truths and guides his house accordingly. House Altara is firmly allied with Asamet, and the white dragons were among the first to kneel to Lazalius when the kingdom was founded. Nimgroth does his best, however, to stay away from the political battleground within Asamet—or at least he does his best to avoid choosing sides. With the other four houses often balanced against each other, House Altara often prospers by sitting on the fence and seizing advantage as the situation dictates. For example, House Altara has often been awarded disputed systems by default when neither side would agree to grant them to a more powerful rival.

The white dragons do not dominate any specific trade or industry. The individual lords pursue commercial interests suited to their natures and ambitions or inherited from their families. As a result, House Altara is perhaps the most economically diversified and decentralized of the royal houses. The Rilion section of the Long Road is almost completely undeveloped, except for the small city of Inglor located at the Malaval Gate and the sprawling military base and checkpoint at the Galador Gate.

POLITICS

The Dragon Empire is the kind of political arrangement that could only have emerged from a crisis. It's irrational and no one who lives under its banner would voluntarily choose it as a form of government. At times, it seems so fragile that it will collapse from within under the slightest pressure.

The Empire has survived for 5,000 years not because it is efficient or just, but because for all its flaws it is preferable to the state of total war that preceded it. The Empire was created solely to put an end to this war and prevent its recurrence, and this overriding objective is responsible for its most unusual features. As irrational, unstable, and fraught with peril as the line of succession is, King Khelorn could devise no other way to secure the support of the dragon lords of Asamet.

The royal houses are truly vast institutions, encompassing thousands of families and millions of dragon lords. It is therefore impossible to identify a house's unified motivations or goals: It probably doesn't have any, and if it does, they're inevitably lost amidst the hundreds of motivations and goals of the individual nobles and families. The houses are given some coherent identity simply by the natures of the dragons they represent, and by the grand dukes who dictate their policies and actions. Nevertheless, each house is a complex tapestry of competing visions and individual endeavors that often work at crosspurposes.

It's said that no one but Khelorn believed the Empire would work, and the only thing that's changed in the last five millennia is that everyone is even more certain that the next emperor will be the last. Early in its history, observers predicted the Empire would fall apart when House Sarava ascended to the Golden Throne. King Khelorn held it together for a thousand years with his charisma and force of will, but it would quickly spin out of control with Emperor Alarion on the throne. Four thousand years and innumerable crises later, the descendants of these observers predicted that Mezzenbone would declare martial law on the throneworlds and set about executing his political enemies as soon as he entered the imperial palace.

King Khelorn's most difficult task was convincing the lords of Asamet to submit to imperial rule. Once the Imperial Charter was in place, however, the chromatic dragons generally had an easier time abiding by its terms than the lords of Qesemet did. As a general rule, the evil dragons have few concerns beyond the power and prosperity of themselves, their families, and their houses. Because the Imperial Charter grants them significant autonomy in the way they administer their domains, most are perfectly happy with the status quo. Even under the rule of Qesemet, they were the master of their domains and suffered few real restrictions on their activities.

The good dragons, however, have faced a more difficult moral challenge. While many are convinced of their superiority to other species, they nevertheless care about the welfare of others. A sense of "noble obligation" toward the non-dragon races of the known galaxy runs particularly strong in House Deserene and House Sarava. These dragon lords believe it is their moral duty to look after the less powerful races in their care. Why else did the gods bestow such bountiful gifts on the dragons if not to shepherd and protect those less fortunate? Others do not share this patronizing attitude but do feel compassion, empathy, and concern for the other races. Grand Duke Kupric of House Golion contemplated breaking the pact rather than give the people of the known galaxy over into Mezzenbone's bloody talons.

For these dragons of good conscience, the question is how they can justify collaborating with the rule of evil beings. If by inaction or active participation they are responsible for the suffering of others, are they not obligated to rebel and attempt to throw down this regime? As might be expected, different dragons have approached these moral questions in different ways. Some, typically the ones in the highest positions of power, believe that the imperial order is necessary to save the people of the known galaxy from far greater suffering and evil. Others believe that the Empire was flawed in conception and corrupt in execution and secretly work with insurgent elements to bring about its demise. No dragon lord has yet tried to openly break away from the Empire, but a few are becoming increasingly daring in their covert resistance.

THE SECRET WAR

The pact that established the Dragon Empire marked the end of open warfare between the Kingdoms of Qesemet and Asamet. It did not bring peace. Indeed, it's unlikely that any agreement could end all hostilities between the metallic and chromatic dragons—they are diametrically opposed to each other and their mutual hatred is so fundamental to them that it is, for most, an inescapable aspect of their natures.

The pact did move the war out of the public spotlight and into the shadows, however. It is now fought on isolated Outlands worlds that few imperial citizens have heard of, or in the private chambers of the Imperial Council, or in the dark alleys of the great metropolises. It is fought not with dreadnoughts and weapons of mass destruction, but with silenced handguns, poisoned daggers, and political propaganda.

This is a covert war that has been ongoing for 5,000 years and for which neither side has a clear objective. Rather, both kingdoms simply *know* they must continue the fight wherever and however they can. Both sides believe they must continue to oppose the enemy lest the war be lost—even if they don't know what would count as winning or losing in this conflict.

THE EMPEROR

Mezzenbone was in his element during the great war that almost exterminated life in the known galaxy. He reveled in the slaughter and destruction, maneuvering to keep himself alive and in position to assume control of the shattered planets that remained in the war's aftermath. Most people viewed the war as a hideous mistake and colossal tragedy that had cost billions of lives. Mezzenbone saw it as a glorious opportunity to serve his dark gods and become like unto a god himself. The Red Dragon lusts for violence and thrives on the pain and suffering of the weak. He has no empathy, compassion, or respect for any living thing—even his own kind.

In Mezzenbone's twisted mind, he is alone at the center of the universe, a single mote of meaning surrounded by slaves to be exploited, tools to be used and discarded, and enemies to be destroyed. These things have meaning only insofar as they enrich or empower him. Those things he cannot control or destroy are a personal affront to him, challenging his sense of self and worldview—which are essentially one and the same. Even the smallest defeat is unthinkable, for it would make him question himself and the unique place in the cosmos that is his alone to occupy.

During the great war, Mezzenbone saw an opportunity to make his personal vision a reality. With the vast

war machine of Asamet at his command, there was nothing he could not destroy, no enemy he could not crush and devour. The five houses would serve his cause until Qesemet had been ground into dust and then they too would join his enemies in oblivion. If he had continued to believe he could win the war, he would never have stopped until he alone remained to rule the void. It was only when it became clear that the great war would inevitably claim him too that he began to explore alternative strategies.

When King Khelorn proposed the creation of an empire ruled by both Asamet and Qesemet, Mezzenbone had found his new strategy. The five millennia of rule under Qesemet would soften the people of the Empire, allowing them to grow weak and complacent. It would also give Mezzenbone time to prepare, marshaling his power and plotting his course to the finest detail. When he took the Golden Throne, he would have a thousand years to strike out against Qesemet and consolidate his control of the remaining houses. This scheme would not afford him any real surprise—he didn't expect the rival dragon lords to trust him—but at least he would be able to attack his enemies from a position of advantage.

Mezzenbone does not intend for House Osorus to inherit the Golden Throne. He will either fulfill the promise of the great war five millennia ago, and thereby fulfill his own destiny, or he will perish in the attempt. The Emperor realizes that a military effort of this scope and scale against an enemy of such might will require magical and technological weapons of enormous power. He needs artifacts capable of slaying the near-immortal dragon lords and scattering the fragments of their souls across the planes. He needs weapons capable of destroying whole worlds and even star systems. And he needs servants willing and able to carry out the difficult and dangerous tasks he sets before them. Mezzenbone is actively gathering artifacts and relics of legendary power on worlds in the Outlands. He's stockpiling weapons and warships in unnamed systems throughout the Domain of Mazorgrim. His legions are being trained and blooded in countless frontier wars.

Mezzenbone does not expect to fight a war in the ordinary sense: He expects the fighting to be over in a matter of minutes, one way or the other. He will either cripple all opposition in his initial assault or he will fail. Even with more than 5,000 years to prepare, he cannot stand against the combined might of the royal houses in a protracted struggle. They must be decapitated and paralyzed by his initial, coordinated attack. Otherwise, they will shrug off any nonfatal wounds and turn on him like a snarling wolfpack.

All of Mezzenbone's actions as Emperor are trained upon this goal. If he proposes a measure to the Imperial Council that would loosen security and increase traffic along the Long Road, it is because he envisions his covert operatives one day destroying the portals and isolating each of the throneworlds. If he cultivates closer trading relationships with the Domains of Qesemet, it is because he needs access to their resources and wants a steady flow of his ships passing through their systems. Mezzenbone's plan is dizzyingly complex, requiring all of his supernatural intellect to develop piece by piece, plot by plot. If it is brought to fruition, darkness may fall at last across the known galaxy.

COMMERCE

Mortal beings are scattered throughout the stars from one end of the known galaxy to the other, and for thousands of years, they've been able to reach out to each other, building relationships and even empires. Most citizens of the Dragon Empire have one thing in common: They need to work for a living. They spend their days growing food, manufacturing goods, and providing services. They trade the sweat of their brow for credits, which they use to purchase the things they want and need. In this respect, the Empire isn't all that different from the countless civilizations of all levels of technological development that have existed throughout the long history of the known galaxy.

While the Imperial Charter allows individual houses—and even individual lords—to set their own trade policies, the imperial economy itself strongly discourages high tariffs and restrictive trade practices. Every planet can benefit from trade and few offer goods or services that are unique in the Empire. If a local lord imposes unusually high tariffs or engages in trade practices that other lords consider unfair, he will quickly find that no one is trading with his planet. As a result, much of the Empire is one vast free-trade zone. Where tariffs do exist, they apply to very narrow market sectors and are just high enough to protect local producers from offworld competition. In systems where specific goods are heavily taxed or restricted, smugglers often move in to satisfy the local demand and reap considerable profits.

Many Outlands worlds are an exception to this rule. A planet with a much less developed technological base has a difficult time integrating with the imperial economy. These worlds offer few goods that are in demand in the Empire, and they can't produce the goods that are in demand as efficiently as the imperial worlds. Likewise, the citizens of the Outlands worlds simply don't have the economic resources to become active consumers in the imperial markets.

These obstacles are dealt with in very different ways within the Domains of Qesemet and the Domains of Asamet. When the metallic dragons colonize a new world, they typically do so at the request of the local rulers. First contact is followed by a steady stream of money, technical expertise, and other resources designed to bootstrap the colony's technology base and economic infrastructure. In short, the houses of Qesemet solve the problem by investing in their colonies and developing them into valuable trading partners. The policies of the houses of Asamet are frequently more severe. In these domains, the relatively abundant natural resources of Outlands colonies are often exploited ruthlessly and the worlds forgotten once their wealth has been exhausted. While this approach is likely inefficient in the long run, it can be extremely profitable in the short run. These huge, short-term profits can be reinvested elsewhere or funneled into the vast treasuries of the royal houses. Because there is a seemingly unending supply of these Outlands worlds, the dragon lords of Asamet have not had to pay the price for their short-term strategies.

The Dragon Empire has always encouraged a healthy capitalism within its borders. Since the reign of Emperor Khelorn, corporations and entrepreneurs have had relatively free markets within which to operate. Taxes have historically been moderate, and they produce sufficient income to support the government infrastructure and public programs. There is a flat 10% tax—known as the Emperor's Tithe—imposed on personal incomes in the Empire. The individual domains also levy their own taxes, ranging from 3% to as much as 8% in the Domain of Osorus.

Of course, despite the generally business-friendly reputation of imperial policy, there are nonetheless whole archives of regulations and laws governing business and trade that have been adopted by the Empire since its founding. These include everything from fair trade laws to environmental and safety regulations. As with tax policy, the individual domains also have the authority to pass additional legislation that is binding within their borders.

Over the past 40 years, Emperor Mezzenbone has been slowly eradicating—under the banner of "policy reform"—much of the legislation regulating corporations and private commercial activities. Laws covering everything from environmental protection to child labor regulations have been significantly weakened or repealed altogether. Observers have noted that these "reforms" unsurprisingly benefit Asamet far more than Qesemet, since the chromatic dragon lords are perfectly willing to take advantage of them at the expense of their citizens. While this motivates those who can afford it to emigrate from the Domains of Asamet, they were probably going to anyway, and most people simply can't afford it. As a result, standards of living on planets within the Domains of Asamet are typically much more stratified than in Qesemet. The rich are richer, the poor are poorer, and that's not ever likely to change.

Mezzenbone's economic reforms have had their most dramatic effects in the Outlands. While newly colonized worlds within the Domains of Asamet have always struggled with their dragon masters, they are now vulnerable to the commercial predations of large, independent corporations as well. Under the rule of the Qesemet Emperors, there were strong laws in place to restrict the activities of private corporations on Outlands worlds. These laws no longer exist.

Once a "new market" is opened to trade, the corporations sweep in to divide the pieces not already claimed by the royal house with dominion over it. In many cases, the corporations have established operations on an Outlands world before the imperial viceroy even arrives. The negotiations that determine the granting of commercial rights in Outlands worlds are complex and secretive. The deals that are made and broken between corporations and royal houses often decide the fortunes of the former and can have a profound impact on the latter.

By the terms of the Imperial Charter, each house is granted colonial rights to every planet within its domain. So long as the house meets its obligations to its kingdom and empire—notably tax revenues—there are very few restrictions on what the house can and cannot do with its colonies. In principle, the royal houses own their colonies as far as imperial law is concerned. They are therefore free to grant, sell, or trade those property rights to other parties, including interstellar corporations, allied lords or houses, or even the native inhabitants of those colonial worlds.

The latter occurs more often than one might expect, even within the Domains of Asamet. When a new colony is established on an Outlands world, it can be extremely beneficial to secure the cooperation of the ruling elites. If the local kings and princes know they will keep their kingdoms, as long as they pay tribute to their new masters, they are much more likely to accept and even embrace the new order.

ARISTOCORPS

Many of the largest interstellar corporations in the Empire are wholly owned private enterprises of the royal houses. Technically, these corporations are legal entities that are indistinguishable from their houses. Families own shares in these companies in proportion to their political and social standing within their house.

These shares are often traded between families or offered as rewards to lower-ranking lords for exceptional service. Together with land grants on the planets themselves, these shares therefore represent the lifeblood of the feudal sector of the imperial economy.

These powerful interstellar corporations are referred to—usually disparagingly—as aristocorps in common speech. Even in Qesemet, the aristocorps have poor reputations among the common citizens. In the daily lives of many citizens, the aristocorps are a more visible symbol of the dragons' rule than the royal houses themselves. They wield an enormous amount of power that almost no one can escape, often determining not only where the common folk can work but what they can buy, where, and for how much.

The management ranks of the aristocorps are filled with the lesser lords of the royal houses. They receive not only generous salaries but also shares in the corporation—which equates to status in their house. After a long career of service to an aristocorp, a dragon lord may have climbed several ranks on the social and political ladder, leaving his descendants with much more status and prestige than he enjoyed.

Dragonblood

Full dragons—the so-called truebloods—hold the highest positions in the aristocorps. Most of the management professionals have at least some dragonblood, and most of the mid- to upper-level executives are sorcerers. Arcane magic provides such an edge on the social and commercial battlegrounds that few can go very far without access to it. Some well-placed lords make do with advisors who can provide the magic they require, but most of the elite have at least some skill in sorcery. These executives typically outperform their ungifted colleagues and certainly enjoy more social prestige. This has led to a division of the non-trueblood nobility into two subcastes: the thickbloods, who can use arcane magic, and the thinbloods, who cannot. The highest-ranking decision-makers in the aristocorps are therefore almost always either truebloods or thickbloods.

Due to the entrenched obstacles and prejudices that confront them in the aristocorps, those who are neither full dragons nor sorcerers often set out on their own to win their fame and fortune, apart from that of their families. These thinbloods' own parents often encourage them to do so, knowing their children have little chance of success in the aristocorps.

This prejudice against thinbloods often seems irrational to outside observers, and most of the lesser nobility—those who are not truebloods—agree. There are

few of these families who have not been touched by the tragedy of thinning blood.

The trueblood dragons are the ones who perpetuate the current class structure. Even the dragons of Qesemet are proud, even arrogant beings who—with some justification—feel they are superior to the other mortal races of the known galaxy. The stratification of society by purity of dragonblood is most severe in the Domains of Osorus and Esmer, the hardline traditionalist houses of Asamet. However, it is present to some extent in all the domains of the Dragon Empire. In fact, Khelorn himself effectively established this class structure when he founded the Kingdom of Qesemet.

Player characters can lay claim to the blood of dragons by their choice of race or class. If the character is a half-dragon, she is considered of lesser nobility by virtue of her birth. If she is recognized by her dragon parent, her status will depend on that of her family. Half-dragons who are not recognized by their dragon parents are called houseless lords. They are treated as members of the aristocracy, but do not gain the status accorded to other members of their family. With effort, ambition, and long service, they may still gain such status on their own merits. Sorcerer characters, regardless of race, are also granted the status of lords, though non-dragon sorcerers are considered the least of the nobility.

Even the lowest of nobles live much better than commoners, but all must serve their house as befits their station. They serve in the aristocorps, governments, and temples of the Empire. For those who strike out on their own, they are truly alone: They keep their title and the privileges that entails, but the wealth and prestige of their families are lost to them. Most aristocratic adventurers have left behind the life of both the idle and the committed nobility. Instead, they have decided to strike out on their own. They may always have friends and family members in their house who they can call upon for assistance, but these heroes are determined to make their mark on their own.

INTERSTELLAR TRADE

The universal laws of supply and demand govern trade between star systems. Goods are purchased on worlds where they are plentiful or inexpensive to produce and transported to worlds where they are rare and expensive. The extremely high cost of star travel, however, places hard limits on the viability of trade. As a general rule, the greater the distance between two systems, the greater the difference in market price required for trade to be financially viable. Of course, skilled and daring pilots can travel from one system to another with fewer jumps, so a cargo that would lose money for one trader might make money for another.

Beyond transport costs, the basic physical properties of the universe often limit the development of interstellar markets. This is especially true of raw materials. The same elements occur everywhere in the known galaxy: If a world discovers that it is relatively poor in gold or uranium, it usually need travel no further than the other planets orbiting its star to find all it needs. It is therefore almost never profitable to transport raw materials across interstellar distances. The only consistent exceptions are materials that are very rare and that do not occur everywhere with the same frequency. These materials are often magical or at least have verifiable mystical properties. The most common examples are mithral and darkwood, but there are countless others in the known galaxy. A cargo of mithral purchased from a dwarven asteroid mine and transported to a developed world lacking the metal can be extremely profitable.

The aristocorps and other giant conglomerates dominate interstellar trade between the core systems of the Empire. These massive corporations have the largest fleets and warehouses, the best access to the markets, and the economic power to secure the most profitable contracts. Beyond the imperial core, as one approaches the Outlands, the situation changes. The distance between colonized systems is vast and the costs of transport correspondingly high. The worlds in these sectors are often poorly developed compared to the core worlds. They sometimes lack strong markets, so that even if a particular cargo is in demand, there may be an extended waiting period before a buyer is found. Law enforcement is sometimes lax in these systems, too, and pirates or planetside gangs can further elevate the costs of shipping cargo.

These distant sectors of the Empire are the domain of free traders and independent merchants. Some own their own freighters, while others captain a ship for an absentee owner. They hire their own crews, decide what cargos they'll carry, and select the systems to transport them to. They operate on tiny margins, counting on their business acumen, skill, and good fortune to net them a worthwhile profit at the end of their runs. They are bold and sometimes even foolhardy, always trying to squeeze a few more light years into every jump to minimize costs and maximize profits. Free traders often earn just enough from a run to maintain their ship and buy their next cargo. While they are always one step away from financial ruin, each one believes he is also one run away from wealth and fortune.

RELIGION

In the **Dragonstar** universe, the existence of gods is not in question. Evidence of their presence can be found everywhere, on every inhabited world in the known galaxy. Clerics can cure the sick, raise the dead, and see the future: No one of sound mind seriously doubts that they are guided by the divine.

However, recognizing the existence of the gods and comprehending their mysteries are two very different things. While most citizens of the Empire worship one or more deities and clerics can even commune with them, no mortal can truly grasp the minds or natures of these divine powers. When it comes to explaining the gods, mortals are forced to make do with finite understandings.

In the Dragon Empire, the Unification Church is one such way of understanding the nature of the gods. For several millennia, it has been the most successful and popular. It is not the only way to understand or make sense of the gods. It is impossible to prove that its doctrines are true in the way that a scientific theory about the physical universe may be proven or disproved. Even in a universe where mortals speak with the gods and wield their magic, some things must be accepted on faith or discarded in favor of a competing belief.

The Unification Church was established in 876 AE by the prophet Nasuit in the holy city of Aani on the planet Maira. The church rose to prominence during an age

in which regular contact and trade between worlds was increasing at a dramatic rate. Qesemet and Asamet had risen to dominate the old Star League, and unification under common causes and banners was the order of the day. In this cultural environment, the Unification Church gained immediate recognition and acceptance. Under its spreading influence, a traveler could find fellow worshippers and a temple to his god no matter where he went. With a shared religion, the Star League finally felt like a single, unified civilization. The symbol of the Unification Church is a stylized spiral galaxy, with each of the twelve spiral arms representing one of the deitypes. In the years leading up to the great war, this became a more recognized symbol in the known galaxy than the flag of the Star League.

Aani remains the religious capital of the Empire, and its ancient temples are still the spiritual and administrative heart of the Unification Church. In its early years, the church was closely aligned with Qesemet, and the Raza system technically lies within the Domain of Deserene. However, the entire system was declared an independent protectorate of both kingdoms before the war, and that tradition is honored to this day.

Orthodox clerics of the Unification Church believe that the thousands and thousands of deities worshipped in the known galaxy are cultural aspects of the

Twelve—the deitypes of the Great Pantheon. According to the strict interpretation of doctrine, this means that there is no *inherent* difference between the Father worshipped by the elves on Aisa and the Father worshipped by the dwarves on Khamar. The only differences are cultural artifacts imposed by the worshippers themselves throughout the centuries or millennia in which their cultures have developed.

Progressive clerics, on the other hand, believe that the gods themselves are not simple, one-dimensional beings, but rather complex, multidimensional entities. To the progressives, it makes no sense to say that the different aspects of the deitypes are not real—they are each as real as anything in the universe, and they are nevertheless all unified into a divine totality: the deitype recognized by the Unification Church. While sometimes difficult to comprehend, this progressive theology has gained greater acceptance for its inclusiveness and respect for traditional religious practices.

This doctrinal schism has usually remained peaceful and scholarly, but it did lead to a more dramatic one. Five hundred years ago, as the Red Age approached and people began to fear a millennial disaster when Mezzenbone took the throne, a splinter sect called Dualism broke away from the Unification Church. Begun by a small group of clergymen, the Dualists claimed that the doctrine of the Unification Church had made it only part way to the truth. According to these heretics, as the Unification Church loyalists described them, there were only *two* deities in the universe. These supreme beings, the Creator and the Adversary, represented all the oppositional forces in the universe: light and dark, positive and negative, good and evil, order and chaos, creation and destruction. Everything in the universe reflected this divine opposition—including the souls of most mortals, which are always in conflict.

Indeed, according to the Dualist Heresy, the Dragon Empire itself is the historical and political manifestation of this opposition writ large across the known galaxy. Two kingdoms dominated by beings of supernatural power, one good and the other evil, almost destroy each other and then unite to form a great empire—an empire in which the pendulum swings back and forth between light and dark over the course of the centuries. The Dualist clerics claim that the Dragon Empire was prophesied in the ancient scriptures of the Unification Church, hundreds of years before the Empire was established. They also claim that the opposition inherent in the Empire will eventually tear it apart, and that the ensuing war will herald the Last Battle between the Creator and the Adversary.

THE TWELVE

THE DESTROYER

Alignment: Chaotic evil
Domains: Chaos, Evil, Destruction, Death, War
Symbol: A black, five-pointed star

The Destroyer is the personification of evil and hate in the universe. He strives to undo all that has been done and bring creation to an end. He is the lord of entropy and the master of the void.

Those who worship the Destroyer believe that life is a cycle of death and rebirth, creation and destruction. It is their duty to tear down what others have built, to destroy what others have created. Through destruction, they hope to renew that which is old and throw off the chains of an orderly universe.

Mezzenbone openly worships the Destroyer, as do many of the lords of his house. This is of grave concern to many, for how can the Emperor uphold the current order when his religion teaches him to tear it down? As a devout follower of the Destroyer, is Mezzenbone's greatest passion not the final destruction of the Dragon Empire and its people?

Clerics of the Destroyer kept a low profile in the Empire until Mezzenbone's ascension to the throne. Now, they worship and spread their faith openly, heralding the last days when the Destroyer will return to the Material Plane and sunder all of creation. These clerics rarely work together to advance their cause, preferring to practice their faith alone or in small and often secretive cults.

The Destroyer appears in countless guises in many different cultures. He may appear as a great, five-headed dragon, a rampaging demon, or a skeletal cancer victim rife with disease. In some cultures, the Destroyer is simply the Void, the nameless, formless manifestation of chaos and entropy. Small, impermanent shrines are more common than formal temples, and they are often dark, foreboding places where worshippers come to pray and leave blood sacrifices for their lord.

THE FATHER

Alignment: Lawful good
Domains: Good, Healing, Law, Knowledge, War
Symbol: A golden sun

The Father is one of the two creator deities within the Great Pantheon, as the 12 deitypes are collectively known. Whereas the Mother represents raw, primal creativity and fertility, the Father is the patron of rules, structure, and the application of science to describe the natural order of things. He is the ultimate lawmaker, the Patriarch of the Gods. In the religions of most cultures, his aspect is responsible for creating the world and for ruling over both gods and mortals.

The Father is often considered the highest authority in a culture or civilization. Clerics of the Father often work closely with the ruling class or government of their culture. In some cases, the clergy and the secular powers are at odds, differing over the rightful division of power. These conflicts have even led to war on countless planets throughout the known galaxy.

Among the short-lived races, the Father typically appears as an aging but strong and vigorous male with a lordly and commanding demeanor. His clothing is often archaic or timeless, usually traditional apparel of the culture's ancient past. Among the long-lived races, the Father is usually depicted as a mature adult in his physical prime with an ageless quality about his features and bearing.

THE JUDGE

Alignment: Lawful good
Domains: Good, Destruction, Knowledge, Law, Protection
Symbol: A balanced scale

In different aspects, the Judge represents mercy and justice, as well as righteous retribution and wrath. The Judge is both the arbiter of fairness and the divine hand wielding the hammer of punishment. In some cultures, lawful neutral aspects of the Judge appear as the impartial, somewhat distant arbitrator who maintains the cosmic balance, judging the good and evil equally. In most civilizations, though, the Judge is viewed as the divine protector of the innocent and righteous and the wrathful punisher of the evil.

The Judge is worshipped by those whose job it is to make, interpret, and enforce the law, including viceroys, magistrates, and police officers. Indeed, her clerics often serve in these capacities in addition to their duties to the church. Many police precincts in the Dragon Empire have chapels dedicated to the Judge, and their chaplains are typically high-ranking officers in the department.

In the Empire, the Judge is often depicted as an elven, dwarven, or human woman. She is blindfolded and bears a balanced scale—a symbol of justice administered fairly and impartially. In other cultures, she may appear as a celestial wielding a flaming sword, a black-hooded humanoid bearing a headsman's axe, or any of countless other forms.

THE LOVER

Alignment: Neutral good
Domains: Animal, Good, Healing, Protection, Water
Symbol: A white dove

The Lover is both the object of ultimate desire and the personification of ideal beauty. She is often represented as the unattainable goal, but she is also the spouse or soulmate with whom you spend your life. In many cultures, she is also the muse, the font of creativity and the artistic impulse. Her aspects can also appear as deities of celebration, festivals, and wine.

Some are drawn to the hedonistic aspects of the Lover, reveling in the satisfaction of the desires of the flesh. She is also worshipped by those searching for love or romance, and she inspires and enriches the creations of bards and artists. Her clerics devote themselves and their temples to the glorification of beauty, art, and romantic love. The ancient temple in the holy city of Aani is one of the Empire's great treasure houses of painting, sculpture, and other fine arts.

The Lover usually appears as a breathtakingly beautiful and seductive nymph, suggestively clothed. She is often depicted wrapped in bedsheets or other diaphanous materials. Her eyes sparkle even in the darkest night, and her scent speaks of exotic and erotic treasures.

THE MAGUS

Alignment: Neutral
Domains: Knowledge, Luck, Magic, Protection, Trickery
Symbol: An open eye

The Magus is the personification of magic, the power to shape reality by the force of will. He is also the god of knowledge, and in some cultures, he manifests darker aspects as the god of secrets or forbidden lore.

The Magus is worshipped by all practitioners of arcane magic. He is the traditional patron of the dragonblooded aristocracy and the divine mentor of sorcerers and wizards. Many bards also offer prayers to the Magus, at least when they are working magic. Many of the common folk honor the Magus and ask for protection from evil magic in their everyday lives.

Clerics of the Magus are rarely involved in the politics of the Dragon Empire. They prefer the privacy of their secluded temples and remote monasteries where they can devote their attentions to the sacred pursuit of knowledge. Many clerics of the Magus are sorcerers as well and a few of the most reclusive are wizards. Indeed, becoming a cleric of the Magus in one of the only ways for a wizard in the Dragon Empire to gain social prestige.

In common renderings, the Magus is usually depicted as an elderly male of any race garbed in black velvet robes embroidered with stars. In the imperial temples that primarily serve the aristocracy, the Magus appears as a trueblood dragon whose scales shift through all the colors of the spectrum.

THE MERCHANT

Alignment: Lawful neutral
Domains: Knowledge, Law, Luck, Travel, Trickery
Symbol: A gold coin

The Merchant is the goddess of commerce, trade, and wealth. She is the goddess of fair contracts and exchanges that benefit both parties, but she is also worshipped by thieves and opportunists. In her gentler aspects, she is the lady of gifts, gift giving, and charity. In many cultures, she is also the traveler and wanderer, the patron of those who journey and explore.

The Merchant is worshipped by traders, entrepreneurs, professionals, smugglers, thieves, corporate executives, and starship captains and crews. Her temples and clerics are often affiliated with commercial enterprises, whether interstellar financial conglomerates or local charities.

The Merchant's clergy are among the staunchest supporters of free enterprise in the Empire. They are always closely involved in imperial politics, pushing for lower taxes, less severe commercial regulations, and more government assistance for independent entrepreneurs. Their own financial institutions often support these enterprises with low-interest loans for factories or starships and other services.

In the Dragon Empire, the Merchant appears as a young female, usually of human or halfling stock. In different depictions, she may wear rugged traveling clothes, a spacesuit, a business suit, or the expensive fashions of the wealthy elite.

THE MOTHER

Alignment: Chaotic good
Domains: Animal, Good, Earth, Protection, Plant
Symbol: A crescent moon

The Mother is the deitype of life. While the Father created the universe, all living things originate with the Mother. She is the personification of nature in all its aspects, from the untouched wilderness to the fiery hearts of the stars. She is the patron of mothers and motherhood, and the goddess of fertility and healing.

The Mother is worshipped by women throughout the Dragon Empire. She is also honored by those who make their living from the land or in the wilderness, especially on the Outlands frontier. She is the lady of gardens, forests, and animals and is especially revered among the elves and other races of the ancient woodlands.

The Mother usually appears as a beautiful matron clothed in the colors of the seasons. She is often draped with plants and flowers, or with a shimmering blanket of snow.

THE REAPER

Alignment: Lawful evil
Domains: Death, Earth, Evil, Law, Trickery
Symbol: A humanoid skull

The Reaper is the embodiment of death. In some cultures, he is the neutral and impartial keeper of the afterlife, to be feared and respected but not hated. In the Dragon Empire, however, he is also the god of murder, the bringer of doom, and the king of the undead.

Most mortals honor the Reaper, but few actually worship him. They offer prayers for the souls of loved ones who have passed but otherwise strive to avoid the Reaper's empty gaze. The death god's rare and secretive followers are drawn from the ranks of necromancers, killers, and the undead. Some pray to the Reaper to grant them the power of his dark realm, while others honor him in a desperate effort to elude his cold grasp just a little longer.

The Reaper's lawful neutral clerics—those who interact openly with mainstream society—honor the dead and provide comfort to the bereaved in their time of grief. Evil clerics of the Reaper are usually reclusive and disorganized, either practicing their dark religion in isolation or forming secretive death cults that haunt the streets of the great cities at night.

The Reaper is commonly depicted as a bleached-white skeleton wrapped in a voluminous robe of impenetrable black. He wields a great scythe that severs souls from their mortal bodies.

THE STORMLORD

Alignment: Chaotic neutral
Domains: Air, Chaos, Destruction, Travel, Water
Symbol: A silver trident

The Stormlord is the deitype of the elemental forces of nature. He is the god of storms, the sea, lightning, and thunder. While the Mother represents the nurturing and life-giving aspects of the natural world, the Stormlord is the personification of its destructive wrath.

The Stormlord is revered by sailors, fishermen, divers, pilots, explorers, and other travelers who live at the mercy of the weather and the elements. The people of island nations and port cities honor him whether or not they live and work at sea. The prosperity of all in such cultures is inextricably tied to the weather and the ocean. Prayers and gifts are offered to the Stormlord in return for the bounty of the sea and his protection from storms.

The Stormlord most often appears as a powerful male giant with long white or sea-green hair and a full beard draped with seaweed and strung with seashells. He often wields a great trident or harpoon in one hand and a conch horn in the other. Inland cultures rarely draw upon the influence of the sea in depictions of the Stormlord. In these civilizations, he is often represented as a great warrior wielding a hammer or lighting bolt, or even as an elemental being of wind, rain, and thunder.

THE SMITH

Alignment: Neutral
Domains: Fire, Knowledge, Magic, Strength, Water
Symbol: An anvil

The Smith is the god of crafts, technology, and the physical sciences. He is the master of technical knowledge and practical magic. In the Dragon Empire, technology touches the lives of almost everyone, and the Smith is one of the most respected and revered deities in the Great Pantheon.

The Smith's worshippers are scientists, engineers, technicians, miners, craftsmen, architects, and others who build, repair, design, or use devices of all varieties. Spellcasters make offerings to him when they craft magic items, and the prayers of a soldier before battle often go to the Warrior to guide his aim, and then to the Smith to bless his gun. The Smith is often the patron deity of pilots, and he is the most commonly worshipped god among those who live and work in deep space.

In the Dragon Empire, the Smith usually appears as a male dwarf wielding a great hammer. His hair is long, red, and braided, and he wears a soot-stained blacksmith's apron and thick leather gloves. Even in human cultures, the Smith shares the coarse hair, eyebrows, and beard, and the stocky, heavily muscled frame that are common characteristics of dwarves.

THE TRICKSTER

Alignment: Chaotic neutral
Domains: Chaos, Knowledge, Luck, Magic, Trickery
Symbol: A fool's scepter

The Trickster is the complex and sometimes seemingly contradictory god of thieves, mischief, comedy, illusion, and secrets both hidden and revealed. He is the patron of cruel humor and biting wit but also of children, laughter, and games.

The Trickster has a reputation as a thief and deceiver, but his pranks and heists often benefit mortals in the traditions of many cultures. In many mythic stories, the Trickster steals things from the gods—such as fire, food, or the sun and moon—and gives them to mortals. These traditions present the Trickster as a fundamentally unpredictable and whimsical god: His actions may be cruel and even evil, or they may just seem that way because mortals cannot see things as he does.

In the mainstream society of the Dragon Empire, clerics of the Trickster emphasize their god's dominion over comedy and good fortune. This Trickster is often the patron of bards, gamblers, and others who live by their wits. Darker sects focus on the Trickster's other face. These clerics are the keepers of dark secrets, thieves in the shadows, and the masters of ill fortune.

The Trickster is often depicted as a humanoid figure of uncertain sex and race. The god's features are usually obscured by a mask, often one with two faces. The Trickster sometimes appears in the jester's motley, but he may just as easily assume the form of a coyote, fox, raven, or other animal. The Trickster is a shapeshifter and illusionist and one can never be certain what form he will take.

THE WARRIOR

Alignment: Lawful neutral
Domains: Law, Luck, Magic, Strength, War
Symbol: A greatsword

The Warrior is the deitype of strength, valor, battle, and warfare. He does not represent battle for the sake of bloodlust or destruction, but rather for defense and preservation or as a test of courage and skill-at-arms. For the Warrior and those who follow him, there is glory to be won in combat but not in slaughter.

The Warrior is worshipped throughout the known galaxy by those who must put their lives in harm's way. He is the patron of soldiers, mercenaries, lawmen, paladins, rangers, and fighting monks. Clerics of the Warrior serve as chaplains in the Imperial Legions and aboard the warships of the Imperial Navy. Non-military common folk rarely worship the Warrior, though they often offer prayers and sacrifices to him when war threatens to touch their lives.

The Warrior appears in many guises in different cultures. In the Dragon Empire, he is most often depicted as a knight clad in archaic armor and wielding his iconic greatsword. He may also appear as a master archer, a bird of prey, a black-clad horseman, or as some other culturally appropriate archetype.

THE DUALIST GODS

THE CREATOR

Alignment: Lawful good
Domains: Any but Chaos and Evil
Symbol: A golden wheel

The Creator is the Dualist god of the positive forces of the universe. He is the deity of good, order, light, peace, and mercy. He fashioned the material universe from the void between the planes and planted the seeds that blossomed into the plants, beasts, and mortal races.

In the Dualist tradition, the Creator is a distant god, a divine mover and lawgiver who rarely intervenes in the affairs of mortals except through his chosen messengers. Clerics of the Creator devote their lives to the benevolent cause of their deity. By striving to attain purity in their own lives, they hope to approach the ideal of purity that the Creator represents. While these clerics never fully succeed in their quest, it nonetheless guides and directs their lives. Temples of the Creator are dedicated to healing, worship, and ministry to the faithful and unfaithful alike. Clerics of the Creator believe it is their duty to guide those who have turned away from it back toward the light.

Dualist purists also honor the Creator, but they do not pattern their lives and actions after his ideal. Rather, they believe they must remain neutral, favoring neither the positive nor the negative, to gain true enlightenment. To comprehend the Creator one must also know the Adversary. These clerics do not devote themselves to "good works," and they seek to remain distanced from material concerns.

THE ADVERSARY

Alignment: Chaotic evil
Domains: Any but Good and Law
Symbol: An open flame

The Adversary is the Creator's dark twin, the divine personification of chaos, evil, destruction, and all the negative forces of the universe. The Adversary's ultimate goal is to corrupt that which is pure, to destroy all that has been created, and to shatter peace with violence.

Only the most evil mortals devote themselves to the Adversary. Their diseased souls are twisted by corruption and their minds are often broken by the dark forces they seek to command. These rare villains willingly sacrifice their souls in return for power, wealth, and the opportunity to satiate their destructive impulses. They have no care for others, except for how they might serve these clerics' evil designs. Clerics devoted to the Adversary sometimes work together, usually when they are thoroughly dominated by a powerful and ruthless leader.

Dualist purists also revere the Adversary, but they do not seek to do his work themselves. They view the Adversary just as they do the Creator, as a necessary manifestation of the universe. The universe was created, but it also decays. It is filled with light but also vast dark spaces. One cannot gain enlightenment by ignoring the negative forces that are just as crucial as the positive to the unfolding of the universe. These purist clerics seek neither to do evil nor to punish it; they only wish to understand it, to incorporate it into the system of knowledge and experience that guides them toward enlightenment.

CHAPTER THREE

ORGANIZATIONS

Thousands of guilds, societies, cults, corporations, orders, and other organizations exist in the Dragon Empire. Some of these are devoted to political or economic gain, others to battling evil, and still others to sewing intrigue and discord. Some of these organizations offer membership to all and operate openly, while others are exclusive and secretive, working quietly in the shadows. Some are associations of the honorable and noble established to serve and protect the common folk. Others are alliances of the evil and ambitious founded on foul agendas and dark designs. This chapter provides an overview of some of the most influential organizations in the **Dragonstar** setting.

ADAMANTINE ORDER

This secretive organization dates to the early years of the war between Qesemet and Asamet. It was established under the auspices of House Noros, but it was staffed and utilized by all of the chromatic dragon clans. Its initial role was as an intelligence-gathering apparatus, but it soon branched out into a variety of covert operations designed to weaken Qesemet's military might and undermine its political base. The victories of the Adamantine Order during the war have become legendary, and it has continued to grow under a perpetual cloud of secrecy and disinformation for five millennia.

When Mezzenbone took the Golden Throne, the Adamantine Order became the Empire's primary intelligence organization. Most of its activities are directed against the Kingdom of Qesemet, but it also runs ongoing operations on many Outlands worlds. Agents of the Adamantine Order have assassinated dragon lords, run disinformation campaigns designed to create political

rifts between rival clans, conducted campaigns of industrial espionage and sabotage against aristocorps, and destabilized governments on Outlands worlds. The order was also responsible for training ISPD officers early in that organization's history, but the drow are increasingly handling this task internally. Select ISPD agents do still train with the Adamantine Order for highly specialized assignments.

Lord Shul, the leader of the Adamantine Order, is a black dragon-halfblood yuan-ti crossbreed. Persistent rumors suggest that a young, up-and-coming Shul was responsible for the death of King Lazalius. Others argue that while Shul has certainly been around a long time, he isn't *that* old, and that his reputation is such that all manner of legendary deeds are attributed to him. Nevertheless, Lord Shul is thought to have the personal favor of the Emperor and he is one of the most feared lords in the known galaxy. Shul is a reptilian humanoid with soft, black scales and the broad, flattened skull of a serpent.

Lord Shul: Male half-dragon/half-blood yuan-ti Rog10/Asn10; CR 30; Medium-size dragon; HD 7d10+21 plus 10d8+30 plus 10d8+30; hp 209; Init +11 (Dex, Improved Initiative, *boosted reflexes*); Spd 40 ft.; AC 32 (+5 Dex, +8 natural, +9 armor); Atk +33/+28/+23/+18/+13 melee (1–6/+12/9–20, scimitar) or +32/+27/+22/+17/+12 (2d10+5, laser pistol) or +30/+25/+20/+15/+10 ranged (4d10+3, assault blaster); SA Breath weapon (60 ft. long line of acid, 6d4, DC 17 for half), poison (Fort save DC 17, 1–6/1–6 temporary Con), psionics, sneak attack +10d6, death attack (Fort save DC 27), poison use; SQ Improved evasion, uncanny dodge (Dex bonus to AC, can't be flanked, +1 Ref save vs. traps), +5 save vs. poison; SR 16; AL NE; SV Fort +14, Ref +23, Will +19; Str 25, Dex 20, Con 17, Int 24, Wis 21, Cha 26.

Skills and Feats: Balance +15, Bluff +18, Climb +17, Concentration +13, Decipher Script +17, Demolitions +21, Diplomacy +22, Disable Device +17, Disguise +18, Escape Artist +15, Gather Information +18, Hide +22*, Innuendo +15, Intimidate +18, Jump +15, Knowledge (imperial history) +12, Knowledge (imperial politics) +12, Listen +20, Move Silently +25, Open Lock +15, Pilot +15, Search +21, Sense Motive +15, Spot +20, Swim +17, Tumble +15, Use Device +17, Use Magic Device +18; Alertness, Blind-Fight, Dodge, Expertise, Improved Critical (scimitar), Improved Initiative, Improved Shot on the Run, Mobile Shot, Mobility, Point Blank Shot, Rapid Shot, Shot on the Run, Technical Proficiency.

* If Lord Shul is using chameleon power, he gains a +8 circumstance bonus on Hide checks.

Spells Prepared (4/4/4/2; DC = 17 + spell level): 1st—*change self, detect poison, obscuring mist, spider climb*; 2nd—*alter self, darkness, undetectable alignment* x2; 3rd—*invisibility* x2, *misdirection, nondetection*; 4th—*dimension door, improved invisibility*.

Possessions: Black Fang: *+5 keen keenblade unholy scimitar of wounding, +5 laser pistol* with laser sight, *+3 assault blaster* with laser sight and electronic scope, *+3 ring of protection, ring of blinking, +3 glamered combat fatigues of heavy fortification and silent moves, +3 amulet of natural armor, boots of speed, cloak of etherealness, dust of disappearance, eyes of charming, medallion of thoughts*, datapad, personal communicator.

Spellware: *Advanced elemental resistance* (fire, electricity), *antitoxin, boosted reflexes, danger sense, darkvision, dermal armor 10/+5, fast healing 2, improved aura mask, low-light vision, telepath, translator*.

BLACKGUARD ORDERS

The sects of the Destroyer and the Reaper support active orders of blackguards. These orders are closely allied with the Kingdom of Asamet and are the mirror image of the paladin orders. The blackguard orders are extremely secretive, operating in the shadows and in isolated regions in the Outlands. Like paladins, they are given advanced instruction in weapons and tactics, but the operations they are trained for have less noble objectives. They are experts in terror, insurgency, and destabilization campaigns, and they are dedicated to the dark causes of their deities.

Typical Eternal Order Blackguard:
Human Ftr5/Rog2/Blk3; CR 12; Medium-size humanoid (human); HD 5d10+10 plus 2d6+4 plus 3d10+6; hp 75 plus 20 (*trauma symbiote*); Init +8 (Dex, Improved Initiative); Spd 30 ft.; AC 22 (+4 Dex, +7 armor, +1 deflection); Atk +13/+8 melee (1–8+2/17–20, masterwork keenblade longsword) or +15/+10 ranged (4d10+1, *+1 assault blaster*); SA Aura of despair, poison use, smite good 2/day (+3 attack, +5 damage), sneak attack +1d6; SQ Command undead 6/day, dark blessing, *detect good*, evasion; AL LE; SV Fort +9, Ref +9, Will +6; Str 15, Dex 18, Con 14, Int 10, Wis 15, Cha 14.

Skills and Feats: Climb +6, Demolitions +5, Diplomacy +6, Disable Device +4, Freefall +4, Gather Information +6, Hide +8, Intimidate +8, Jump +6, Knowledge (religion) +4, Listen +6, Move Silently +8, Pilot +8, Search +5, Spot +7, Swim +6, Use Device +4, Use Magic Device +6; Autofire, Cleave, Improved Initiative, Point Blank Shot, Power Attack, Precise Shot, Rapid Shot, Sunder, Technical Proficiency.

Spells Prepared (2; DC = 12 + spell level): 1st—*endure elements, protection from good.*

Possessions: +1 assault blaster with laser sight, +1 combat fatigues, +1 ring of protection, masterwork keenblade longsword, *dermpatch of cure serious wounds*, datapad, personal communicator, medkit.

Spellware: Darkvision, enhanced Dexterity, extra smite, ranged smite, trauma symbiote.

THE ETERNAL ORDER OF NIGHT

This blackguard order dedicated to the Reaper is steeped in seemingly archaic, mystic traditions. Its organization and procedures are more reminiscent of a secret society than a modern military unit. The Eternal Order is closely allied with House Osorus, acting under its authorization and protection. The paladins of the order are believed to be the bitter enemies of not only the paladin orders but also the Adamantine Order, the Imperial Secret Police Directorate, and the Hell Hounds. All of these organizations are effectively controlled by the Emperor, and the Eternal Order is firmly entrenched in the Asamet faction made up of hardline conservatives and traditionalists.

The order is the militant arm of the sect of the Reaper and is used to spread fear and awe of the Lord of Death throughout the dark corners of the Empire. The Eternal Order of Night was founded shortly before the great war in response to the creation of new paladin orders. During the war, blackguards of the Eternal Order served as assassins, targeting high-ranking nobles, generals, and industrialists identified as enemies of the Kingdom of Asamet. After the war, the religious leaders assumed more control of the order, using its members to directly advance the cause of their deity. Traditionally, these missions have involved the accumulation of power in the hands of those leaders.

Blackguards of the Eternal Order worship death and dedicate themselves to murder. They assassinate targets selected by their leaders, whether lords of Qesemet, enemy paladins, or political rivals. They train, equip, and sometimes even lead evil forces on Outlands worlds, harvesting the souls of millions for the glory of their dark god. They explore lost cities and venture into forgotten dungeons in search of dark artifacts to empower themselves or their masters. In their secret shrines and sanctuaries, they perform dark rituals and sacrifices in honor of the Reaper, strengthening their unholy faith and initiating new blackguards into their profane traditions.

THE HELL HOUNDS

Officially part of Mezzenbone's infamous Red Legion, the Hell Hounds are an order of blackguards dedicated to the Destroyer. The Red Legion is an elite unit of shock troops used to break enemy opposition when and where it is able to resist the Emperor's con-

ventional forces. The Hell Hounds are known as a "cleaner" unit specifically trained in scorched earth tactics. They are only sent into a combat zone when the lord marshal commanding the Red Legion—or the Emperor himself—decrees that nothing is to be left alive or intact. The Hell Hounds drop in, terminate all hostiles, and leave the combat zone in flames.

There is rarely any military justification for the kind of operational overkill the Hell Hounds are trained for. Any opposition sufficient to warrant it would be more efficiently neutralized by orbital bombardment or air power. In most cases, the unit is used as a political weapon. When the Hell Hounds are unleashed on a resistant city or stronghold on some unsuspecting Outlands world, they make a statement that even the most stubborn rebels find hard to ignore.

The Hell Hounds are based on Arangorn, the throneworld of House Mazorgrim. The Emperor shares their devotion to the Destroyer, and he is said to have handpicked some of the unit's highest-ranking officers. These officers are hard and often cruel, and the Hell Hounds take pride in reports that the majority of new recruits are killed during the year-long initiation period. Based on these reports and others like them, critics of the Hell Hounds—most of them within House Osorus—claim the unit is wasteful and irrational, and lacks any real military role. Mezzenbone dismisses such criticisms, pointing out that efficiency and rationality have little place in true service to the Destroyer.

When not in training, the Hell Hounds wear black and red dress uniforms. They are equipped with powered armor and combat vehicles on many missions, and these devastating weapons only reinforce their terrifying legend on the Outlands worlds they have visited. The unit's symbol is a black hell hound's head with glowing red eyes.

THE BLACK HOLE SYNDICATE

The Dragon Empire is a place of enormous wealth and tremendous opportunity, and such places always attract the criminal element. Most crimes are committed either by ordinary people in the heat of the moment or by petty crooks who are destined to spend most of their adult lives incarcerated. While these small-time hoods can be dangerous to a citizen out on the streets late at night, they don't even register on the Empire's radar screen. They are the problem of the local Imperial Police precincts; the Empire's real hooks are designed

Bazzrit: Male rakshasa Rog13; CR 23; Medium-size outsider; HD 7d8+28 plus 13d6+52; hp 157; Init +11 (Dex, Improved Initiative, *boosted reflexes*); Spd 50 ft.; AC 35 (+6 Dex, +9 natural, +8 armor, +2 deflection); Atk +17/+12/+7/+2 melee (1–4+4/15–20, dagger) or +22/+17/+12/+7 (3d8+3, blaster pistol); SA Detect thoughts, sneak attack +7d6, spells; SQ Alternate form, spell immunity, vulnerable to blessed crossbow bolts, damage reduction 20/+3, improved evasion, uncanny dodge (Dex bonus to AC, can't be flanked, +1 Ref save vs. traps), skill mastery; AL LE; SV Fort +15, Ref +21, Will +15; Str 13, Dex 22, Con 19, Int 21, Wis 18, Cha 26.

Skills and Feats: Balance +12, Bluff +21*, Climb +11, Concentration +14*, Decipher Script +15, Diplomacy +18*, Disable Device +15, Disguise +22*, Escape Artist +16*, Gather Information +18, Hide +16*, Innuendo +11, Jump +11, Listen +11, Move Silently +15*, Perform +17, Pilot +16, Search +15, Sense Motive +20*, Spellcraft +7, Spot +12, Swim +11, Tumble +16, Use Device +15, Use Magic Device +17; Alertness, Dodge.

* Mastered skills

Spells Known (6/8/8/6; DC = 18 + spell level): 0—*daze*, *detect magic*, *detect poison*, *mage hand*, *open/close*, *ray of frost*, *read magic*; 1st—*charm person*, *endure elements*, *identify*, *shield*, *true strike*; 2nd—*blur*, *cat's grace*, *protection from arrows*; 3rd—*nondetection*, *suggestion*.

Possessions: +3 blaster pistol with laser sight, +8 bracers of armor, +2 ring of protection, datapad, personal communicator.

Spellware: *Antitoxin*, *boosted reflexes*, *danger sense*, *darkvision*, *elemental resistance* (fire, electricity), *fast healing 2*, *low-light vision*.

for bigger fish.

The Black Hole Syndicate is probably older than the Star League. Some believe it followed the Forongorn Confederation to the stars like a parasite riding along on its host. It is a vast, interstellar network of criminals that thrives on the illegal acquisition and trade of a dizzying variety of goods and services. The Syndicate backs and controls pirate rings operating along the Outlands frontier. It finances and coordinates smugglers running contraband to and from the imperial core worlds. It even traffics in the flesh of sentient beings, buying and selling slaves for pleasure or labor throughout the Domains of Asamet.

The Syndicate's coordinated activities and complex enterprises suggest a single, unified command structure or organization. However, the Imperial Police have never been able to determine who gives the orders even at a planetary level. The Syndicate appears to be organized into individual cells, called gangs or crews, capable of operating autonomously for extended periods of time. In most cases, a crew's leader does not even know the identity of the superior he reports to. This tangled, secretive organization makes investigating the Syndicate an almost impossible proposition.

The truth is the Black Hole Syndicate is only an "organization" in the loosest sense of the word. It has survived for so long simply because it can operate effectively on its own inertia with almost no control from the top. In some cases, decades have passed in which there was no overall leadership of the Syndicate at all. The individual crews continued operating and reporting up the ladder, but only the highest-placed Syndicate bosses knew that their massive, tentacled monster had no head. Usually, these bosses were undertaking a secret war amongst themselves to determine the next overboss. In other cases, the organization has been guided by multiple, competing bosses all struggling to gain sole control.

For the last 70 years, the overboss of the Black Hole Syndicate has been a rakshasa lord named Bazzrit. The rakshasa immigrated to the Material Plane more than a century ago, and tirelessly wormed his way into the heart of the organization. Drawing upon outsider sources of information, he identified the current over-boss, assassinated him, and took his place without any of the other bosses learning that anything was amiss. In the ensuing decades, his empire has thrived and Bazzrit rules it like a decadent king. He has no permanent residence, preferring to move around and constantly change legal identities to keep the authorities—and his rivals—off his trail.

DRUIDIC SOCIETY

This secretive organization is at least as old as the Star League. Scholars suggest that it may have been established by forest gnomes on Aranal—the world that gave birth to the Forongorn Confederation, and eventually, to interstellar civilization. Others believe it emerged on one of the first technologically primitive planets the confederation contacted. Regardless, it has been a quiet champion of nature working to control the unchecked expansion of technology and industry for millennia.

The modern Druidic Society is a sophisticated organization with an educated and intelligent membership. It draws many of its recruits from the life science fields, including botany, zoology, ecology, and many others. Upon entering the Druidic Society, these young scientists are initiated into the mysteries of the ancient tradition, taught its ways and codes, and instructed in the responsible and effective mastery of its primal magic. When their training is complete, novitiate druids are sent back out into the world to resume their normal lives. They rarely reveal their membership in the secret society to any but other druids. The Druidic Society has no permanent headquarters. Convocations attended by thousands of druids are held biannually on Draconis Prime's summer and winter solstice. The locations of these convocations change every year and are a closely guarded secret of the membership.

For the last several centuries, the Druidic Society has become increasingly divided. The organization is split between two factions opposed to each other on fundamental philosophical grounds. The so-called traditionalist faction rejects technology, industrialization, and urbanization in all its forms, even in their own personal lives. They strive to live simple lives without modern conveniences through which they strengthen their spiritual bond with the natural world. Some traditionalists hail from Outlands worlds, while others are imperial citizens who have turned their backs on technological civilization.

The progressive or liberal faction of the Druidic Society considers the traditionalists impractical and even deluded radicals and idealists. This majority faction believes that the only way to protect nature is to work within the social and political system to bring about change. They live their lives much like other imperial citizens, using the countless technological resources available to make their lives easier and more enjoyable.

This division within the Druidic Society has become rather bitter. The factions compete with each other for recruits and even try to recruit members from the opposing faction. They often strive to thwart each other's initiatives and projects, and their political influence is often neutralized because they cannot present a united front. There have even been instances of sabotage and violence between members of the two factions. If this trend continues, the traditionalists may eventually split off from the Druidic Society to form a splinter group.

IMPERIAL LEGIONS

Military power and defense are delicate issues in the Dragon Empire. On the one hand, everyone wants a strong military to keep the peace and protect the Empire from outside threats. On the other, no one wants too much power to be controlled by one dragon lord or even one house. The Imperial Charter addressed these issues by incorporating a number of checks and balances into the organization of the Dragon Empire's primary military force: the Imperial Legions.

The Imperial Legions are ultimately commanded by the Emperor. However, the forces stationed within each domain are under the immediate command of an officer appointed by the ruling house of that domain. For example, while the Legions stationed in the Domain of Deserene are ultimately under the command of Mezzenbone, Lord High Marshal Finwyr, the nephew of King Khelorn, is the local commander-in-chief of the Imperial Legions stationed in the Domain of Deserene. The lord high marshal is obligated to execute any orders passed down from the imperial command but is otherwise responsible for training his troops, selecting his officers, and maintaining the military readiness of his forces.

This system works, for the most part, because there are legal and political limits on the orders an emperor can issue to the lord high marshals. As a general rule, the only orders Mezzenbone can issue to the Imperial Legions stationed in the Domain of Deserene are those "necessary and conducive" to the defense and security of the domain. While Mezzenbone can and does endeavor to stretch the meaning of this section of the Imperial

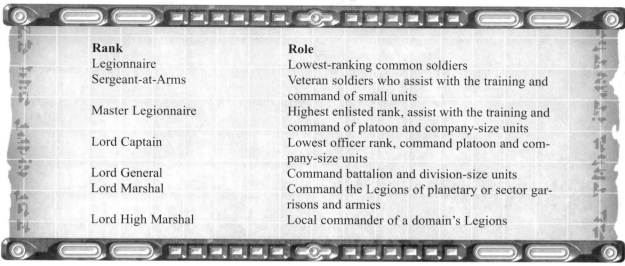

Rank	Role
Legionnaire	Lowest-ranking common soldiers
Sergeant-at-Arms	Veteran soldiers who assist with the training and command of small units
Master Legionnaire	Highest enlisted rank, assist with the training and command of platoon and company-size units
Lord Captain	Lowest officer rank, command platoon and company-size units
Lord General	Command battalion and division-size units
Lord Marshal	Command the Legions of planetary or sector garrisons and armies
Lord High Marshal	Local commander of a domain's Legions

Charter, there's a hard limit on his ability to use the Imperial Legions in the Domains of Qesemet against the wishes and interests of the metallic dragons.

Nevertheless, this heavily politicized command structure creates a pervasive tension in the Legions. Mezzenbone has fueled the flame by assigning ISPD operatives to many units, especially those campaigning in the Outlands. The ISPD is a legal extension of the Emperor's authority, and it is difficult for many Legion officers to stomach their orders, interference, or even their mere presence.

The justification of Mezzenbone's Outlands campaign was conveniently provided by a number of incidents since he assumed the throne. Mind flayer raiders operating out of the Dark Zone have attacked several imperial colonies in the Rimward Barrens. Piracy and smuggling—much of it controlled by the Black Hole Syndicate—is on the rise throughout the Outlands. And several independent Outlands worlds have themselves presented a threat to the security of the imperial frontier, usually as a result of uncontrolled outsider activity.

Each planet controlled by the Empire has at least a minimal Legion garrison in addition to any local forces it may support. Recruits are drawn from every world in every domain, and the numbers of conscripts drawn from annexed Outlands worlds are on the rise. These conscripts usually have little or no military training, and most have no understanding of or familiarity with modern weapons and battlefield tactics. They must undergo intensive training programs before they can be expected to contribute as soldiers in combat. Under the guiding hand of the ISPD, however, many of these conscripts never receive this training. Instead, they are essentially used as unskilled labor, digging trenches, building fortifications, working the kitchens, and performing other menial tasks in support of the combat troops.

The command and rank hierarchy of the Imperial Legions is infused with the semi-feudal social and political structure of the Empire. Enlisted personnel are drawn from all parts of society, but officers must be of noble birth or granted title. The above table lists the various ranks and their duties.

Typical Legionnaire: Human War5; CR 6; Medium-size humanoid (human); HD 5d8+10; hp 36 plus 20 (*trauma symbiote*); Init +2 (Dex); Spd 30 ft.; AC 21 (+2 Dex, +9 armor); Atk +8 melee (1–4+1/17–20, masterwork keenblade dagger) or +8 ranged (3d10, masterwork assault laser); AL LN; SV Fort +6, Ref +3, Will +1; Str 13, Dex 14, Con 14, Int 10, Wis 11, Cha 10.

Skills and Feats: Climb +4, Demolitions +4, Freefall +4, Intimidate +2, Jump +4, Pilot +4, Swim +4; Point Blank Shot, Precise Shot, Rapid Shot, Technical Proficiency.

Possessions: masterwork assault laser with laser sight, masterwork keenblade dagger, combat armor, personal communicator.

Spellware: Trauma symbiote.

IMPERIAL SOCIETY OF ARCANE MAGIC

The Imperial Society is the largest organization of wizards in the Dragon Empire. Its labyrinthine headquarters complex in the cloud city of Vespar on Aelding is home to more than 500 wizards of varying levels of power and accomplishment. The Vespar Academy of the Art, established, supported, and administered by the Imperial Society, is the most well known and highly regarded institute of arcane scholarship in the known galaxy. While wizards are looked down upon by the aristocracy—including the lords of House Sarava—the Imperial Society is nevertheless an influential and respected presence on the silver dragon throneworld.

The Imperial Society is dedicated to advancing the art and status of wizardry in the Dragon Empire. It trains novice wizards at the Vespar Academy and other colleges of arcane magic throughout the Empire. The society provides grants and arcane laboratory facilities to wizards conducting valuable research. Most visibly, the Imperial Society sponsors a number of public relations

and political campaigns designed to foster social acceptance of wizards and enhance their political clout on the throneworlds and Draconis Prime.

Regardless of its many initiatives on their behalf, most wizards pay their dues to the Imperial Society for one reason: To gain access to the thousands of spells in the society's online database. This resource is believed to be the largest archive of spell formulas in the known galaxy. By paying their dues and remaining in good standing, wizards are able to constantly update their selection of spells as their needs, research efforts, or circumstances dictate.

Dues are 1,000 cr per caster level per standard year. Only those who can cast arcane spells and prepare them as a wizard are eligible for membership. The spell database can only be accessed from one of the throneworlds, as the InfoNet depends on the landlines that run under the Long Road. A wizard downloading spells must follow the rules for copying spells detailed in the *Starfarer's Handbook* (see page 136), and his spellbook software must have sufficient capacity to store the spell.

IMPERIAL SPECIAL POLICE DIRECTORATE

Shortly after his coronation as the new emperor, Mezzenbone created a new division within the Imperial Police. The ISPD is a secret police organization tasked with a broad range of intelligence, counterintelligence, and security duties. Its primary mission is to identify and neutralize both internal and external threats to the Empire. The ranks of the ISPD are dominated by drow, and they have gained a formidable reputation with imperial citizens.

The ISPD has been most visible when working inside the Empire. The agency is essentially a political inquisition designed to root out and neutralize "treasonous activity." The ISPD seems to define this as any political opposition it can safely target: dissident citizens with no significant political or legal protection, lesser lords of both kingdoms, and so on. Given the broad authority Mezzenbone has granted the ISPD, its operations and methods are perfectly legal and the scope of its powers is truly terrifying to lords and commoners alike.

The ISPD is also active in the Outlands. The agency is responsible for coordinating and executing the Emperor's campaign along the frontier. ISPD agents are often assigned to the Imperial Legions fighting in the Outlands, either to "encourage morale" or even to take command of specific operations.

The explanation for the ISPD's presence within the Legions is simple: Only they know what Mezzenbone truly wants from the Outlands worlds. They are responsible for locating and retrieving the artifacts of power that the Emperor is amassing to destroy the other dragon clans and force the known galaxy into slavery and submission. This is the ISPD's primary mission in the Outlands, and its agents often compromise the objectives of military missions to fulfill it.

The internal organization of the ISPD follows a traditional command hierarchy. The lowest-ranking field officers are called special agents, and their superiors are lieutenants and captains. There are many other titles for officers working in support positions, such as analysts and researchers. The director of the ISPD is Avix Vazenorn, a female drow of exceptional ruthlessness and cunning who was a veteran agent in the Adamantine Order before being assigned to head Mezzenbone's secret police.

Typical ISPD Special Agent: Drow Rog3/Sor2; CR 8; Medium-size humanoid (elf); HD 3d6 plus 2d4; hp 18 plus 20 (*trauma symbiote*); Init +7 (Dex, Improved Initiative); Spd 30 ft.; AC 19 (+3 Dex, +6 armor); Atk +5 melee (1–4/17–20, keenblade dagger) or +7 ranged (3d8, masterwork blaster pistol); SQ Drow traits, light blindness (negated by spellware), spell-like abilities; SR 16; AL CE; SV Fort +1, Ref +6, Will +4; Str 11, Dex 16, Con 10, Int 14, Wis 11, Cha 15.

Skills and Feats: Balance +4, Bluff +6, Concentration +2, Cryptography +3, Diplomacy +8, Disguise +3, Freefall +3, Gather Information +8, Hide +6, Knowledge (arcana) +4, Listen +6, Move Silently +6, Open Lock +4, Pilot +4, Profession (police officer) +6, Scry +4, Search +5, Sense Motive +6, Spellcraft +4, Spot +4, Urban Lore +6, Use Device +4; Improved Initiative, Point Blank Shot, Technical Proficiency.

Spells Known (6/5; DC = 12 + spell level): 0—*daze, detect magic, mage hand, open/close, read magic;* 1st—*change self, charm person.*

Possessions: Masterwork blaster pistol, masterwork keenblade dagger, *+1 armor vest, dermpatch of cure serious wounds,* datapad, scrollware (1st-level spells, 2nd-level caster): *endure elements, expeditious retreat, shield, true strike),* personal communicator.

Spellware: Light tolerance, trauma symbiote.

THE INSURRECTION

The Dragon Empire was established 5,000 years ago as a unilateral action of the dragon clans of Asamet and Qesemet. None of the other races and member worlds of the old Star League were consulted. As a courtesy, representatives of King Khelorn asked these worlds and groups for their voluntary support, but it was always clear that submission to the newly formed Empire would not ultimately be optional. Most systems recognized the benefits of an end to the devastataing war and membership in a prosperous and secure empire, but many individuals—and even whole worlds—refused to submit to the dragon's rule. There has therefore been a long tradition of stubborn, if usually quiet, opposition to the Dragon Empire.

This opposition has become louder and more visible in the years since Mezzenbone took the Golden Throne. Many citizens who supported the Empire under the rule of Qesemet have become vocal opponents in the face of five millennia of rule under the evil dragon clans. Dissident groups on many worlds in the Domains of Qesemet have become more outspoken, expressing their opposition to the Dragon Empire and its inequities in the media and in political rallies attended by hundreds or even thousands of like-minded people. Opposition in the Domains of Asamet, where the ISPD operates more freely, is usually more subtle and covert.

Most of the many dissident groups and movements that have formed in the last few decades are organizations of law-abiding citizens whose activities never go beyond impassioned speeches and peaceful demonstrations. Some dissidents, however, have started to take a more active hand in trying to inact change. These rebels are beginning to quietly organize, meeting in secret to plan operations whose ultimate goal is the replacement of the current regime with a more democratic and equitable form of government. On countless worlds, these groups are starting to make contact with each other, and a larger umbrella network is gradually forming. Many groups have ties with legitimate political organizations, and they use these connections to generate funding, gather intelligence, and communicate with each other more freely.

To date, the activities of this fledgling insurrection have been rather modest in scope and objectives, designed primarily to publicize their cause. They publish underground newspapers or maintain radical sites on the InfoNet that speak out against the injustices of the draconic regime. They decorate the walls of public buildings with political graffiti and circulate their pro-

paganda at legitimate rallies and assemblies. They have also begun preparing for more ambitious efforts: making contact with sympathetic dragon lords, purchasing black market weapons and explosives, and training their members in combat and covert operations.

Currently, the insurrection is very loosely organized. It is more a network of independent groups and cells than a single coherent organization. Contact and communication between these cells is growing, however, and a central leadership is beginning to form. Morgan Vestans, a half-human, half-gold dragon from Serenity III has emerged as the charismatic, high-profile spokesman of the insurrection. Vestans turned his back on his draconic heritage and publicly disavowed the Empire, earning instant credibility with radical dissidents who believed that no dragon would ever sacrifice his own status and position in the cause of justice. The young half-dragon has called for the dismantling of the draconic regime with the consent and cooperation of its current masters. Failing that, the people of the galaxy should "come together as a righteous army to tear down the corrupt empire."

Vestans's current whereabouts are unknown, but he is believed to be in hiding somewhere in the Domain of Golion.

PALADIN ORDERS

The sects of the Father, the Judge, the Mother, and the Warrior maintain paladin orders. In **Dragonstar**, paladins are elite sacred soldiers trained to fight the forces of evil on their own turf. They are trained in commando tactics, provided with cutting-edge weapons and spellware, and given the spiritual guidance they need to fortify their souls and harden their faith. Paladins are the rarely seen, almost legendary champions of the benevolent deities of the Great Pantheon.

SPECIAL OUTLANDS ARMY RECON

SOLAR is the most renowned paladin order in the Empire. It was founded by Lord Hendaran, a lesser half-dragon lord of House Deserene and paladin of the Father, in 864 AE. The order's primary mission is the defense of Qesemet and its colonies against evil forces along the Outlands frontier. SOLAR paladins have been called on to fight guerilla actions against humanoid armies, clear out undead infestations of remote outposts, and contain flare-ups of outsider activity on isolated colony worlds. The order's unit insignia, a silver sword on a blazing golden sun, represents sacred battle in righteous service to the Father.

Like all paladin orders, SOLAR never recruits its soldiers. Paladins who heed the call seek out the order on their own. Some are Legionnaires granted sacred visions in the midst of battle, while others are mere children who claim to have always known their destiny. Prospective paladins are required to pass a rigorous series of physical, mental, and spiritual challenges during their initiation. These tests are not designed to measure strength or skill-at-arms, but rather the potential for these qualities that can be nurtured by the order. The initiate's faith is what is truly challenged: So long as the would-be paladin never loses faith in himself or the Father, he will be victorious in his trials.

SOLAR units are typically assigned to high-threat situations in the Outlands that lesser soldiers are simply not prepared to handle. In most of these situations, evil supernatural beings such as undead or outsiders are the

Typical SOLAR Paladin: Human Pal5; CR 7; Medium-size humanoid (human); HD 5d10+10; hp 42 plus 20 (*trauma symbiote*); Init +3 (Dex); Spd 30 ft.; AC 21 (+3 Dex, +8 armor); Atk +8 melee (1–8+1/17–20, masterwork keenblade longsword) or +10 ranged (3d10+1, *+1 assault laser*); SA Smite 2/day (+2 attack, +5 damage), turn undead 5/day; SQ Detect evil, divine grace, aura of courage, remove disease, lay on hands (10 hp/day); AL LG; SV Fort +6, Ref +4, Will +2; Str 13, Dex 17, Con 14, Int 10, Wis 13, Cha 14.

Skills and Feats: Climb +4, Freefall +5, Heal +4, Jump +3, Knowledge (religion) +4, Knowledge (undead) +1, Listen +4, Spot +4, Swim +3; Point Blank Shot, Precise Shot, Rapid Shot, Technical Proficiency.

Spells Prepared (1; DC = 11 + spell level): 1st—*protection from evil*.

Possessions: *+1 assault laser* with laser sight, masterwork keenblade longsword, masterwork battle armor, *dermpatch of cure serious wounds*, datapad, personal communicator.

Spellware: *Darkvision*, *extra smite*, *ranged smite*, *trauma symbiote*.

root of the crisis. Because they are viral threats—they can multiply themselves effectively without limits—Qesemet takes these "hot zones" very seriously.

Like the wandering knights of old, SOLARs are often charged with open-ended solo missions. On these missions, the paladin must be prepared to take the initiative and act on his own authority, isolated from the normal chain of command. Much of a SOLAR's early training focuses on preparations for these missions, instilling in the paladin the sense of independence and self-reliance he needs to operate effectively outside his unit.

ROYAL MARSHAL SERVICE

The RMS is an order of paladins in service to the Judge. It is also the elite law enforcement agency of the Kingdom of Qesemet. While SOLAR is devoted to battling evil on the front lines and beyond, the Royal Marshal Service is charged with maintaining law and order within the Domains of Qesemet. The individual domains, star systems, and planets have their own local police forces, but the RMS focuses on high-profile crimes and organized criminal activity. The badge of the Royal Marshal Service is a silver shield engraved with the scales of justice.

Most royal marshals worked in law enforcement before receiving their call to service. If their application to the order is accepted, they become cadets at the Royal Marshal Academy in Betherian on Galador. Graduates become rookie officers in the RMS. The standard curriculum at the academy includes the martial training paladins require for defense of both themselves and innocent civilians, instruction in the law, and spiritual guidance designed to strengthen and enrich their bond with the Judge. Royal marshal characters gain Knowledge (imperial law) as a bonus class skill.

The RMS is charged with investigating severe or violent crimes in the Kingdom of Qesemet. The royal marshals also have jurisdiction on cases involving organized crime or threats to the security of the kingdom, such as espionage and terrorism. The RMS sometimes investigates cases in Outlands colonies within the Domains of Qesemet, but the marshals rarely venture into the Deep Outlands. Royal marshals are often called upon to work undercover, and they often have levels in the rogue class to represent their training in the skills necessary to interact with and survive in the criminal underworld.

TASK FORCE SANCTUARY

This order of paladins dedicated to the Mother specializes in search, rescue, and recovery operations. Members of Task Force Sanctuary are trained to operate in both wilderness and urban environments, and to offer emergency assistance and trauma care to those in need. The paladins of Task Force Sanctuary are highly skilled soldiers and combat medics. They specialize in hostage

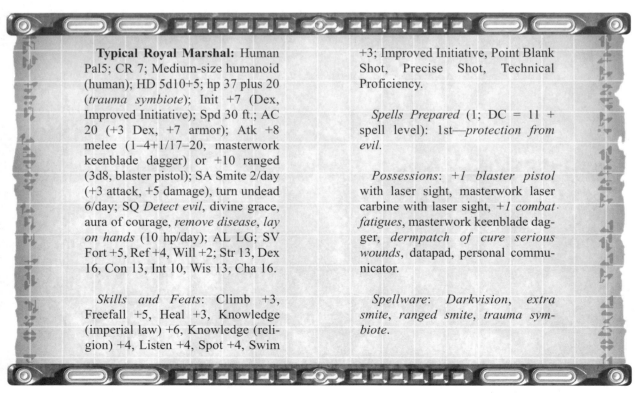

Typical Royal Marshal: Human Pal5; CR 7; Medium-size humanoid (human); HD 5d10+5; hp 37 plus 20 (*trauma symbiote*); Init +7 (Dex, Improved Initiative); Spd 30 ft.; AC 20 (+3 Dex, +7 armor); Atk +8 melee (1–4+1/17–20, masterwork keenblade dagger) or +10 ranged (3d8, blaster pistol); SA Smite 2/day (+3 attack, +5 damage), turn undead 6/day; SQ *Detect evil*, divine grace, aura of courage, *remove disease, lay on hands* (10 hp/day); AL LG; SV Fort +5, Ref +4, Will +2; Str 13, Dex 16, Con 13, Int 10, Wis 13, Cha 16.

Skills and Feats: Climb +3, Freefall +5, Heal +3, Knowledge (imperial law) +6, Knowledge (religion) +4, Listen +4, Spot +4, Swim +3; Improved Initiative, Point Blank Shot, Precise Shot, Technical Proficiency.

Spells Prepared (1; DC = 11 + spell level): 1st—*protection from evil*.

Possessions: +1 blaster pistol with laser sight, masterwork laser carbine with laser sight, +1 combat fatigues, masterwork keenblade dagger, *dermpatch of cure serious wounds*, datapad, personal communicator.

Spellware: Darkvision, extra smite, ranged smite, trauma symbiote.

Typical TFS Paladin: Human Pal4/Rgr1; CR 7; Medium-size humanoid (human); HD 4d10+4 plus 1d8+1; hp 36 plus 20 (*trauma symbiote*); Init +5 (Dex, *boosted reflexes*); Spd 40 ft.; AC 20 (+3 Dex, +7 armor); Atk +8 melee (1–4+1/17–20, masterwork keenblade dagger) or +11 ranged (3d10+1, laser rifle); SA Smite 2/day (+3 attack, +5 damage), turn undead 6/day; SQ *Detect evil*, divine grace, aura of courage, *remove disease*, *lay on hands* (10 hp/day); AL LG; SV Fort +5, Ref +4, Will +2; Str 13, Dex 16, Con 13, Int 10, Wis 14, Cha 15.

Skills and Feats: Climb +2, Freefall +4, Heal +9, Hide +5, Intuit Direction +4, Jump +4, Knowledge (religion) +2, Listen +4, Move Silently +5, Search +4, Spot +4, Swim +2, Wilderness Lore +6; Far Shot, Point Blank Shot, Precise Shot, Skill Focus (Heal), Technical Proficiency, Track, Weapon Focus (laser rifle).

Spells Prepared (1; DC = 12 + spell level): 1st—*cure light wounds*, *endure elements*.

Possessions: +1 laser rifle with laser sight, +1 combat fatigues, masterwork keenblade dagger, *dermpatch of cure serious wounds*, datapad, personal communicator, medkit.

Spellware: *Boosted reflexes*, *extra smite*, *ranged smite*, *trauma symbiote*.

---

rescue operations and field care of soldiers in extremely dangerous battlefield environments. Task Force Sanctuary works closely with other paladin orders and conventional military units. The assignment of a TFS paladin or team to a unit provides an instant boost to morale, because every soldier knows it increases his chances of survival dramatically.

The headquarters of Task Force Sanctuary is on Endagar, the throneworld of House Handor, and in fact, it shares a military base with the famous War College. The order is a good partner to the college, training cadets in special operations and tactics, search and rescue, and participating in war games and maneuvers. The paladins and clerics of Task Force Sanctuary also serve at the base's infirmary. The unit's insignia is a crescent moon and three silver stars representing the compassion to pursue good, the will to uphold law, and the power to defeat evil.

THE CELESTIAL GUARD

This order devoted to the Warrior began as a hand-picked cadre of paladins who served as the palace guard for King Khelorn and his family. Over the centuries, its status changed as its membership increased and it assumed a broader range of duties. Today, the paladins of the Celestial Guard are known throughout the Kingdom of Qesemet as the deadliest and most dedicated soldiers in the known galaxy. A small, elite cadre is still selected from the ranks of the Celestial Guard to serve in the palace on Galador.

Paladins of the Celestial Guard served the armies of Qesemet as elite shock troops in the great war against the forces of Asamet. In many of the most terrible battles of the war, they were the first in and the last out, taking or holding positions crucial to Qesemet's war effort. For the last five millennia, their duties have shifted more and more to the Outlands as the Imperial Charter limited armed conflict between Qesemet and Asamet. Many Outlands worlds colonized by Qesemet are threatened by evil forces, whether powerful necromancers, dark artifacts uncovered by new excavation, or armies of giantkind united under a charismatic king. In some cases, contact with the Empire has given these forces access to technological weapons, greatly enhancing the threat they pose to innocent civilians and colonists.

The Celestial Guard is committed to the ideals of courage, valor, and righteous glory in battle. Its paladins devote themselves not only to martial prowess, but also to the rules and traditions of honorable combat. They always respect their adversaries, even if they hate the evil and corruption that defiles their souls. They recognize a common bond that unites not only their fellow paladins but their enemies as well. All who serve the Warrior, no matter how misguided they may be, know what it is to take life and face death on the battlefield. The insignia of the Celestial Guard is a celestial eagle clutching a longsword in its talons.

NOETIC ORDER

There are many monastic orders in the Dragon Empire. Some are devoted to the gods of the Unification Church or the Dualist Heresy, while others are dedicated to obscure philosophies that are incomprehensible to all but their most enlightened members. The Noetic Order is perhaps the most secretive and mysterious of these organizations.

The Noetic Order is devoted to understanding and developing the potential of the sentient mind. It was founded during the reign of Emperor Kupric by an elven psion named Henivol the Seeker. The elf believed that the true, underlying nature of the universe was *thought*. He taught his disciples that what mortals perceived as matter and energy were actually the manifested thoughts of the gods. By learning to attune oneself to these divine thoughts, and eventually to shape and mold them, the noetic would gain enlightenment and eventually become one with the Divine Consciousness of the universe.

The order's members are monks, psions, psychic warriors, and others devoted to comprehending and harnessing the powers of the mind. The Noetics lead a highly ordered and disciplined lifestyle, and it sometimes becomes too regimented and constraining to the order's more independent members. These Noetics often leave the monastery and wander the known galaxy, teaching the Noetic philosophy to others or pursuing their own individual path to enlightenment.

The Noetic Order believes that the concerns of ordinary mortals—wealth, power, love, hate, personal ambition, etc.—are distractions that lead the seeker astray in his quest for truth. As a result, the Noetics take no part in the politics of the Empire and avoid contact with the unenlightened as much as possible. When he founded the order, Henivol purchased a near-derelict orbital station in the Kulas system from the aristocorp of House Aranath. The Noetic monks spent decades restoring the station and creating an isolated monastery where they could pursue enlightenment without interference.

Of course, no one lives in an orbital station surrounded by hard vacuum without at least a little contact with the outside world. The Noetic monks provide for themselves and their order by crafting power stones, dorjes, crystal capacitors, and other psionic items. These rare and valuable items are sold to independent traders in exchange for the necessities the order requires for survival. Psionic items created by the monks of the Noetic Order have an excellent reputation for quality and are highly sought after by psionicists throughout the Dragon Empire.

ROYAL EXPLORATORY SERVICE

In 583 AE, King Khelorn ordered the establishment of an organization devoted to discovering and exploring the seemingly infinite frontier worlds beyond the borders of civilized space. The Royal Exploratory Service was created as an official agency of the Kingdom of Qesemet with its headquarters in the wilds of Meneer, the throneworld of House Golion. The RES attracted rangers, pilots, scientists, and other experts in many different fields.

For more than 5,000 years, the Royal Exploratory Service has been pushing the boundaries of the known galaxy. In that time, it has grown to become a massive organization with many diverse interests and programs. It is best known for the Explorer Teams and Contact Teams it organizes and supports. These teams are charged with charting unknown star systems, exploring new worlds, and making first contact with the countless cultures and civilizations sprinkled throughout the Outlands. The RES also sponsors Science Teams that follow the Explorer Teams to systems and worlds with unusual or intriguing characteristics, from rare stellar phenomena to particularly diverse or exotic biospheres.

The Royal Exploratory Service is not devoted entirely to exploration and scientific discovery. Since just before the great war, it has also been one of the primary intelligence arms of the Kingdom of Qesemet. Under the guise of Explorer Teams, Contact Teams, and Science Teams, intelligence agents are active throughout the Outlands gathering information that helps the kingdom react effectively to threats and crises. Few planets in the Outlands are any kind of technological threat to Qesemet or the Empire, so these operations usual target supernatural threats and incidents.

These covert teams identify and thwart the machinations of powerful spellcasters who use their power for evil. They also investigate reports of outsider activity, and often coordinate with the paladin teams, such as SOLARs, who are brought in to neutralize or contain these threats. Frequently, the paladins are operating on intelligence that was originally gathered "in the field" by RES agents. Many of these missions occur on worlds that have not been formally contacted by the Empire, and the agents must operate while concealing their true natures and blending in with a strange culture.

CHAPTER FOUR

THE PRIMOGEN SYSTEM

The rules in the *Starfarer's Handbook* give your players everything they need to create dramatic d20 System characters appropriate for galaxy-spanning fantasy adventure. The previous chapters of this book provide you with information on the known galaxy and the Dragon Empire that will help you create a campaign fitting for such heroes. In short, you and your players are just about ready to enter the Serpent's Eye galaxy and make it your own.

The next two chapters present extended examples of adventure locations that can play a major role in your **Dragonstar** campaign. This chapter provides extensive background details of a star system that offers a suitable launching pad for your game: the Primogen system.

HOW TO USE THIS SYSTEM

The Primogen system is designed as a possible starting point for any **Dragonstar** campaign. It's set on the border between the Outlands and the Dragon Empire, but with a bit of tweaking you could easily place it anywhere you like in the known galaxy. The actual location of the Primogen system isn't all that important. We recommend that you place it somewhere within the Domains of Asamet to maintain its desperate, gritty feel, but other than that, you can put it anywhere that works best for your campaign.

STARTING A NEW CAMPAIGN

If you're starting a new campaign with a clean slate—meaning you have no characters you're bringing over from an existing d20 System fantasy game—using the Primogen system is easy. If you like, you can simply set

your first few adventures in the Primogen system, probably on Primogen II itself. Some of the characters might even be native to the system, giving you a good reason to come back to this location again and again.

If all of the characters hail from some other part of the galaxy, you might need to create a good reason for them to be in the system. For some ideas on how to do this, see "Adventuring Opportunities" later in this chapter. As DM, you don't have to do all the work yourself, though. You can always ask the players to come up with their own reasons for why their characters are in the Primogen system. You have veto power over any suggestions, of course, but having several minds work on the situation at once can make coming up with a solution much easier. This may also help the players to develop their characters' backgrounds and goals, determining where they've been, what they've done, and what their plans and goals are.

STARTING A LEGACY CAMPAIGN

In **Dragonstar**, a legacy campaign is one that features characters, places, or situations from an existing d20 System fantasy game. Those elements you retain from the original campaign are the legacy you carry over into the next.

In a legacy campaign, the first thing you need to do is introduce your characters to the concept of the Dragon Empire. There are extensive guidelines for handling this introduction in Chapter 9: Dragonstar Campaigns.

Perhaps the star system where your existing campaign world is located is relatively close to the Primogen system. Maybe that world is newly colonized and relatively undeveloped, and Primogen is the closest system with an established imperial presence. This would make the Primogen system a natural staging point for the charac-

OVERVIEW

Primogen is a yellow star located on the nebulous border between the Dragon Empire and the Outlands. Imperial astronomers long considered Primogen to be a common system, one with a handful of planets that might someday be useful for colonization and commercial exploitation. There were literally hundreds of similar systems in the neighborhood, however, and so Primogen went unexplored for centuries—until a private exploration company discovered life on Primogen II.

When Captain Seanian first brought his ship, the *Mettle*, into the Primogen system, he immediately realized he'd made the find of his life. While most of the system's planets were barren, the second planet from the sun not only supported life but also an advanced civilization. It wasn't long before the *Mettle* made planetfall, heralding the imminent arrival of the Dragon Empire on its heels.

That was more than 20 years ago. Today, Primogen II is one of many worlds recently colonized by the Dragon Empire. This new status has caused a lot of friction among its varied peoples, many of whom have mightily resisted submission to the Empire. From the Empire's perspective, Primogen is yet another market to expand into, and offers the added benefit of a planet whose remnants of an ancient civilization offer untold riches both magical and mundane. The native inhabitants of the planet are of little importance to those who stand to gain the most from the exploration and exploitation of Primogen II.

ters to take their first steps into the Dragon Empire. From there, they can move on to other locations and new adventures, but they will always remember the Primogen system as their first encounter with **Dragonstar**.

DETAILS

The details of the Primogen system are intentionally left incomplete. First, it would be impossible to describe in depth an entire solar system in a full book, much less the space we have here. With many d20 System campaign settings, publishers have filled entire shelves with books describing the people and places of a single continent. Imagine how much more could be done with not just a full planet but a whole solar system.

Second, this allows you to put your own creative touches on the system and its worlds, tailoring it to the tastes of both you and your players. You know much more than we do about the kinds of games you and your friends like to play. That's one of the major strengths of your campaign, and you should always use it to your advantage. Take the framework we are giving you here and create something you can call your own.

THE SYSTEM

Primogen is a standard yellow star. There are five planets in the system. Imperial astronomers call them Primogen I, II, III, IV, and V, although the people of Primogen have their own names for the celestial bodies, of course. There's also a large and mineral-rich asteroid belt spinning between the orbits of Primogen III and IV. Each of these planets is described in brief below.

Primogen I

This small, barren planet is like a tiny, glowing cinder. Its orbit spins far too close to Primogen, making the place inhospitable to all but the hardiest forms of life. A creature immune to fire and heat might be able to withstand the hellish inferno, but few others could.

Primogen I has no atmosphere, and any water that might have once existed on the surface has long since boiled away. The planet's crust is little more than molten

THE PRIMOGEN SYSTEM

System Type: Single yellow star
Planets: 5

PRIMOGEN I

Planet Type:	Terrestrial
Size:	Small
Gravity:	Low
Atmospheric Density:	Vacuum
Atmospheric Composition:	None
Geology:	Standard
Hydrosphere:	No water
Biosphere:	Very scarce
Population:	None
Technology:	None
Magic:	None

PRIMOGEN II

Planet Type:	Terrestrial
Size:	Medium
Gravity:	Standard
Atmospheric Density:	Standard
Atmospheric Composition:	Breathable
Geology:	Standard
Hydrosphere:	Dry
Biosphere:	Scarce
Population:	Low
Technology:	Imperial
Magic:	High

PRIMOGEN III

Planet Type:	Terrestrial
Size:	Small
Gravity:	Low
Atmospheric Density:	Vacuum
Atmospheric Composition:	None
Geology:	Rugged
Hydrosphere:	Very dry
Biosphere:	No life
Population:	Very low
Technology:	Imperial
Magic:	High

PRIMOGEN IV

Planet Type:	Gas giant
Size:	Very large
Gravity:	Extreme
Atmospheric Density:	Very dense
Atmospheric Composition:	Hostile
Geology:	Flat
Hydrosphere:	Very dry
Biosphere:	Very scarce
Population:	None
Technology:	None
Magic:	None

PRIMOGEN V

Planet Type:	Terrestrial
Size:	Small
Gravity:	Low
Atmospheric Density:	Vacuum
Atmospheric Composition:	None
Geology:	Rugged
Hydrosphere:	Very dry
Biosphere:	None
Population:	Very low
Technology:	Imperial
Magic:	Low

lava featuring hundred-foot waves of liquid rock rising up and then crashing down as the planet is tormented by the gravitational effects of three moons and the nearby sun.

Primogen I remains undeveloped, though a survey team equipped with hostile environment gear was recently dispatched to explore and map the surface. The primary goal of this survey mission was to assess the planet's suitability for mining efforts, but it remains incomplete. The last radio trasmission from the surface of the planet indicated that the survey team was being attacked by some unknown life form and all contact was lost soon thereafter. The Viceroy of Primogen II has considered hiring an independent team to investigate but hasn't yet found anyone qualified or properly equipped.

Primogen II

Primogen II is the jewel in the Primogen crown. It is the only planet in the system that's capable of sustaining life without technological assistance.

In the ancient past, Primogen II was teeming with sentient life nearly from pole to pole. At some point in the world's history, however, a cataclysm wracked the planet and shifted it on its axis, causing global temperatures to rise to levels only barely within the habitability zone. Desertification claimed much of the planet's tropical and temperate zones, and people gradually began to retreat to the planet's warming poles.

From space, Primogen II looks like a mottled brown sphere capped on the top and bottom with crystal blue and lush green. Only near the poles can most of the planet's denizens survive for long. Much of the planet's land area has been abandoned to the infernal winds and shifting sands of the great equatorial deserts.

Primogen's axial tilt is pronounced enough that the southern and northern latitudes periodically experience long periods of day or night. In the middle of summer, it is common for the peoples of Primogen to face literally weeks of nearly constant sunlight. In the winter, it is just the opposite, with weeks passing with only the dimmest gray light to warm the frigid air.

The vast majority of Primogen II's sentient inhabitants live in narrow bands encircling the planet's north and south poles. The small amount of land that is hospitable on the planet has been a source of conflict among the peoples of Primogen II for centuries, and dozens of wars have been fought as the populations migrated to the poles. This near-constant state of battle suppressed the development of technology on the planet, as the ongoing wars claimed whole generations and resources were constantly diverted to the fighting. The immediacy of the neverending conflict made it nearly impossible

for anyone to concentrate on anything else, and the ravages of the wars upon the peoples and their planet meant that questions of basic survival often took precedence over more esoteric pursuits like science and engineering. This history of conflict actually dates to the time before the cataclsym that almost destroyed Primogen II. Indeed, the cataclysm itself was one consequence of this centuries-long war.

Once every year, Primogen II is plunged into shadow for about a month by the partial eclipse of the sun caused by the passing of Primogen I. This has occurred at different times over the years, due to the vagaries of the planetary orbits. However, for the past several generations, the month of shadow has always fallen during the equinox—spring to the northerners, and fall for the southerners.

Primogen II has a single, large moon that is close enough to the planet to actually create tides in the dunes of the great desert that encircles the planet's waist. While these are far less pronounced and noticeable than ocean tides, they do have a measurable effect on the always-changing topography of the great deserts. Centuries of this tidal activity and the inexorable work of the wind have buried the ruined cities of ancient Primogen II under a sea of sand. The same forces can just as easily expose a ruin that had previously lain hidden for centuries.

Most of the major races are well represented on Primogen II. There are dwarves, elves, halflings, gnomes, orcs, and humans. Different cultures are scattered all across the narrow temperate bands of the planet's northern and southern hemispheres.

The planet is also populated with a great number of wild creatures. Monsters are common in the deserts and in the wastelands and badlands that border them. These creatures have long been a menace to frontier settlements. The unquestioned masters of the great deserts in pre-contact times were the blue dragons, but they have since left their wilderness homes and been welcomed into the Dragon Empire aristocracy.

Primogen III

Primogen III is a small, airless rockey planetoid. The black veins that run through its gray surface are visible signs of the high levels of adamantine found in the crust, and they can even be identified from orbit. This precious metal is abundant throughout the mountains and twisted landscape of the rugged planet.

This wealth of adamantine was what first drew explorers to the Primogen system. It's only when Captain Seanian found an inhabited planet in the system

that he realized he had truly stumbled upon a fortune waiting to be claimed.

Deep-space mining operations are always difficult to set up and maintain. Getting people to work in such isolated and hostile conditions can be challenging, though dwarves are usually more willing than most. The presence of a hospitable world like Primogen II makes the operation must simpler. Instead of having to wait months or even longer for supplies or fresh workers, mine administrators can acquire new goods and personnel from the nearby planet whenever they are needed. Primogen II also offers the miners a pleasant diversion during their brief vacations, and this has had a tremendous impact on both safety and morale.

The mining operation on Primogen III is maintained by Noros Interplanetary, the leading aristocorp of the black dragon clan. The Empire taxes the adamantine mines of Primogen III heavily, but the aristocorp has already recouped its initial investment and the operation is one of its most profitable sources of revenue.

Primogen III has two large moons, each of which is rich in iron and other minerals. The moons have no atmosphere and are completely devoid of life. Noros Interplanetary has established smaller mining operations on these moons to exploit its mineral weath. While these mines are much less profitable than the adamantine mines on Primogen III, their proximity to the larger concern allows them to be operated efficiently. Cargo ships deliver supplies and new workers to all three mining operations at the same time, and iron and other ores from the moons is used to fill out the holds of freighters loaded with adamantine.

The Asteroid Belt

Beyond the orbit of Primogen III and millions of miles from the orbit of the gas giant in the system's fourth orbit, a massive asteroid belt is scattered across interplanetary space like pebbles on a beach. The Primogen asteroid belt is believed to be the remains of a planet that either never fully formed during the birth of the system or that was destroyed billions of years ago by some celestial impact or collision. Millions of asteroids from tiny shards to massive planetoids tumble through space at varying speeds in their neverending orbit of the sun.

Given the mineral wealth of the inner system, the asteroid belt might never have attracted extensive mining operations. The presence of a habitable world in the system made this far more feasible an undertaking. Primogen II offers both a reliable source of supplies and personnel, as well as a developing market for the raw materials mined from the asteroids. The asteroid belt's riches, however, were not sufficient to motivate Noros Interplanetary, and the massive conglomerate instead sold mineral rights to independent concerns.

Private mining companies and individual prospectors purchase claims from the aristocorp. Usually, these claims cover a single rock, though some of the largest host several claims owned by competing companies and prospectors. The miners work their claims and usually transport their ore to Primogen II where it is sold at the new Mineral Exchange in Praxilus. Ore haulers occasionally dock at one of the larger asteroids in the belt to fill out their holds before teleporting out of the system, but these visits are typically few and far between. As a result, most independent miners have to maintain their own starship and only make the jump in system when they've harvested enough ore to make a profitable round trip to Primogen II.

Most ships entering and leaving the Primogen system take care to avoid the asteroid belt altogether. Most teleport in to the outer fringe of the system, pause to calculate new coordinates, and teleport to their final destination in system—usually Primogen II or Primogen III.

The asteroid belt is home to several families of asterwraths, and legend has it that a star dragon claims a lair in one of the larger rocks. If this is true, no one who has ever found the rumored lair and lived to tell the tale. Still, the rumor alone spurs many enterprising starship captains to lead their crews into the very heart of the asteroid belt in the desperate hope of locating the star dragon's lair—hopefully while it isn't home.

Primogen IV

Primogen IV is a massive gas giant, about 100 times the size of Primogen II. No explorers have yet penetrated deep into the atmosphere of the planet. However, there is a permanet orbital station that is home to a scientific team charged with investigating the miles of impenetrable gas and cloud that perpetually shroud the planet. A second orbital serves as a supply and refueling station for starships passing through the system. Hydrogen and helium are harvested from the gas giant

to provide fuel for the fusion drives that provide conventional propulsion for these ships.

With nine moons of various sizes orbiting it, Primogen IV has the most natural satellites of any planet in the system. Most of these moons are icy balls of rock, but one is actually inhabited. A powerful elven wizard named Galiad Molentrian has carved a fortress out of Primogen IV's seventh moon.

Molentrian is a noted recluse, unhappy with visitors of any kind. The less expected they are, the less welcome. The fortress is protected by security measures of all kinds, both magical and technological. Few people have actually ever seen Molentrian, which often gives rise to rumors that the wizened elf is dead, leaving his fortress open to exploration by intrepid adventurers. So far, no one has visited the fortress and returned to confirm these rumors. Perhaps the wizard lives and punished them for their intrusion, or maybe the elf really is dead but his fortress's defenses continue to guard his secrets.

Primogen V

Primogen V is a relatively small rocky planet, about half the mass of Primogen II. It has no moons, but it is encircled by a banded ring of dust and ice. When these minute particles catch the light of the distant sun, the rings look like a sparkling belt of diamonds and gold.

Primogen is a frigid, airless place with little or no valuable minerals trapped within its frozen crust. It is occasionally used as a base of operations for a group of pirates plying their trade in the Primogen system, but it is also the occasional nesting place of a space kraken native to the system. The beast has chased off most of the pirates, forcing them to find new bases further in system.

One pirate ship seems not to have any problems with the space kraken, though. This is the *Dark Thrasher*, a ramshackle freighter under the command of an orc by the name of Kraxt. This Kraxt's all-orc crew apparently reveres the space kraken as a god or some kind of personal totem. Whether the prayers the orcs offer up to the beast—or maybe just dumb luck—have saved their lives, the massive creature has thus far ignored the orc freebooters.

Kraxt has long taken advantage of this fact. When being pursued by faster ships, Kraxt usually runs directly for Primogen V, hoping that the legends of the space kraken might be enough to scare off those giving chase. If this isn't enough, Kraxt goes hunting for the kraken, hoping he can survive long enough to find the creature and convince it that the ship trailing the *Dark Thrasher* would make a more appetizing feast.

HISTORY

Like most systems in the Dragon Empire, Primogen is a comparatively young system, having formed from the interstellar dust four or five billion years ago. It lies on the border of the Outlands hundreds of light years from Draconis Prime. Of course, its location has had no effect on the native inhabitants save to explain the timing of the system's discovery and colonization by the Dragon Empire.

Imperial astronomers have known of Primogen's existence since the founding of the Empire. They didn't, of course, know about the potential riches the system guarded. Even using powerful magic and advanced technology, stellar analysis hasn't progressed to the point where the details of a system can be identified across light years of space. Astronomers can predict whether or not planets might be found orbiting a star, and can sometimes even identify them using powerful space-based telescopes. They usually cannot, however, determine with any certainty the number of planets in a system. They can usually determine whether or not the planets they've identified are rocky terrestrial worlds or gas giants, but they can provide few other details. Only explorers who actually make the journey to the system can gather this kind of hard data. This is one of the factors that make the Empire's exploration of the galaxy so painstakingly slow. There is no faster means of thoroughly cataloging the assets of the billions of star systems in the galaxy.

Primogen II is far and away the greatest of its system's treasures. Not only does the planet boast extensive mineral wealth, but it is also the home to thousands of species of creatures, including dozens of sentient life forms that are cousins to those found elsewhere in the Dragon Empire. The gods once smiled upon this planet and gifted it with life, though it has since experienced more tragedy than triumph. In fact, before contact with the Empire, many of the peoples of Primogen II were beginning to lose faith in their ancient gods.

PRE-EMPIRE

In ancient days, long before even the Empire was born, Primogen II was a rather ordinary world typical of those scattered across the known galaxy. It had several large continents separated by massive oceans, and its polar regions were capped in ice. The equatorial belt of the planet was so warm that it was inhospitable to most life forms, and most creatures avoided the great deserts for the cooler temperate regions.

These were the glory days of Primogen II. The peoples of the planet were wise and healthy, and there always seemed to be plenty to go around. There were conflicts, of course, but most of these were based on greed or desire rather than true need.

In those days, the major cities of Primogen were on the edge of the great deserts, large ports from which trade expeditions and caravans were regularly launched to sail the sea of dust, linking the far-flung realms into a common civilization. These realms were rich in arcane lore and many of their masters wielded powerful magic.

At some point thousands of years ago, a being known as the Faceless Man appeared on Primogen II and unified the evil races—mostly goblinoids—under a common banner. A series of wars between the armies of the Faceless Man and the desert realms ensued, and at first it appeared that the goblinoids would be defeated. The masters of the desert realms used their magic to vanquish their foes and the great cities themselves were never truly threatened. Always, however, the evil armies seemed to grow, and each subsequent attack would be a greater threat than the last. Each time, the masters of the desert realms would turn still-greater magics against their foes. Too late, they realized they'd been caught in a trap. Eventually, they were faced with an army so vast that the magic required to defeat it would inevitably tear the world assunder. The desert realms had always relied on their magic, and they had no other weapons with which to fight this battle. Faced with a terrible choice, they prayed to their gods for mercy and forgiveness and unleashed titanic arcane forces to destroy the Faceless Man's host.

Their efforts were successful. The evil army was destroyed and the Faceless Man himself was either vanquished or banished to another plane of existence. Unfortunatley, the magics the masters of the desert realms unleashed were also catastrophic. Mountains were thrown down, new ones were raised from tortured earth, and oceans were vaporized in an instant. The planet itself shifted on its axis, causing titanic storms that swept across the land destroying everything in their path. The great civilizations of the desert realms were lost, though many of its people were able to escape the destruction.

The cataclysm irrevocably altered the planet's delicate ecological balance. In the aftermath, Primogen II grew warmer and the great deserts began to expand into once-temperate regions. The polar caps—never very thick to begin with—started to melt, and the people gradually migrated further toward the poles, doing their best to escape the infernal heat and aridity that had claimed their ancestral homelands.

The encroaching sand and dust eventually consumed the ruins of the great cities that once guarded the borders of the great deserts. The citizens of these once-brilliant

jewels took with them what they could and fled. The ruins of the proud cities stood empty and quickly vanished beneath the ever-shifting dunes.

As the people from one land moved into another, this inevitably led to competition over space, food, and water. The survivors of the desert realms also encountered the remnants of the goblinoid nations that had once served the Faceless Man as they both fled the destruction. Inevitably, this competition led to a continuation of the ancient war.

Now, however, the war was fought on a small scale, between desperate families and small bands of refugees with stickes, stones, and what weapons they recovered from the ruins of the old cities. The battles were horrible, pitting the survivors of the desert realms—humans, elves, dwarves, halflings, and gnomes, predominantly—against the remnants of the goblinoid nations—goblins, orcs, hobgoblins, bugbears, and others.

Some races had been decimated by the cataclysm. The continuing wars finished off some of them, leaving them with only a handful of survivors to carry on the legacy of their fallen kin. It looked like the rest of the peoples might follow in the footsteps of the lost races, and sooner rather than later. The ravages of war had reduced these desperate refugees to the point where conflict over

territory was no longer necessary. Most of them nevertheless continued out of habit and an unquenchable thirst for revenge.

Most of the leaders on both sides realized they were facing extinction. Every year, their numbers were thinned and their quality of life plummeted lower. The end of the world was clearly drawing near.

Then the first starship arrived.

ENTER THE EMPIRE

When the *Mettle* landed at Praxilus, the people of Primogen II had no idea how their lives were about to change. Praxilus was then—and is today—the largest city on the planet, situated almost exactly on Primogen II's northern pole. Captain Seanian and his crew—elves and humans, mostly—looked like the Primogenians themselves, not some strange aliens from beyond the stars. They spoke the same languages and worshipped similar gods.

At first, the people of Primogen believed that the *Mettle* must have come from the now-legendary Southern Hemisphere of the planet. Travel between the two regions was extremely hazardous, so it would only make sense that their long-lost kin would be the ones to visit in a craft that came from the sky.

It quickly became clear, however, that the truth was far stranger than even these wild imaginings.

With the arrival of the newcomers, conflicts in the North ceased almost immediately. At first, the Primogenian leaders weren't pleased to learn of a star-spanning empire that would treat their planet as the most recent of many new colonies, but eventually both greed and good sense won out over these concerns. Before long, these leaders were knocking each other over as they jockeyed for the best position with the newcomers, each of them wanting to be the Empire's primary liason with the native inhabitants of the planet.

The Empire took to Primogen II like a hungry man to a roasted pig. Despite its ecological and political problems, this was a planet that was ripe for the picking. In fact, the ruins of the ancient desert realms gave the imperial plunderers hope of finding all sorts of powerful artifacts and wondrous lore buried deep beneath the sand.

The Primogenians were perhaps unfortunate that their star system was located within the Domain of Noros. Had they found themselves in one of the Domains of Qesemet, their transition would have certainly gone easier. The metallic dragon lords would have first turned their attentions toward finding some peaceful resolution to the centuries-old disputes between the peoples of Primogen II. Instead, the representatives of the black dragons moved in, declared martial law, and began to pursue their own interests in Primogen II, leaving the native inhabitants of Primogen II to fend for themselves.

Almost immediately, Praxilus became the center of the imperial presence on Primogen II. While much of the city continued to look like the ramshackle frontier town it was before contact with the Empire, a gleaming imperial enclave began to grow at its center. This enclave became in effect a city within a city. The streets of the enclave were paved with smooth concrete and new buildings were quickly raised using advanced materials. High technology, though hard to come by at first, made life as comfortable as possible for the imperials who came to live on this Outlands world.

Beyond the enclave's borders, rickety buildings constructed of unpainted wooded clapboards and ancient stone flanked muddy, unpaved streets. The natives of Primogen II continued to flock to Praxilus hoping to benefit from the wealth of their new masters. The city quickly became overcrowded, as both the children of the desert realms and the goblinoids recognized that the enclave in the city's heart offered their best chance for survival. Almost overnight, the city became the new battleground for their age-old struggle. Despite the declaration of martial law, militias formed to protect each group from attacks by the other. These militias were lit-tle more than gangs of armed thugs, and they did nothing to curtail violence. The small garrison of Imperial Legionnaires that eventually arrived on the planet did nothing to stop the conflict, either, and in fact rarely even ventured outside the borders of the imperial enclave. The city was eventually partitioned into halves by an informal border called the Green Line. The eastern districts were controlled by the goblinoid militias, called the Army of the Faceless Man, or just AFM, in Common speech. The militas loyal to the descendants of the desert realms, called the Free Nations, controlled the western half of the city.

This situation continues in Praxilus to this day. Much of the city looks like a warzone, with burned cars choking the streets, bombed-out buildings marring the skyline, and refugee camps that create a vast sea of tents completely encircling the city. Praxilus is one of the most dangerous places to live in the Dragon Empire, as armed gangs rule the streets and no authorities are present who are interested in controlling the violence.

WELCOME TO THE EMPIRE

Primogen II is one of the newest additions to the Dragon Empire. Despite this—or perhaps because of it—the planet still has a frontier feel. The imperial enclave in Praxilus is still fairly small, supporting about 5,000 imperial citizens. Even in the enclave, some high-tech conveniences are in short supply, and beyond its borders, high technology is almost non-existent. Devices can occasionally be found second hand from the dealers and scavengers that supply the gray and black markets of Praxilus. The AFM and Free Nations militias usually snatch up any weapons and armor that become available, however.

Primogen's colonization was exceptionally rapid by historical standards. Captain Seanian and his crew were the first imperials to enter the system, and they landed on Primogen II almost immediately. There was no lengthy period of investigation by either the RES or the ISPD and there was no need for an invasion or protracted conflict. As soon as Seanian reported his discovery to House Noros authorities on Morngond, imperial ships began arriving in orbit around Primogen II on a regular basis. Imperial Police officers, agents of the ISPD, and a small garrison of Legionnaires were among the first to arrive.

PRIMOGEN'S POLITICS

Long before the arrival of the Empire, the people of Primogen II had divided into two major factions: the descendants of the desert realms and the survivors of the Faceless Man's armies. As noted earlier, both factions are concentrated in the city of Praxilus and the sprawling refugee camps that encircle it. The streets of the city are effectively in a state of anarchy, and the two militias—the AFM and the Free Nations—are too deeply involved in their ongoing guerrilla war to provide any law and order. The Viceroy has established a state of martial law, but the imperials are generally content to hide between the walls of their enclave and ignore the violence tearing the city apart.

The AFM is led by the orc Warlord Yaruk. Its headquarters is in the old stonework gatehouse on the eastern edge of the city. Orcs and goblins make up the majority of the AFM's membership, though many other evil humanoid races are represented as well. Gangs armed with archaic melee weapons and an occasional firearm man the checkpoints along the Green Line, patrol the streets of AFM-controlled territory, and launch occasional raids into Free Nations territory. The goblinoids also frequently raid the refugee camps on the western side of the city. The refugees in this area—mostly humans and elves—rarely enjoy any protection from the Free Nations militias, who usually stick to the relative safety of their territory within the city.

The Free Nations militias are led by Wileth Narlion, an elf sorcerer. While the AFM enjoys the reputation of their evil natures, Narlion is no less ruthless than Warlord Yaruk. Goblinoids—whether militia thugs or innocent civilians—who are caught on the west side of the Green Line by Narlion's gangs are killed with no questions asked and no possibility of quarter. Narlion's brutal tactics were forged over years of bloody conflict, and while some among his advisors attempt to moderate them, his hatred for his enemies is legendary and knows no mercy.

Not only have the imperials done nothing to control the violence between the AFM and the Free Nations, there is even evidence that they are encouraging it. The Praxilus Hotel in the imperial enclave has become the headquarters for journalists from across the Empire. Media coverage of the urban warfare is improving, and reports are starting to filter out that the ISPD is arming both militias with firearms and explosives. Commenting on the increasing levels of violence in the city, one journalist described Praxilus as "A cocktail party where half the guests hate the other half and want to kill them…And there's an ISPD agent standing at the front door handing out guns to those going inside."

Warlord Yaruk is growing old, and dozens of his lieutenants are jockeying for his position once he is either removed or succumbs to old age. Only a handful of these ambitious soldiers actually have any chance at claiming Yaruk's power, including Yaruk's eldest son, Garuk.

Among the Free Nations, Narlion has done his best to forge strong ties with Baron Udorhil, the black dragon who has been appointed viceroy of the planet by Mezzenbone. Narlion had some qualms about allying himself with such an evil creature, but he believes it is the only way he can maintain his power over his people and continue his war against the AFM.

To many of the peoples who have fought for decades under Narlion's banner, the imperial enclave is a symbol of a better life and a brighter future. They are eager to end the war with the AFM and build new lives for themselves in this new world. Narlion, however, remains unwilling to give up the fight. He has developed an unlikely friendship—or at least mutual respect—with Methenes, the captain of the ISPD contingent in Praxilus. Narlion has encouraged Methenes to harass his own allies in order to convince them that the Free Nations militias are still necessary to ensure their security and that of their families and friends.

Narlion has also developed ties with Slivern, the black dragon who is Noros Interplanetary's highest-ranking executive on Primogen II. While Lord Udorhil wields absolute political power on the planet, Lord Slivern effectively controls all of the wealth that flows in and out of the Primogen system. In many ways, this makes him a more powerful ally than Udorhil. Slivern knows that Narlion is trying to play him against the Viceroy, but the dragon generally ignores these petty designs of a provincial lord with no real power.

If Narlion loses the favor of either Slivern or Udorhil, either one of them could topple him from power—or even destroy the Free Nations entirely. For now, while many of his followers hope for change, they realize that Narlion is currently their only safeguard. Even if peace were made with the AFM, they might find themselves targeted by the ISPD or other imperial factions without the elf's connections to protect them.

Of course, the Primogenians recognize a despot when they see one. They have had no direct contact with the Emperor, but Viceroy Udorhil is himself a sufficiently black-hearted tyrant to breed animosity and resentment. There are other dragons on the planet—creatures who have suddenly gained immeasurable status with Primogen's colonization by the Empire—and the planet's natives know of the chromatic dragons' evil natures. They are not fooled by the mantle of civilization and sophistication worn by Udorhil and his draconic entourage, and no "principle of active morality" will ever persuade them that a black dragon has their best interests at heart.

OTHER CITIES

While the city of Praxilus is unquestionably the heart of the imperial presence on Primogen II, there are several other cities scattered across the Northern and Southern Hemispheres. Many of these are, like Praxilus, strange hybrids of the archaic and the modern. Stone walls encircle prefabricated buildings of plastic and composite, steel and glass. Modern hovercraft motor noisily down narrow, cobblestone streets barely wide enough for horse-drawn carts. Radio antennas and satellite dishes bristle from ancient villas appropriated by the imperials.

The Dragon Empire's wealth has inevitably trickled down to some of the native inhabitants of the planet. A privileged few, such as Yaruk and Narlion, now live in accommodations with conveniences that would have been unthinkably luxurious to them prior to contact. On the other hand, many people have not gotten a share of this new prosperity. Thousands of people still live much as they did before the arrival of the Empire. The only thing that has changed is that the gap between the lowest classes and the highest has become almost immeasurable.

Some of the more isolated towns and remote settlements are almost untouched by the Empire and its advanced technology. In these places, the lives of ordinary people have not changed at all, and the only evidence they have of the changes elsewhere on Primogen II are the contrails and sonic booms with which imperial aircraft and spacecraft mark the distant sky.

THE GREAT DESERTS

Primogen II's equatorial and temperate regions are girded by vast, seemingly endless seas of sand and rock. These wastelands are home to monstrous creatures, savage storms, and infernal temperatures. Adventurers who can survive these dangers may also discover great treasures. The ruins of the great cities of the ancients still lie buried beneath the dunes, and the treasures they guard have long been forgotten by the descendants of those who once lived within them.

As is often the case, freelance adventurers quickly followed the first imperial representatives to arrive on Primogen II. While many of them use Praxilus as a base of operations, a string of frontier towns has sprung up along the edges of the great deserts. Most of these towns boast only a handful of permanent residents, and they owe their existence entirely to the adventuring groups

they support. These towns usually boast a small inn, a trading post, and a few modest dwellings that are home to those who live and work in the town. Adventurers use these towns to rest, recuperate, and resupply between expeditions into the desert.

ADVENTURING OPPORTUNITIES

As presented, there are dozens of opportunities for adventure in the Primogen system. Some of these are outlined below, but we encourage you to create your own based on the unique preferences of both you and your players.

Exposing Narlion's relationship with Captain Methenes. To maintain his grasp on his people, Narlion is helping Captain Methenes harass rival leaders—and even his own lieutenants—among the Free Nations militias. Once the characters learn of this conspiracy, what they should do with their knowledge is up to them. Will they provide evidence of the conspiracy to one of the investigative journalists stationed at the Praxilus Hotel, or will they use the information to blackmail the elf leader?

Investigating the secrets of the great deserts. The tides and winds that shift the sands of the great deserts often expose the ruins of ancient cities and fortresses. The characters could launch an expedition to explore such a ruin before the sands bury it once again. They would have to contend with the hazards of the tomb, the limited amount of time they have, and rival groups of explorers trying to beat them to its treasures.

Making contact with the wizard Galiad Molentrian. The characters may decide they need to meet with the mysterious wizard of Primogen IV's seventh moon. Perhaps they need a special service—or maybe it's for one of Primogen II's rulers instead. Either way, the characters must travel to the moon, enter the wizard's citadel, penetrate his defenses, and discover whether he is truly alive or dead.

Bringing in the pirate Draxt. There's a bounty of 50,000 credits on the head of Draxt, which should be enough incentive for most characters to go after the pirate. An attack upon their ship or the ship of a friend could make this bounty hunt a personal vendetta instead.

Helping out with a mining strike on Primogen III. The executives of Noros Interplanetary are driven by a single motivation: profits. Slivern has been notoriously stingy with wages in the mines of Primogen III. While this had led to record profits, the miners are extremely dissatisfied with their lot. The characters can sign on as agitators (working with the miners) or freelance enforcers and security (keeping the miners in line and hard at work).

Rescuing a mining crew stranded in the asteroid belt. A mining crew is occasionally stranded in the asteroid belt, usually as the result of some industrial accident or life support failure. Maybe a ship was destroyed by a collision with an asteroid. Perhaps pirates boarded the craft and abandoned the crew at an old mining outpost. Or maybe an asterwrath attacked the ship. Whatever the case, the characters' own ship is in the vicinity when they receive a distress call. The spacer's code obligates them to lend assistance, but what if the danger hasn't entirely passed?

Joining the Free Nations in their fight. Heroic characters may feel obligated to aid the people of the Free Nations in their centuries-long struggle against their goblinoid enemies. Many of these people are innocent refugees who have been preyed upon by the evil humanoids their entire lives. Of course, once they become involved in the struggle, the characters will soon realize that the situation is much more complicated than they'd at first assumed. For starters, Narlion seems more concerned with accumulating power and privilege than he does with protecting his people or improving their lives. And what of the mad orc shaman that wanders the streets muttering nearly incomprehensible prophecies of the Faceless Man's return?

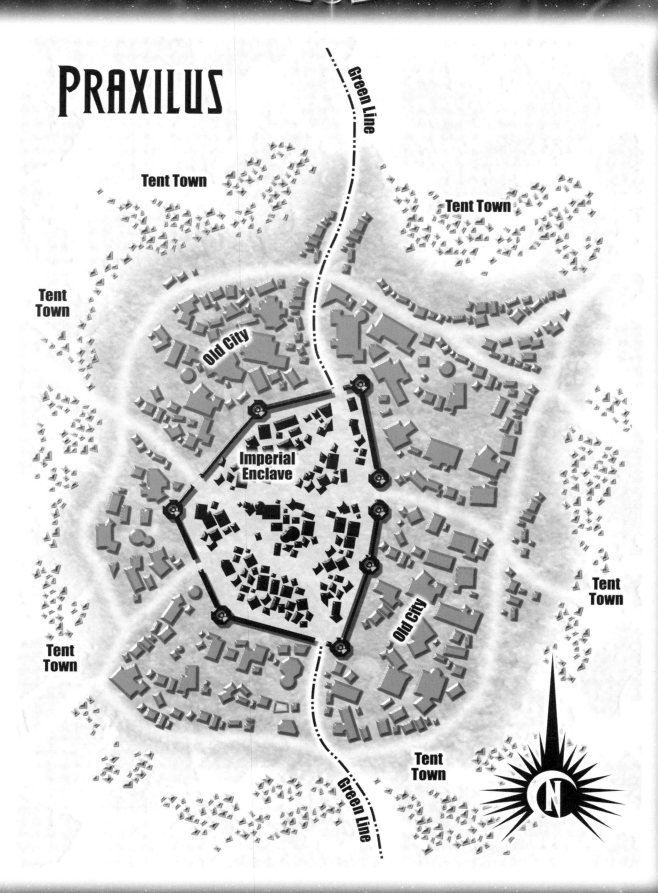

PRAXILUS

Green Line

Tent Town

Tent Town

Tent Town

Old City

Tent Town

Imperial Enclave

Old City

Tent Town

Tent Town

Green Line

N

CHAPTER FIVE

OUTLANDS STATION

By now you have enough of an overview of the known galaxy to run an exciting **Dragonstar** game. The only thing missing is a place to start. The previous section offered details of a star system and planet you can use to begin your party's adventures.

If you already have a world of your own in mind, however, the details of the Primogen system might be of limited use to you. This section, on the other hand, details an adventure location that can be plugged in to just about any **Dragonstar** campaign. It is a unique deep-space facility called *Outlands Station*.

WELCOME TO *OUTLANDS STATION*

Outlands Station is the only existing prototype of a new concept developed during the reign of the previous Dragon Emperor. In many ways, it is similar to other orbital stations. It is a convenient supply point and repair depot for starships and efficient production and research facility for industries that depend on microgravity and vacuum.

The difference between *Outlands Station* and other orbital facilities is dramatic, however. *Outlands Station* is not just a single facility, it is actually a series of space stations separated by hundreds of light years but linked together by a network of teleportation portals. This network is similar to the one that connects the Long Road, and it allows near-instantaneous travel from one side of the Empire to the other.

Ten different facilities in all make up *Outlands Station*. Each is located along the frontier of one of the 10 imperial domains. Unlike the Long Road, which is linear, Outlands Station is a true nexus through which you can travel to any domain from any other. A network of conveyor tracks that runs throughout the docking sections of the station even allows small spacecraft to be moved through the teleportation portals from one sector to another.

HOW TO USE *OUTLANDS STATION*

Outlands Station can be used in just about any **Dragonstar** campaign. You can place the different sectors in any Outlands systems you choose, and it offers an excellent base of operations for characters ranging from free traders, to mercenaries, to explorers. Of course, most adventurers use the station as a staging point for expeditions into the Outlands. If you're using the Primogen system described in the previous section, you could even put one sector of *Outlands Station* in orbit around Primogen II.

Alternatively, you could place a sector of *Outlands Station* in orbit around the world that is home to your traditional fantasy campaign. It may be a recent addition to this newly colonized world and offer your characters an exciting introduction to the strange civilization of the Dragon Empire.

Wherever you locate the 10 sectors of *Outlands Station*, you should be able to make good use of the details in this section. They are designed to be self-contained and as fully modular as possible. When you integrate the station into your own campaign, you'll want to create stronger ties to local planets, systems, and people. This will bring the station to life and entrench it as a fully realized location in your campaign.

OVERVIEW

Outlands Station is a sprawling orbital complex under the direct authority of the Dragon Empire. Its mission is to serve as a supply and staging point for trade and exploration in the Outlands and as a convenient bridge between the imperial domains. In the 75 years since its construction, *Outlands Station* has become one of the most popular destinations in the Empire for adventurers, traders, and explorers testing their fortune along the frontier.

Today, *Outlands Station* is under the command of Captain Dredda Salvort, a half-dragon/half-human who is distantly related to the Emperor himself. Captain Salvort rules over the space station with an iron fist, hampered only by the fact that the people under her aren't nearly as competent as she is.

Captain Salvort's mission, as she sees it, is to get law-abiding citizens in and out of her space station quickly as possible—as long as she is able to extort certain "docking" fees from them in the process. Despite her larcenous tendencies, Salvort is otherwise a fine commander and a real stickler for the rules. Those who have crossed her in the past often remark that the only reason she cares about the rules is so that she can levy more and larger fines upon any transgressors.

In any case, Captain Salvort runs a tight space station. The crew and station personnel are generally content, as long as they don't incur the captain's wrath by provoking her notoriously short temper. Two particularly recalcitrant employees were found floating in a depressurized airlock, but in both cases the station's physician ruled the deaths accidental.

Most passengers and pilots pass through *Outlands Station* without incident. Knowledgeable pilots pay the requisite bribes and are sent quickly on their way. Of course, not everyone is so lucky.

The 10 independent facilities that are linked together to form *Outlands Station* are called sectors. The name of each sector is taken from the imperial domain it occupies: Deserene Sector, Golion Sector, Mazorgrim Sector, Noros Sector, etc. The entire station is under a single unified command, that of Captain Salvort, and the same laws and regulations are in place for each sector. Nevertheless, each sector possesses something of the feel and culture of its domain: Deserene Sector is a bright and cheery place populated with disciplined and industrious people, while Noros Sector is dark, somewhat gritty, and frequented by those of low reputation.

In each sector, there is a teleportation portal leading to each of the other sectors. Despite the well-marked cor-

ridors and frequent electronic map terminals, navigating inside *Outlands Station* can be a disorienting task for many newcomers. There are security checkpoints at each portal and travelers must pay a 100 cr fee each time they pass through. Crew members and authorized personnel have badges that let them traverse the portals as often as they need to without paying. However, the semi-permanent residents of the station tend to avoid the fees by restricting their activities to a single sector.

The station was conceived by the engineers of House Golion and the copper dragon's sector was the first constructed. It also houses the station's overall administration and command facilities, including the bridge. For this reason, Golion Sector is traditionally known as the Hub and most veterans of the facility come to think of it as the heart of *Outlands Station*.

The station was constructed as a gesture of good faith between the royal houses as the time for Asamet to assume the Golden Throne drew near. Its principle mission is to facilitate the exploration and development of the Outlands frontier. The station has already achieved this objective by providing a convenient bridge for both transportation and communication between the far-flung reaches of the domains' most isolated regions. While the station has occasionally been the focus of political disputes, the royal houses for the most part have been content to leave it alone and see what happens. Though it is less than 100 years old, every indication is that *Outlands Station* will prosper.

IMPORTANT PEOPLE

The following NPCs live and work on *Outlands Station*. Each is described in some detail here. Their game statistics appear in the section at the end of this chapter.

CAPTAIN DREDDA SALVORT

Dredda Salvort is tall and lithe, with more draconic features than human ones. Her scarlet scales are flecked with hints of gold, and she wears her uniform proudly. Her reptilian eyes betray her cold demeanor, and her haughty attitude deprives her of the fierce beauty she might otherwise enjoy.

Captain Salvort is the illegitimate daughter of a half-dragon father and a human mother. She was raised in the foreign sectors of the subterranean warrens below hellish Arangorn, the throneworld of House Mazorgrim. Many times during her childhood, Dredda and her mother went to watch the great dragons assembling at the royal court, and her mother would spend hours

Captain Dredda Salvort

telling Dredda about her father's people.

Once she came of age, Salvort went to her father and demanded that he recognize her as his kin. Tests confirmed Salvort's claims, but rather than take his daughter in, the dragon arranged for her to find a high-ranking post in the Imperial Legions instead. With Mezzenbone on the Golden Throne, this was a choice assignment, though it prevented Salvort from gaining the recognition she so craved.

Although Salvort is "stuck in this gods-forsaken tin can" for the foreseeable future, she has decided to make the most of it. She is channeling bribes, kickbacks, and extortion money into private accounts, and sending a substantial stipend to her mother on Arangorn. She's not sure what she'd have to do to win her way into the court of House Mazorgrim, but she figures money is a decent place to start.

FIRST MATE POLISTO

Polisto is a broad and tubby human with short-cropped brown hair and a generally jolly demeanor. Always ready with a friendly word and a charming smile, he is the antithesis of his captain.

First Mate Polisto

Polisto is an ex-lieutenant in the Imperial Legions, where he served at several locations throughout the Domain of Esmer. The lords of House Esmer are notorious draconic supremacists, but Polisto will cheerfully explain that he never pays any attention to imperial politics. The young Polisto was conscripted by the Legions when he came of age, and he found that he took well and easily to military life. Since being assigned to *Outlands Station*, however, he has grown somewhat soft. Salvort cares little for Polisto, but she demands even less of him. He spends most of his time in the Coffin Nail, a tavern in the Hub, chatting up the owner, Thefra Wisten.

LIEUTENANT FASILA DURLEXIS

Durlexis is a female drow, but a rare childhood disease left her body stunted and twisted. Despite her physical challenges, she is nonetheless as ruthless as any other in the galaxy. She is all too aware of her malformed physique and is painfully sensitive about it. If a stranger makes disparaging comments about her appearance, Durlexis refuses to show her hurt. However, she takes her revenge upon the person at the earliest opportunity.

As head of security for *Outlands Station,* Durlexis is capable of providing a lot of misery to those she dislikes, and she has a long memory for those who slight her. She is extremely good at her job, despite her emotional nature, and she has become a bane of the smugglers who have tried to move contraband through the station.

While Captain Salvort commands the facility's personnel, Durlexis is likely the most powerful person aboard *Outlands Station*. She is backed by the full authority of the ISPD, and therefore, by the might of the Emperor himself. In matters of the security of the station, the Empire, or the Emperor, Durlexis has the authority to step in and assume command of the facility. While she has yet to exercise this authority, everyone aboard—especially Captain Salvort—knows she could at any time if she considers it justified.

Like most ISPD agents, Durlexis is responsible for intelligence and counter intelligence in addition to traditional security duties. The high level of traffic on *Outlands Station* makes it an excellent resource for gathering information on the activities of the royal houses, aristocorps, and many private organizations and individuals. No one knows more about what is happening aboard *Outlands Station* than Lieutenant Durlexis.

Lieutenant Fasila Durlexis

Doctor Haldo

CHIEF ENGINEER FALLYNOCK

Fallynock is a wizened gnome from Aranal. Only a scant 13 months from retirement, he has seen more of the galaxy than he normally cares to talk about. If he gets a few ales in him, though, he can spin tales of far-ranging adventure guaranteed to keep a listener's attention well into the night.

Old Fallynock is short, even for a gnome. He claims to have shrunk several inches over the years, particularly during the stint he did on Chamus IV, a high-g world that did its best to smash him flat for the two years he was stationed there.

Fallynock is a fantastic engineer. He's a bit leery of all the different folks that pass through the station. He knows that if anything goes wrong with the station's system, he'll be the first one to suffer for it. All he wants to do is make it through to his retirement in one piece, and every day he prays to the Father to grant his wish. He hopes to open a little robotics shop on Aranal once his tour is finished.

Chief Engineer Fallynock

DOCTOR HALDO

Doctor Haldo is a halfling from Primogen II. As a youth, before the planet was contacted by the Empire, Haldo trained as a healer at a monastery. First contact introduced him to a whole new universe of science and medical technology. From the moment he first gained access to modern scientific references, Haldo began absorbing information on the life sciences and medicine.

Haldo's passion did not go unnoticed. He was conscripted by the Legions and assigned to the medical corps where he distinguished himself as a quick learner and ready student of modern technologies and methods. Haldo had hoped to see the galaxy during his tour with the Legions, but he never got any farther than *Outlands Station*. While the assignment is far less hazardous than that of a combat medic, Haldo is nonetheless a bit disappointed about the lack of adventure in his life. He consoles himself with the thought that his request for a transfer must go through sooner or later.

Thefra Wisten

LIEUTENANT KRUUSAX

Kruusax is the kind of half-orc blessed with a face that even his own mother couldn't love. Indeed, Kruusax was abandoned by his human father shortly after birth, as his mother couldn't stand the sight of the "squalling ball of soft pink flesh." As port master, he's often the first person people see as they step into the space station, which is as Captain Salvort likes it. She feels it sets the proper tone for any visit.

Kruusax may have a gruff manner that matches his features, but underneath it all there is a heart of gold. He keeps a cat in his quarters, and he loves this creature above all else. He goes a long way to keep his pet happy, and veteran pilots docking at the station often bribe him with catnip and toys to win his favor.

While Kruusax succumbs to the occasional bribe, he is never willing to just look the other way. He makes random spot inspections of the ships that dock at his station, and no amount of graft can persuade him not to report any serious or hazardous infractions to Captain Salvort.

Lieutenant Kruusax

THEFRA WISTEN

Wisten is a handsome female dwarf considered pretty even by human standards. Many of her patrons deem her to be the biggest attraction in the Coffin Nail, the tavern that she runs in the Hub. By all accounts, it certainly isn't the flavorless food or the watered-down ale she serves.

Miss Wisten, as her regulars call her, runs her place well, but she has little incentive to improve her offerings. There are few enough taverns on the station, and she knows her clientele keeps coming back for the atmosphere and companionship, rather than the quality of her food and drink. Besides, her offerings are better than the synthetic stuff most ship crewmen and adventurers get their fill of.

More than anything else, Wisten is an accomplished conversationalist. She always has a kind and easy word for everyone who stumbles through her door, and she's an even better listener. If anyone on the station wants advice on social or personal matters, the Coffin Nail is usually their first stop.

THE CREW

The hundreds of personnel under Captain Salvort's command are mostly low-level crewmembers. They come from worlds scattered throughout all of the imperial domains, from developed worlds to new Outlands colonies. Many of them, especially those in security, are in the middle of tours with the Imperial Legions.

LOCATIONS

Each of the major locations on *Outlands Station* is described in some detail below. Most of the habitation sections of the station are equipped with antigravity generators that provide a consistent 1g environment. The docks and industrial areas of the station have no gravity. Artificial gravity is expensive, so it is only used in areas where it is especially convenient or useful.

DAY AND NIGHT

Because it connects different locations throughout the Empire, *Outlands Station* has established its own day-night cycle. Timekeeping on the station is matched to the imperial clock on Draconis Prime. The station therefore enjoys a standard 24-hour cycle, with 12 hours of "day" and 12 hours of "night." The station remains fairly active around the clock, however, and there is little apparent difference between the two.

SECURITY

Many areas of the space station are designated as off-limits to all but authorized personnel. This includes Captain Salvort, First Mate Polisto, Lieutenant Durlexis, Doctor Haldo, Chief Engineer Fallynock, Lieutenant Kruusax, and any of the security officers assigned to *Outlands Station*.

Private quarters, of course, are off-limits to anyone but the people who reside in them. Captain Salvort, First Mate Polisto, Lieutenant Durlexis, and Chief Engineer Fallynock have the authority to override access security on private quarters.

THE BRIDGE

Gravity: 1g

This is the command center for the entire network of linked stations. It is located in the central habitation module of Golion Sector, also known as the Hub. Captain Salvort spends most of her time here. When she is not on duty, First Mate Polisto can usually be found on the bridge coordinating the activities of the crew. The

space station's major systems, including communications and life support, are controlled from the bridge. Engineering has its own set of parallel controls as well. The bridge is off-limits to all but authorized personnel.

There are windows set into the bulkheads on the bridge, but it also features a massive electronic screen that displays schematics of the station's interior and the region of space around each sector.

An operator at a terminal on the bridge can unlock, lock, open or close any door in the entire complex remotely. This requires the proper passcodes or some other way of accessing the computer-control systems (Use Device DC 40).

THE BRIG

Gravity: 1g

This location in the Hub is where prisoners are held until they can be transferred to the custody of the local domain authorities or the Imperial Police. On rare occasions, Captain Salvort herself can convene a military court to pass judgment on the personnel under her command. This includes the crewmembers and security personnel described in this section, with the exception of the civilian Thefra Wisten.

The walls of the brig are made of four-inch-thick composite, while the sliding door is two-inch-thick steel. The door can only be opened by Captain Salvort, First Mate Polisto, Lieutenant Durlexis, Chief Engineer Fallynock or authorized security officers by means of a voiceprint and a retinal scan (Open Lock DC 35).

The station gets a lot of visitors, and the brig is almost always occupied by at least a couple of prisoners. The turnover rate is high, however, as they are processed and transported to planet-side detention facilities as quickly and efficiently as possible.

Lieutenant Durlexis's office is just outside the brig. She is usually here when she is not sleeping, patrolling the station, or helping Lieutenant Kruusax inspect incoming ships.

SICKBAY

Gravity: 1g

This is the domain of Doctor Haldo and his medical staff. The small facility is located in the Hub, on the deck directly below the bridge, and features 40 beds, an operating room, a critical care ward, a quarantine ward, and several autodocs for emergency care of critically injured or ill patients.

The doctor is here intermittently during daylight hours. When he has no patients, he spends his time doing research on the computer terminal in his office, but he can just as often be found hanging around at the

Coffin Nail. Even when he isn't around, some of his staff are always on duty in sickbay, and the doors are always open to walk-in patients.

ENGINEERING

Gravity: 1g

This is where Chief Engineer Fallynock spends most of his time. This complex is located on one of the lowest decks in Golion Sector, near the docking bays. It is filled with the tools and machines necessary to keep the station in top working order.

The maintenance and repair infrastructure for spacecraft is all located in the station's docking and repair bays. Outlands Station doesn't have sufficient resources for Fallynock to repair severely damaged spacecraft—extensive repairs and refits require a fully equipped spacedock.

Th engineering section is only accessible to authorized personnel. Fallynock is only here about half the time during the daylight hours. He spends a good part of each day supervising repairs and routine maintenance throughout the station. The door to the engineering section is kept locked whether or not Fallynock is around.

Fallynock can also be found here on occasion in the evenings, tinkering with one or more of his own personal projects. However, he's even more likely to be found socializing at the Coffin Nail.

THE COFFIN NAIL

Gravity: 1g

The Coffin Nail is the most popular tavern on *Outlands Station*, and is the destination of choice in the Hub for crewman on leave from their ships. The food served at the Nail is of notoriously mediocre quality, usually some frozen packaged dinner heated up by Thefra Wisten or one of her three regular employees: Balterra (a young, female halfing), Eltra Finnegat (a female human), or Timot Velentra (a male half-elf). The food is only a few steps above cardboard with regards to both taste and nutrition, but many people aboard the space station manage to choke it down rather than having to cook for themselves.

Captain Salvort and Lieutenant Durlexis are the only two members of the crew who do not regularly visit the Coffin Nail. They normally dine in their own quarters, alone.

The Coffin Nail is always dimly lit, except during the breakfast rush. Wisten likes to call it "mood lighting." The walls of the tavern are decorated with trophies and knickknacks recovered from explorers and traders on countless Outlands worlds. These decorations include a wide variety of archaic weapons, a collection of gobli-

noid tribal masks, an array of hand-drawn maps, and many other souvenirs of the regulars' travels to distant lands.

The Coffin Nail's drinks are usually watered down, but the spacers who frequent the establishment are often happy to find any source of strong spirits. And despite the bad food and watered-down drinks, most of the regulars would never be found anywhere else.

DOCKING BAYS

Gravity: 0g

There are several docking bays in each sector of *Outlands Station*. These bays are situated at regular intervals around the outer ring of each sector.

For permission to dock at the station, a spacecraft must contact the Sector Controller's Office and be transmitted the appropriate navigational and docking codes. No ship whose shields or weapons are powered up is allowed to dock at the station.

Guided by the controller, a spacecraft drifts slowly through the bay doors and lines up with the assigned docking port. Magnetic couplings secure the ship to the docking cradle, connecting one or more of the ship's airlocks with the station. The docking bays for smaller ships are fully pressurized once the bay doors have been closed and resealed. The massive bays designed for larger ships are never pressurized, requiring the crew to enter the station through the airlocks. Umbilical lines for air and fuel extend to the ship and maintenance crews and robots enter the docking bay to attend to the ship's technical needs.

A network of conveyor tracks runs from the smaller docking bays into the heart of each sector. These tracks are equipped with magnetic couplings that can lock on to Colossal or smaller spacecraft. The tracks lead through interior bay doors into a network of massive corridors that crisscross each sector. Teleportation portals are constructed at various locations throughout this network of access tunnels, and this allows relatively small spacecraft to be transported almost instantly from one side of the Empire to another. A ship can dock at *Outlands Station* in the Domain of Deserene and emerge a short while later from a docking bay in the Domain of Altara.

This feature of *Outlands Station* is extremely useful for the free traders and explorers who use it most, but it isn't free. Transferring a ship between sectors costs 2,000 cr for Gargantuan and smaller vessels and 5,000 cr for Colossal vessels. While steep, these prices are nonetheless much less expensive than the multiple *teleports* it would take a starcaster to cross the Empire from one Outlands frontier to another.

NPCs

Game statistics for the major NPCs of *Outlands Station* are listed below.

Captain Dredda Salvort: Female half-dragon/half-human Sor7; CR 11; Medium-size dragon; HD 7d6+14; hp 41 plus 20 (*trauma symbiote*); Init +6 (Dex, Improved Initiative); Spd 30 ft.; AC 22 (+2 Dex, +4 natural, +6 armor); Atk +7 melee (1d6, bite), +7 melee (1d4, claw), +5 ranged (3d8, blaster pistol); SA Breath weapon (cone of fire, 6d10, DC 19); SQ Low-light vision, darkvision 60 ft., immune to *sleep* and paralysis, immune to fire; AL LE; SV Fort +4, Ref +4, Will +6; Str 18, Dex 14, Con 15, Int 11, Wis 12, Cha 22.

Skills and Feats: Concentration +6, Knowledge (arcana) +4, Profession (spacer) +4, Scry +4, Spellcraft +4; Combat Casting, Improved Initiative, Point Blank Shot, Technical Proficiency.

Spells Known (6/7/7/5, DC = 16 + spell level): 0—*daze, detect magic, detect poison, disrupt undead, mage hand, read magic, resistance*; 1st—*cause fear, charm person, comprehend languages, sleep, true strike*; 2nd—*detect thoughts, locate object, invisibility*; 3rd—*dispel magic, gaseous form*.

Possessions: Blaster pistol, *+2 armor vest, dermpatch of cure critical wounds*, datapad, personal communicator.

Spellware: *Enhanced Charisma, trauma symbiote*.

First Mate Polisto: Male human Ftr5; CR 7; Medium-size humanoid; HD 5d8+10; hp 36 plus 20 (*trauma symbiote*); Init +5 (Dex, Improved Initiative); Spd 30 ft.; AC 16 (+1 Dex; +5 armor); Atk +9 ranged (3d8, blaster pistol); AL CG; SV Fort +6, Ref +2, Will +2; Str 15, Dex 13, Con 14, Int 10, Wis 12, Cha 13.

Skills and Feats: Freefall +4, Jump +4, Listen +3, Spot +3, Pilot +4; Alertness, Improved Initiative, Point Blank Shot, Precise Shot, Technical Proficiency, Weapon Focus (blaster pistol), Weapon Specialization (blaster pistol).

Possessions: Masterwork blaster pistol with laser sight, combat fatigues, *dermpatch of cure light wounds*, datapad, personal communicator.

Spellware: *Trauma symbiote*.

Lieutenant Fasila Durlexis: Female drow Rog5: CR 8; Medium-size humanoid; HD 5d6+15; hp 35 plus 20 (*trauma symbiote*); Init +5 (Dex, Improved Initiative); Spd 30 ft.; AC 16 (+1 Dex; +5 armor); Atk +6 ranged (3d8, blaster pistol); SQ +2 saves vs. enchantments, +2 on Will saves vs. spells, SR 16, spell-like abilities, darkvision 120 ft., light blindness, find secret doors; AL NE; SV Fort +4, Ref +5, Will +2; Str 15, Dex 13, Con 16, Int 12, Wis 12, Cha 11.

Skills and Feats: Bluff +6, Climb +7, Diplomacy +8, Disable Device +6, Freefall +6, Gather Information +8, Intimidate +5, Jump +7, Listen +8, Pilot +6, Search +6, Spot +8, Use Device +6; Alertness, Improved Initiative, Technical Proficiency.

Possessions: Blaster pistol, *+1 armor vest*, datapad, personal communicator.

Spellware: *Trauma symbiote*.

Doctor Haldo: Male halfling Exp3; CR 3; Small humanoid; HD 3d6; hp 13; Init +5 (Dex, Improved Initiative); Spd 20 ft.; AC 13 (+2 Dex, +1 size); Atk +5 ranged (1d10, holdout laser); SQ +2 saves vs. fear; AL NG; SV Fort +2, Ref +4, Will +5; Str 9, Dex 14, Con 11, Int 15, Wis 12, Cha 12.

Skills and Feats: Bluff +3, Climb +4, Freefall +2, Heal +8, Hide +6, Jump +4, Listen +4, Move Silently +4, Pilot +2, Profession (surgeon) +6, Use Device +8, Sense Motive +4, Spot +4; Improved Initiative, Skill Focus (Heal), Technical Proficiency.

Possessions: Holdout laser, medkit, datapad, personal communicator.

Chief Engineer Fallynock: Male gnome Exp6; CR 6; Small humanoid; HD 6d6+6; hp 30; Init +1 (Dex); Spd 20 ft.; AC 12 (+1 Dex, +1 size); Atk +4 ranged (1d10, light autopistol); SQ Low-light vision, +2 saves vs. illusions, +1 to attacks vs. kobolds and goblinoids, +4 dodge vs. giants; AL N; SV Fort +2, Ref +4, Will +5; Str 9, Dex 13, Con 13, Int 13, Wis 10, Cha 10.

Skills and Feats: Alchemy +3, Freefall +7, Hide +5, Listen +4, Pilot +4, Navigate +7, Repair +13, Search +9, Sense Motive +9, Spot +9, Use Device +14; Born Spacer, Gearhead, Low-G Tolerance, Technical Proficiency.

Spells: 1/day—*dancing lights, ghost sound,* and *prestidigitation*; treat as if cast by a 1st-level caster.

Possessions: Light autopistol, datapad, personal communicator, masterwork toolkit.

Thefra Wisten: Female dwarf Exp3; CR 2; Medium-size humanoid; HD 3d6+3; hp 16; Init +0; Spd 20 ft.; AC 10; Atk +2 melee (1d6 plus

stun, stun baton); SQ Darkvision 60 ft., stonecunning, +2 saves vs. poison, +2 saves vs. spells, +1 to attacks vs. orcs and goblinoids, +4 dodge bonus vs. giants; AL CG; SV Fort +2, Ref +1, Will +6; Str 11, Dex 11, Con 13, Int 10, Wis 13, Cha 14.

Skills and Feats: Bluff +6, Freefall +2, Gather Information +4, Hide +4, Listen +4, Move Silently +2, Pilot +2, Use Technology +2, Research +2, Search +2, Sense Motive +4, Spot +4; Information Junkie, Iron Will, Technical Proficiency.

Possessions: Stun baton, datapad, personal communicator.

Lieutenant Kruusax: Male half-orc Ftr3: CR 5; Medium-size humanoid; HD 3d10+6; hp 27 plus 20 (*trauma symbiote*); Init +5 (Dex, Improved Initiative); Spd 30 ft.; AC 16 (+1 Dex; +5 armor); Atk +6 ranged (3d8, blaster pistol); SQ Darkvision 60 ft.; AL CN; SV Fort +5, Ref +2, Will +2; Str 17, Dex 13, Con 14, Int 10, Wis 12, Cha 8.

Skills and Feats: Demolitions +3, Freefall +3, Jump +4, Listen +5, Search +2, Spot +5, Pilot +3; Alertness, Improved Initiative, Point-Blank Shot, Technical Proficiency, Weapon Focus (blaster pistol).

Possessions: Blaster pistol with laser sight, combat fatigues, dermpatch of cure light wounds, datapad, personal communicator.

WEAPONS STATIONS

Gravity: 0g

Each sector of *Outlands Station* maintains weapon emplacements for the defense of the sector facilities. These weapon stations feature standard laser and plasma cannons. The gun platforms are on automated turrets, giving them the widest possible fire arcs. The stations are kept weightless to allow the gunners quick and easy mobility. The station's offensive capability is fairly limited and certainly not sufficient to hold off a determined attack by one or more warships. It is, however, an effective deterrent for pirates and armed smugglers. The weapons stations are open only to authorized personnel.

ENGINE ROOMS

Gravity: 0g

This is where each station sector's reactors are located. Under normal circumstances, the reactors only provide power to the sectors. However, simple drive systems provide enough thrust to move each sector at low velocities over short distances. These areas are open only to authorized personnel.

STORAGE BAYS

Gravity: 0g

Each sector maintains expansive storage areas adjacent to the docking bays where goods, supplies, replacement parts, and repair machinery are kept. Ship captains can rent space in these bays for their cargoes, though this mandates a second round of inspections by the security team. Lieutenant Kruusax is extremely careful about security for these areas, as it is his primary responsibility.

HABITATION SECTIONS

Gravity: 1g

Each sector boasts an extensive section that offers comfortable private quarters to visitors. The station's population at any given time is often far in excess of its capacity, however, and there is usually a long waiting list for these facilities. Most newcomers to the station discover that they must continue living on their ship when they arrive at *Outlands Station*. Rooms, when they are available, are 100 cr per night, 500 cr per week, or 1,800 cr per standard month. Given these outrageous rates for sparsely furnished, cramped quarters, most visitors don't mind sleeping aboard ship.

CHAPTER SIX

MAGIC ITEMS

Magic items play as big a role in a **Dragonstar** campaign as they do in traditional fantasy settings. Your character can win magic items in battle with Imperial Legionnaires, discover them in lost cities on forgotten planets, or liberate them from the hoards of terrible monsters.

Some of these items are truly ancient and are usually recovered from Outlands worlds: wood-carved wands and staves, weapons of stone, iron, and steel, alchemical potions in quaint glass or ceramic vials. Other magic items were produced using the high technology of the Empire: Wands and staves may be manufactured with plastic or carbon fiber, while weapons are forged with titanium or other high-strength alloys. While these items are often more technically sophisticated than their counterparts found in the Outlands, they are never mass-produced. Magic items must be created by individual spellcasters working long hours and sacrificing some measure of their own life energy. Even in the Empire, you won't find such people working on assembly lines.

Magic items of all the types listed in the d20 System core rules are available in **Dragonstar**: armor and shields, weapons, potions, rings, rods, scrolls, staffs, wands, and wondrous items. In addition, two new classes of magic items are introduced in this chapter that are unique to **Dragonstar**: vehicle enhancements and spellware.

ARMOR

Magic armor is as common in the Dragon Empire as it is on most Outlands worlds. However, the high-tech armor manufactured in the Empire provides even more protection when enhanced with magic. As in the core rules, enhancement bonuses for armor range from +1 to +5 and stack with normal armor bonuses. All magic high-tech armor is masterwork, either mass-produced brands of exceptional quality or custom armors crafted by master armorsmiths. As a result, the armor check penalties for all magic armors are reduced by 1. Magic high-tech armors may also be given special abilities, as described in the core rules. Shields are extremely uncommon in the Dragon Empire, and magical shields are almost never crafted. Magic shields are still abundant on many Outlands worlds and are occasionally carried by adventurers who acquired them in the course of their travels.

RANDOM ARMOR TYPE

d%	Armor	Armor Cost*
01–10	Heavy clothes	+155 cr
11–20	Flight suit	+200 cr
21–35	Armor vest	+225 cr
36–50	Combat fatigues	+250 cr
51–60	Battle suit	+500 cr
61–70	Battle armor	+650 cr
71–75	Combat armor	+900 cr
76–80	Shock armor	+2,150 cr
81–85	Combat exoskeleton	+3,650 cr
86–90	Assault exoskeleton	+5,150 cr
91–95	Combat hardsuit	+10,150 cr
96–100	Assault hardsuit	+15,150 cr

All magic armor is masterwork armor (with an armor check penalty 1 lower than normal).

* Add to enhancement bonus and reference core rules (DMG 180) to determine total market price.

MAGIC ARMOR SPECIAL ABILITIES

Most magic armors only have enhancement bonuses. However, armors can also have any of the special abilities listed in the core rules, as well as the new special abilities listed here. An armor with a special ability must have at least a +1 enhancement bonus.

Antigravity: This useful special ability is a favorite of Legionnaires stationed aboard warships in the Imperial Navy. It negates all gravity check modifiers, allowing the wearer to move and act as if in standard gravity. (The armor's armor check penalty still applies normally).

Caster Level: 13th; *Prerequisites*: Craft Magic Arms and Armor, *reverse gravity*; *Market Price*: +4 bonus.

Fire Evasion: This special ability protects the armor's wearer as if he had the evade fire monk class ability. Once per round when he would normally be struck by a ranged weapon, he can make a Reflex saving throw (DC 20). If the ranged weapon has an enhancement bonus, the DC increases by that amount. If the character succeeds, the armor deflects the attack. The character must be aware of the attack and not flat-footed. Attempting to evade a ranged attack doesn't count as an action.

Caster Level: 7th; *Prerequisites*: Craft Magic Arms and Armor, *shield*; *Market Price*: +3 bonus.

Radiation Resistance: A suit of armor with this special ability is often black or safety orange, depending on its original design profile. It is often decorated with the universal symbol for radiation and is often worn by military personnel working around nuclear reactors or stationed near blast sites. The armor protects against the first 10 points of damage from radiation each round and provides a +10 circumstance bonus on Fortitude saves to resist the effects of radiation (similar to a hostile environment suit).

Caster Level: 5th; *Prerequisites*: Craft Magic Arms and Armor, *resist radiation*; *Market Price*: +3 bonus.

Underwater Action: A suit of armor with this special ability is often green or blue in color. It is a favorite of marines and adventurers who routinely operate below the surface of the ocean. The wearer is treated as unarmored for the purposes of Swim checks and is able to breathe underwater indefinitely.

Caster Level: 9th; *Prerequisites*: Craft Magic Arms and Armor, *freedom of action*, *water breathing*; *Market Price*: +4 bonus.

Weightless Moves: This armor is magically constructed to equalize the wearer's sense of direction and balance, allowing him to move freely and effectively in zero-g. It adds a +10 circumstance bonus to the wearer's Freefall checks. (The armor's armor check penalty still applies normally).

Caster Level: 5th; *Prerequisites*: Craft Magic Arms and Armor, *freedom of action*; *Market Price*: +1 bonus.

SPECIFIC ARMORS

The following armor types are usually crafted with the specific qualities described here.

Ace Pilot's Flight Suit: This durable *+2 flight suit* features additional enhancements that make it a favorite of pilots throughout the Dragon Empire. The armor magically enhances the pilot's ability to control his craft, providing a +10 circumstance bonus on Pilot checks. The armor also allows the wearer to *feather fall* once per day as the spell cast by a 5th-level caster.

Caster Level: 5th; *Prerequisites*: Craft Magic Arms and Armor, *feather fall*; *Market Price*: 11,200 cr; *Cost to Create*: 5,700 cr + 220 XP.

Airborne Combat Armor: This *+2 combat armor* is favored by Legionnaires in airborne and special operations units. The rigid components of the armor are slim and light, and the armor can be worn under normal clothing without attracting attention. It is considered light armor, and has a maximum Dexterity bonus of +6, an armor check penalty of –1, and an arcane spell failure chance of 10%. It allows characters to move freely with no penalty to their base speed. The armor also allows the wearer to *fly* on command as the spell once per day.

Caster Level: 5th; *Prerequisites*: Craft Magic Arms and Armor, *fly*; *Market Price*: 24,900 cr; *Cost to Create*: 12,900 cr + 480 XP.

Arcanist's Vest: This *+1 armor vest* is incredibly light and extremely thin and can be worn under normal clothing without revealing its presence. The armor has a 0% chance of arcane spell failure, and this makes it a sought-after item among arcane spellcasters.

Caster Level: 5th; *Prerequisites*: Craft Magic Arms and Armor, *mage armor*; *Market Price*: 4,225 cr; *Cost to Create*: 2,225 cr + 80 XP.

Dragon Powered Armor: This *+4 combat hardsuit* is custom designed for the elite shock troops of the Imperial Legions and is crafted to give the wearer a draconic appearance. The integral combat helmet is created to look like a horned dragon head, and the wearer looks out through a narrow, slanting faceplate. The armor allows the wearer to make claw attacks that deal 1d10+4 (x2 critical) points of damage, strike as +1 weapons, and affect the target as if he had been struck by a *slow* spell (Will negates DC 14).

Caster Level: 11th; *Prerequisites*: Craft Magic Arms and Armor, *slow*; *Market Price*: 61,150 cr; *Cost to Create*: 35,650 cr + 1,020 XP.

Elven Battle Suit: The durable polymers of this battle suit are laced with a weave of light mithral fibers.

The battle suit is treated as light armor, has maximum Dexterity bonus of +8, an armor check penalty of 0, an arcane spell failure chance of 5%, and allows the wearer to move freely with no penalty to his base speed. The elven battle suit weighs about 8 lb.

Caster Level: —; *Prerequisites*: —; *Market Price*: 4,500 cr.

WEAPONS

As in traditional fantasy campaigns, weapons are among the most common and valued magic items in **Dragonstar**. As with armor, magic weapons have enhancement bonuses ranging from +1 to +5, and these bonuses apply to both attack and damage rolls in combat. All magic weapons are masterwork weapons, but their masterwork attack bonuses do not stack with their enhancement bonuses. However, the +1 bonus to attack rolls granted keenblade melee weapons does stack with magic enhancement bonuses.

As in the core rules, enhancement bonuses for magic ranged weapons and magic ammunition do stack. However, the "ammunition" for high-tech energy weapons cannot be enchanted, nor can it be enhanced by weapon special abilities (such as the flaming or pulsing

HIGH-TECH WEAPON TYPE DETERMINATION

d%	Weapon Type
01–20	Melee weapon*
21–60	Simple ranged weapon
61–90	Martial ranged weapon
91–100	Explosive weapon

* For tables listing random common and uncommon melee weapons, see the core rules (DMG 184).

SIMPLE RANGED WEAPONS

d%	Weapon	Weapon Cost*
01–10	Ammunition	
01–10	Arrows (50)	+350 cr
11–20	Bolts, crossbow (50)	+350 cr
21–60	Bullets (25)	+350 cr
61–80	Shells, shotgun (15)	+350 cr
81–100	Taser darts (15)	+350 cr
01–05	Autopistol, heavy	+700 cr
06–10	Autopistol, light	+600 cr
11–15	Blaster carbine	+1,200 cr
16–25	Blaster pistol	+900 cr
26–30	Blaster rifle	+1,300 cr
31–35	Crossbow, automatic	+500 cr
36–40	Holdout laser	+500 cr
41–45	Holdout pistol	+450 cr
46–50	Hunting carbine	+650 cr
51–55	Hunting rifle	+750 cr
56–60	Laser carbine	+1,000 cr
61–70	Laser pistol	+800 cr
71–75	Laser rifle	+1,100 cr
76–80	Longbow, compound	+500 cr
81–85	Screamer pistol	+750 cr
86–90	Screamer rifle	+950 cr
91–95	Shotgun	+700 cr
95–100	Taser pistol	+400 cr

MARTIAL RANGED WEAPONS

d%	Weapon	Weapon Cost*
1–10	Assault blaster	+2,300 cr
11–20	Assault carbine	+950 cr
21–30	Assault laser	+1,800 cr
31–40	Assault rifle	+1,050 cr
41–45	Blaster cannon	+5,300 cr
46–50	Flamethrower	+1,300 cr
51–55	Laser cannon	+4,300 cr
56–65	Machinegun, heavy	+1,800 cr
66–75	Machinegun, light	+1,300 cr
76–80	Plasma cannon	+7,800 cr
81–85	Plasma rifle	+3,300 cr
86–90	Sniper rifle	+1,100 cr
91–100	Submachine gun	+800 cr

EXPLOSIVE WEAPONS

d%	Weapon	Weapon Cost*
01–10	Ammunition	
01–05	Grenade, adhesive	+350 cr
06–15	Grenade, concussion	+400 cr
16–20	Grenade, flash-bang	+350 cr
21–30	Grenade, fragmentation	+400 cr
31–40	Grenade, incendiary	+400 cr
41–45	Grenade, nausea	+350 cr
41–50	Grenade, smoke	+330 cr
51–60	Grenade, stun	+350 cr
61–70	Missile, HE	+800 cr
71–75	Missile, HEAP	+1,050 cr
76–80	Missile, AA	+1,300 cr
81–90	Rocket, HE	+550 cr
91–95	Rocket, HEAP	+700 cr
96–100	Torpedo	+1,300 cr

EXPLOSIVE WEAPONS (CONT.)

d%	Weapon	Weapon Cost
1–20	Grenade launcher	+800 cr
21–40	Missile launcher	+7,800 cr
41–45	Missile launcher, multishot (4)	+12,300 cr
46–50	Missile launcher, multishot (8)	+15,300 cr
51–55	Missile launcher, multishot (16)	+20,300 cr
56–60	Missile launcher, multishot (24)	+30,300 cr
61–80	Rocket launcher	+5,300 cr
81–100	Rocket launcher, multishot	+6,800 cr

All magic weapons are masterwork weapons.

* Add to enhancement bonus and reference core rules (DMG 180) to determine total market price.

special abilities). Ammunition for projectile weapons such as slug-throwers and needlers are often enchanted with magic enhancement bonuses and special abilities.

MAGIC WEAPON SPECIAL ABILITIES

Most magic weapons only have enhancement bonuses. However, weapons can also have any of the special abilities listed in the core rules, as well as the new special abilities listed here. A weapon with a special ability must have at least a +1 enhancement bonus.

Defensive Fire: This special ability can only be granted a ranged weapon. The enchantment allows the wielder to make ranged attacks with the weapon in a threatened area without provoking attacks of opportunity.

Caster Level: 5th; *Prerequisites*: Craft Magic Arms and Armor, *shield*; *Market Price*: +1 bonus.

Energy Flux: Only ranged energy weapons can have this special ability. It allows the weapon to alter the energy form of its attacks. Before each attack, as a free action, the wielder can choose whether the weapon deals fire, electricity, or sonic damage. The weapon's other characteristics remain unchanged.

Caster Level: 10th; *Prerequisites*: Craft Magic Arms and Armor, *fireball*, *lightning bolt*, *shatter*; *Market Price*: +2 bonus.

Precision Targeting: This special ability can only be granted a ranged weapon. Cover bonuses to AC are halved against attacks made by the weapon. If the wielder has the Crack Shot feat, cover bonuses to AC are eliminated altogether.

Caster Level: 8th; *Prerequisites*: Craft Magic Arms

and Armor, *true strike*; *Market Price*: +2 bonus.

Pulsing: Upon command, a pulsing weapon is sheathed in electromagnetic energy. The weapon deals +2d6 points of bonus electricity damage to robots, soul-mechs, vehicles, and technological devices that require electrical current. Projectile weapons with this special ability bestow this electromagnetic energy upon their ammunition.

Caster Level: 10th; *Prerequisites*: Craft Magic Arms and Armor, *power down*; *Market Price*: +1 bonus.

Rapid Fire: This special ability can only be granted a fully automatic ranged weapon that fires three-shot bursts. The enchantment enables the weapon to fire up to five shots with each burst. The weapon's other characteristics remain unchanged.

Caster Level: 5th; *Prerequisites*: Craft Magic Arms and Armor, *haste*; *Market Price*: +1 bonus.

SPECIFIC WEAPONS

The following weapons are usually crafted with the specific qualities described here.

Antimatter Cannon: This devastating *+2 weapon* fires a stream of magically contained antimatter particles that are released on contact with a target. Armor and enhancement bonuses do not apply to the AC of the target and objects do not receive the benefits of hardness, as the particles react explosively to normal matter. Indeed, the attack gains bonus damage equal to the armor bonus of any armor the target is wearing and deals double damage to objects. In all other respects, including rate of fire, damage, critical threat range and multiplier, range increment, energy type, and magazine

capacity, the weapon is identical to a plasma rifle.

Caster Level: 13th; *Prerequisites*: Craft Magic Arms and Armor, *gate, sunburst*; *Market Price*: 52,300 cr; *Cost to Create*: 27,800 cr + 980 XP.

Assassin's Rifle: This is a sleak, black *+3 sniper rifle* in a compact bullpup configuration. It is the favored weapon of military snipers and assassins throughout the Dragon Empire. Once per day for every five character levels, the wielder can make a sneak attack or death attack at a distance up to the first range increment of the weapon, adjusted for any modifiers (Far Shot feat, electronic scope, etc.).

Caster Level: 13th; *Prerequisites*: Craft Magic Arms and Armor, *true strike*; *Market Price*: 73,100 cr; *Cost to Create*: 37,100 cr + 1,440 XP.

Negative Energy Rifle: This terrifying *+2 energy weapon* disrupts organic tissue at the cellular level and can even drain the life force of its targets. The weapon shares the same characteristics as a conventional blaster rifle, except the damage it deals is treated as acid damage. If the attacker scores a critical hit with the weapon, it bestows a negative level in addition to its normal damage.

Caster Level: 17th; *Prerequisites*: Craft Magic Arms and Armor, *Melf's acid arrow, energy drain*; *Market Price*: 33,300 cr; *Cost to Create*: 17,300 cr + 640 XP.

Spell Warheads: Explosive weapons, including grenades, missiles, rockets, and torpedoes, can be enchanted to discharge spell effects when they are detonated. These spell effects replace the weapon's conventional damage. The market price of spell warheads is equal to the caster level multiplied by the spell level multiplied by 50 cr. The warhead's base cost is based on the type of explosive weapon used:

Weapon	Base Cost
Grenade	+100 cr
Missile	+800 cr
Rocket	+550 cr
Torpedo	+1,300 cr

Spell warheads are used for a variety of purposes in combat. Grenades imbued with non-lethal spells such as *stinking cloud* and *web* can be used to subdue the enemy and are especially useful in crowded situations where innocents might otherwise be in harm's way. Spell warheads on heavier weapon systems, such as rocket launchers, missile launchers, and starship torpedo systems, are often used to penetrate the magical defenses of enemy vehicles. For example, *disintegrate* torpedoes are often used by warships to counter *walls of force* and other such obstacles. Spell warheads can be launched from any system capable of launching a normal weapon of that type (e.g., grenade launcher, missile launcher, etc.).

Caster Level: variable; *Prerequisites*: Craft Magic Arms and Armor, by spell effect; *Market Price*: caster level x spell level x 50 cr, plus base cost of weapon.

Star Laser: This *+1 laser rifle* features an oversized design that makes it easy to operate by a wielder wearing a bulky vacuum suit and thick gloves. It is a favored weapon of marines in the Imperial Navy and others who often fight in airless environments. In outer space or in any conditions of hard vacuum, the *star laser* gains a +3 enhancement bonus. The weapon also deals 1d6 points of bonus fire damage on a successful hit against a creature with the space subtype (see Chapter 7: Monsters).

Caster Level: 9th; *Prerequisites*: Craft Magic Arms and Armor, *flame arrow*; *Market Price*: 19,100 cr; *Cost to Create*: 10,100 cr + 360 XP.

POTIONS

A wide variety of potions and oils are available in the **Dragonstar** universe. Few potions are the imbibed liquids found on Outlands worlds. In the Dragon Empire, most potions are created as dermpatches. These small, plastic tabs feature an adhesive backing on one side that allows the dermpatch to be quickly and easily attached to exposed skin. Once attached, the potion is absorbed through the skin directly into the user's bloodstream. Dermpatches are identical to liquid potions in all respects, except they only require a move-equivalent action to apply. Like liquid potions, dermpatches can be identified by taste by seasoned adventurers.

POTION DESCRIPTIONS

Dermpatches imbued with any spells of 3rd level or lower can be created using the standard Brew Potion feat. Dermpatches featuring higher-level spells may be possible if creators have access to non-core item creation feats. New potions are described below.

Oil of Repair Light Damage: This oil is specifically crafted to be effective when applied to an object or construct, including robots and soulmechs. The oil repairs 1d8+3 points of damage, as the spell *repair light damage* cast by a 3rd-level spellcaster. The oil has no effect if applied to the skin of an organic being.

Caster Level: 3rd; *Prerequisites*: Brew Potion, *repair light damage*; *Market Price*: 150 cr.

Signature Mask: This dermpatch allows the user to alter his chemical signature, from pheromones to DNA. The user can control his odor, completely nullifying the ability of a creature to locate or track him with the Scent feat. The dermpatch grants the user a +10 circumstance bonus on Disguise checks if he is trying mask his own chemical profile or match that of another person. The *signature mask* also renders devices that use chemical analysis for identification ineffective against the user. The dermpatch's effect lasts for one hour.

Caster Level: 3rd; *Prerequisites*: Brew Potion, *alter self*; *Market Price*: 300 cr.

RINGS

Magic rings crafted in the Dragon Empire are identical in all respects to those created on Outlands worlds.

Ring of Freefall: This unadorned silver ring provides the wearer with a +10 circumstance bonus on Freefall checks.

Caster Level: 7th; *Prerequisites*: Forge Ring, *freedom of movement*; *Market Price*: 2,000 cr.

Ring of Vacuum Protection: This titanium band allows the wearer to survive without breathing, and protects him from all other effects of exposure to hard vacuum. The wearer is also immune to the extreme cold and lethal radiation of outer space. This ring is only effective in vacuum and in space. It does not allow the wearer to survive underwater or to endure the freezing temperatures of an arctic environment on a planetary surface.

Caster Level: 9th; *Prerequisites*: Forge Ring, *total protection*; *Market Price*: 14,000 cr.

RODS, STAFFS, AND WANDS

These items are identical in most respects to their archaic counterparts found on Outlands worlds. In the Dragon Empire, however, most rods, staffs, and wands are crafted from carbon-fiber composites, and this makes them much sturdier and resistant to physical damage. A typical rod has an AC of 9, 35 hit points, and a hardness of 18. A typical staff has an AC of 7, 40 hit points, and a hardness of 18. A typical wand has an AC of 7, 25 hit points, and a hardness of 18.

Rod of Electromagnetism: This rod pulses in the wielder's hand and points to the largest mass of metal within 30 feet, just as a *rod of metal and mineral detec-*

tion. The *rod of electromagnetism* cannot be used to identify specific metals or minerals, however. Once per day on command, the rod can also discharge a powerful electromagnetic pulse that has a devastating effect on any devices within 30 feet that use an electrical current or circuits. This includes datapads, personal communicators, robots, and most firearms. Devices within the area of effect cease functioning for 1d4 rounds. If a device is in a character's possession or directly under his control, the character can make a Reflex save (DC 14) to avoid the effect.

Caster Level: 12th; *Prerequisites*: Craft Rod, *power down*; *Market Price*: 18,000 cr.

Staff of the Technomancer: This gray composite staff is banded with adamantine and tipped with a silver sphere that glows with blue and golden light from within. It allows the use of the following spells:

cause light damage (1 charge, DC 14)
cause critical damage (2 charges, DC 16)
demolish (3 charges)
instant reboot (1 charge, DC 15)
power down (1 charge, DC 15)
refuel (1 charge)

Caster Level: 11th; *Prerequisites*: Craft Staff, *cause light damage, cause critical damage, demolish, instant reboot, power down, refuel*; *Market Price*: 75,000 cr.

Staff of Repair: Crafted of carbon fiber, this staff is tipped with a smooth iron ball. It allows the use of the following spells:

restore (1 charge)
recreate (2 charges)

Caster Level: 17th; *Prerequisites*: Craft Staff, *recreate, restore*; *Market Price*: 164,250 cr.

SCROLLS

Scrolls are as common in the Dragon Empire as in the Outlands worlds. They can be created as either archaic paper scrolls or digital scrollware.

WONDROUS ITEMS

These magic items come in as many diverse forms in the Dragon Empire as in the Outlands.

Ansible: In the **Dragonstar** universe, nothing can travel faster than light without the aid of magic. This inescapable fact makes faster-than-light communication by technological means impossible. While small courier ships transport messages and data between star systems for a fee, the lack of any real-time communication between systems is a real obstacle to the development of a star-spanning Empire.

The *ansible* acts as a sort of interstellar telegraph that links the scattered systems of the Dragon Empire. It is a small, silvery sphere about six inches in diameter, very similar in appearance to a miniature starcaster. Anyone who touches the sphere gains the ability to send a short message to another location, no matter how distant, as the *sending* spell. The message can be directed at a specific person or a specific *ansible*. The *ansible* does not allow the transmission of complex data, including visual images and graphics, but it is the most effective means of FTL communication in the known galaxy.

Caster Level: 7th; *Prerequisites*: Craft Wondrous Item, *sending*; *Market Price*: 56,000 cr; *Weight*: 1 lb.

Grav Boots: This magical footwear looks like the durable utility boots commonly worn with a spacer's jumpsuit aboard ship. The boots negate all gravity check modifiers, allowing the user to move normally in even crushing gravity. Grav boots also provide a +10 circumstance bonus to the user's Freefall checks.

Caster Level: 7th; *Prerequisites*: Craft Wondrous Item, *freedom of movement*; *Market Price*: 58,000 cr; *Weight*: 1 lb.

Scope of Sure Aim: This powerful electronic scope can be attached to any firearm of Medium-size or greater. When the user spends one full-round action viewing a target through the *scope of sure aim*, his next attack roll suffers no range penalties as long as the target is within 10 range increments. The attacker must have line of sight to the target and must be able to see the target when sighting through the *scope*.

Caster Level: 3rd; *Prerequisites*: Craft Wondrous Item, *true strike*; *Market Price*: 6,000 cr; *Weight*: 1 lb.

VEHICLE ENHANCEMENTS

Magic is a pervasive and inescapable presence in the Dragon Empire. Vehicles can be engineered to withstand the elements and the wear and tear of daily use, and military vehicles can be augmented with armor and other defenses against physical attacks. Even the most powerful combat vehicles, including starships, can be extremely vulnerable to magic, however. As a result, a wide variety of magical enhancements for vehicles have been developed. Some simply augment a vehicle's existing capabilities, while others protect vehicles from spellcasters and magical attacks.

Magical vehicle enhancements are created with the Craft Wondrous Item feat. Market prices are based on the size of the vehicle the enhancement is designed for, as described below.

VEHICLE ENHANCEMENT DESCRIPTIONS

The following magical enhancements are relatively common in the Dragon Empire.

Armor Enhancement: The bodies or hulls of vehicles can be given enhancement bonuses to Armor Class, just like a suit of armor designed for a character. Magical armor enhancement bonuses are uncommon on all but cutting-edge military vehicles where the high cost of the enhancement is often justified. As with conventional armor, the minimum caster level required to craft the enhancement is three times the enhancement bonus of the armor. Enchanting vehicle armor requires customized modifications to the vehicle's structure and is covered by the Craft Wondrous Item feat rather than the Craft Weapons and Armor feat. The market price of

MARKET PRICE OF VEHICLE ARMOR ENHANCEMENTS

Size	+1	+2	+3	+4	+5
Medium-size	1,000 cr	4,000 cr	9,000 cr	16,000 cr	25,000 cr
Large	1,500 cr	6,000 cr	13,500 cr	24,000 cr	37,500 cr
Huge	2,000 cr	8,000 cr	18,000 cr	32,000 cr	50,000 cr
Gargantuan	2,500 cr	10,000 cr	22,500 cr	40,000 cr	62,500 cr
Colossal	3,000 cr	12,000 cr	27,000 cr	48,000 cr	75,000 cr
Colossal II	3,500 cr	14,000 cr	31,500 cr	56,000 cr	87,500 cr
Colossal III	4,000 cr	16,000 cr	36,000 cr	64,000 cr	100,000 cr
Colossal IV	4,500 cr	18,000 cr	40,500 cr	72,000 cr	112,500 cr
Colossal V	5,000 cr	20,000 cr	45,000 cr	80,000 cr	125,000 cr
Colossal VI	5,500 cr	22,000 cr	49,500 cr	88,000 cr	137,500 cr

armor enhancements is based on the enhancement bonus and the size of the vehicle.

Gravlift: This vehicle enhancement uses levitation magic as an alternative suspension system for surface vehicles. A gravlift vehicle floats about three feet off the ground and can temporarily elevate even higher to circumvent obstacles and rough terrain. A gravlift vehicle's magical suspension is much more effective than wheels, tracks, or the air cushion system used in conventional hovercraft. Gravlift vehicles gain a +1 bonus to their acceleration and handling ratings. However, gravlift vehicles are somewhat more difficult to brake, and they receive a −1 penalty on their deceleration rating. Only surface vehicles of Huge size or smaller can be outfitted with gravlift systems.

Caster Level: 3rd; *Prerequisites*: Craft Wondrous Item, *levitate*; *Market Price*: 12,000 cr (Medium-size), 18,000 cr (Large), 24,000 cr (Huge); *Weight*: 10 lb. (Medium-size), 15 lb. (Large), 20 lb. (Huge).

Force Shield Generator: This powerful but expensive enhancement is typically only given to combat vehicles and starships. Sophisticated sensors identify incoming projectiles, whether bullets, shells, missiles, torpedoes, or kinetic-kill weapons. The sensors activate

the generator, which creates a *wall of force* around the vehicle. This force shield is invisible and moves with the vehicle. It otherwise functions just as the spell: It is immune to physical damage and most spells. The *force shield generator* is effective against physical projectiles, no matter how advanced, but it provides no defense against energy weapons. Attacks from these weapons travel at the speed of light and the sensors cannot identify and assess them quickly enough to activate the *force shield generator*.

Caster Level: 9th; *Prerequisites*: Craft Wondrous Item, *wall of force*; *Market Price*: 90,000 cr (Huge), 110,000 cr (Gargantuan), 130,000 cr (Colossal), 150,000 cr (Colossal II), 170,000 cr (Colossal III), 190,000 cr (Colossal IV), 210,000 cr (Colossal V), 230,000 cr (Colossal VI); *Weight*: 100 lb. (Huge), 200 lb. (Gargantuan), 400 lb. (Colossal), 800 lb. (Colossal II), 1,600 lb. (Colossal III), 3,200 lb. (Colossal IV), 6,400 lb. (Colossal V), 12,800 lb. (Colossal VI).

Spell Resistance: The body or hull of a vehicle can be enchanted to make it resistant to magic. This works just like the spell resistance special ability, and the cost depends on the level of SR and the size of the vehicle.

Caster Level: 9th; *Prerequisites*: Craft Wondrous Item, *spell resistance*; *Market Price*: varies; *Weight*: —.

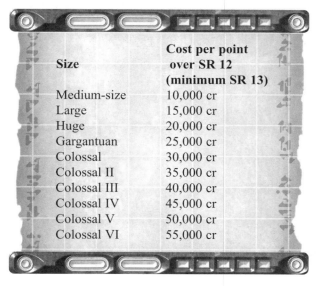

Size	Cost per point over SR 12 (minimum SR 13)
Medium-size	10,000 cr
Large	15,000 cr
Huge	20,000 cr
Gargantuan	25,000 cr
Colossal	30,000 cr
Colossal II	35,000 cr
Colossal III	40,000 cr
Colossal IV	45,000 cr
Colossal V	50,000 cr
Colossal VI	55,000 cr

Teleport Supressor: Starships can be particularly vulnerable to spellcasters with the ability to *teleport*. In principle, there's nothing to stop a sorcerer from teleporting onto a ship, casting a spell or delivering some devastating weapon, and then teleporting away again. Because a spellcaster can teleport from one point to another anywhere on the same plane, even light years of distance would not be an obstacle. This enhancement surrounds the vehicle with a specialized antimagic zone that completely blocks teleportation, ethereal travel, and related methods of magical travel or movement. *Teleport suppressors* prevent the functioning of starcasters, so the device must be deactivated before a starship can teleport.

Caster Level: 11th; *Prerequisites*: Craft Wondrous Item, *antimagic field*, *teleport*; *Market Price*: varies; *Weight*: 50 lb.

STARSHIPS

Starships use magical artifacts called starcasters to teleport from one system to another. Because they allow transportation and communication across light years of space, these devices make a star-spanning empire possible. However, the extraordinary cost of crafting and recharging a starcaster is a powerful incentive for the development of alternatives.

ASTRAL DRIVES

The Astral Plane connects the material universe with the other planes of existence, binding the cosmos together. It brushes against the Material Plane, and the right magic allows you to enter it and move through it. The laws of the material universe do not apply to the Astral Plane, and arcane engineers have discovered a way to turn this to the advantage of star travelers throughout the Dragon Empire.

Astral drives are similar to starcasters in many respects. They are powerful artifacts and the secret of their construction is known only to a few. The devices are cylindrical in shape and constructed of a dark metal formed through a complex alchemical ritual utilizing adamantine, mithral, and other rare substances with known arcane properties. Astral drives are created almost exclusively by the aristocorps and other large, wealthy organizations. They are rarely sold to independent buyers, but their market price would be at least 5,000,000 cr.

Despite this exhorbitant cost, astral drives have two advantages over starcasters that make them a very appealing alternative. First, they can only be constructed on the Astral Plane and the process requires complex arcane rituals that take weeks to complete. However, the device actually absorbs and infuses itself with the unique arcane energy of the Astral Plane as it forms. The fortunate result of this phenomenon is that the spellcasters who craft the artifact need not invest their own life forces into its creation—and indeed, it would have no effect on the device if they did. This means that there is no XP cost to create an astral drive. Second, the astral drive operates continuously and does not need to be recharged. Thus, while the cost to construct the drive is several times that of a starcaster, the operating costs are dramatically lower.

The visible effect when an astral drive is activated is very similar to that of a starcaster. A shimmering field of light appears around the starship and an instant later it appears to recede from view, regardless of the angle or angles from which it is observed. It dwindles to a pinpoint of light in the span of a microsecond and then winks out of existence. The ship appears on the Astral Plane and is magically propelled through it at tremendous speeds. The relativistic effects that make faster-than-light travel impossible in the material universe do not apply on the Astral Plane. Starships powered by astral drives can travel a distance corresponding to 10 light years on the Material Plane in a standard day. This makes astral drives much slower than starcasters—it would take a ship using an astral drive more than three months to travel from one edge of the Empire to the

found in the *Starfarer's Handbook* (see page 81). The standard DC for navigating between star systems in known space is 40. However, remember that a navigator with access to a standard ship's computer receives a +20 circumstance bonus on the check. Failure indicates that the ship deviates from the proper course by as much as 10% of the total distance traveled. Given sufficient time, the navigator can take 10 or take 20 on this check. Due to the same gravity phenomena that affect starcasters, a ship should be at least 100,000 miles from a massive body before engaging an astral drive. Activating the drive within this range imposes a –10 penalty on the Navigate check.

Astral drives are still relatively rare in the Dragon Empire, limited mainly to the warships of the Imperial Navy and the deep-space explorers of the Royal Exploratory Service. They are becoming more common, however, as several aristocorps have launched ambitious production programs. The biggest limiting factors—besides the cost, of course—are the relative scarcity of qualified spellcasters to craft the devices and the logistical challenges of conducting arcane rituals and development on the Astral Plane. Nevertheless, the first few corporate ships are in service and several designed for private concerns are on the way.

ELVEN LIVESHIPS

The elves enjoy a closer bond with the natural world than any of the major races of the Dragon Empire. Their magnificent liveships are only one example of the ways they have benefited from this bond as they adapted themselves to life in a starfaring civilization.

Liveships are organic starships owned by wealthy and powerful elven families. They are equipped with standard starcasters, but the devices are powered by the life forces of generations of the family members who captain them on their voyages among the stars. When the captain of a liveship dies aboard his ship, the liveship is imbued with his spirit. The ship uses this spiritual energy to power its starcaster. For every year a captain serves with his liveship, the starcaster gains 10 charges. Given the life span the elves enjoy, a liveship usually has thousands of charges stored when a new captain takes command of the vessel.

Liveships have a rudimentary sentience, and they share an empathic link with members of their families that is identical to the connection between an arcane spellcaster and his familiar. A family member aboard the ship can feel what the ship feels and can communicate telepathically with it. Most elven liveships are of the explorer, free trader, or freighter classes. In addition to those listed above, they gain the following benefits:

other—but the cost efficiency more than offsets the lack of speed for many purposes.

The Astral Plane is a timeless realm and this creates interesting implications for ships using astral drives. The crews of ships traveling through the plane do not age or suffer from hunger or thirst. They do still experience the passage of time, and these functions resume when they return to the Material Plane. However, this creates a kind of time dilation that can have a dramatic impact on the lives of starship crews. Because they do not age while on the Astral Plane, the lifespans of spacers may be artificially extended by many years relative to their friends and loved ones who remain behind on the Material Plane. Astral drives have not been around long enough for these effects to manifest in any significant way, but they will begin to in the near future. Already, the crews of astral ships seem to distance themselves from others, knowing that the years they spend traveling the Astral Plane will result in their living long after those bound to the Material Plane have passed away.

Because the geometry of the Astral Plane reflects that of the Material, navigation using an astral drive is actually relatively simple. A course can be plotted before the ship makes the jump to astral space. This requires a Navigate check, and the rules covering this skill can be

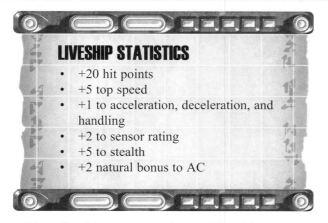

LIVESHIP STATISTICS

- +20 hit points
- +5 top speed
- +1 to acceleration, deceleration, and handling
- +2 to sensor rating
- +5 to stealth
- +2 natural bonus to AC

Elven liveships are grown in an orbital shipyard from large, gnarled, and very hard seeds. The growth process is infused with both arcane and divine magic, and the details of these rituals are a closely guarded secret of the liveship families. They claim that the liveships are a personal gift from the Mother reserved for them alone. When mature, a liveship is usually a mottled brown and gray with a hard, smooth texture similar to the shell of a coconut. The interior bulkheads of the ship are of similar material, and airlocks are usually muscular, self-sealing membranes. Little besides the hull and superstructure of a liveship is truly organic, and devices such as sensor clusters, fusion drives, starcasters, computers, and most furniture and life support systems must be grafted in as the ship matures. Nevertheless, the liveship families are careful to maintain the organic aesthetics of their ships in the design of these accessories.

Liveships are never sold outside the elven families who control their manufacture. Debate rages about the costs of constructing them. Some engineers insist that the ships must cost two or three times as much as conventional ships of similar classes. Others believe that liveship seeds are discovered in nature and that the process of growing them is relatively inexpensive.

LIQUID MITHRAL

The greatest disadvantage of starcasters is that they can only be recharged at a very high price. Several spellcasters must usually infuse the artifact with a significant portion of their life forces, and those who are both willing and able to do this are rare and expensive. This often results in long delays between the time when a starcaster's charges are expended and the needed spellcasters are gathered to peform the recharging ritual. In the case of military ships, this can create a serious security issue as warships are out of service for extended periods of time. It can also be disastrous for commercial ships because they must constantly be producing revenues to maintain their starcasters.

Fortunately, nature has provided at least a partial solution to these problems. Mithral can be transmuted into a liquid form through a specific alchemical processs. The infusion of this liquid mithral into the starcaster during the recharging ritual produces arcane energy that offsets the XP cost of the recharging. For every 1,000 cr worth of liquid mithral used in the ritual, the XP cost of the recharging is reduced by 100. Thus, if the cost of the recharging is increased to 14,000 cr per charge, the XP cost is reduced to 0. For the Imperial Navy, and even most commercial operations, the extra credits are much easier to come by than spellcasters willing to expend their life forces.

The applications of liquid mithral in starcaster recharging have made the metal one of the most valuable commodities in the Dragon Empire. Explorers survey Outlands worlds searching for new sources of the precious substance, while independent prospectors scour remote asteroids for small veins that could secure their fortunes. Mithral is the favored cargo of independent ship captains, as they can keep a supply of the metal to recharge their ships when the time comes and sell the rest on imperial markets for a healthy profit. Mithral has become so valuable that some observers consider it the economic lifeblood of the Empire. Outlands worlds have been invaded for it and there are constant rumors of claim wars on isolated asteroids between greedy and desperate miners. Of course, ships with holds full of mithral are also favored targets of pirates, and supplies of the ore can often been found on the black markets of backwater worlds all along the frontier.

SPELLWARE

In addition to conventional magic items, **Dragonstar** introduces a new category of magic items. Spellware is a form of arcane biomodification, a process of imbuing magical effects not in inanimate objects but in living, organic beings. Using spellware, characters in **Dragonstar** can enhance their existing abilities or gain new ones they could never otherwise possess.

In some ways, spellware works just like other magic items. For instance, spellware can be suppressed by certain spells and effects (e.g., *dispel magic*, *antimagic field*). In other ways, spellware is very different from conventional magic items. When it is implanted in a patient, spellware becomes an integral part of that character or creature. It cannot be damaged directly and never has to make item saving throws to resist damage. Of course, if the character's body is destroyed, the spellware is irrevocably destroyed, whether or not the character is subsequently raised or resurrected. Finally, while there is a limit on the type and number of conventional magic items a character can use at one time, there is no limit on the number of spellware enhancements a character can receive.

CREATING SPELLWARE

Just as with other magic items, creating spellware requires spellcasters to invest time and money into the project. They must also have a new item creation feat, called Implant Spellware (SHB 88). The creator must also have ranks in Profession (surgeon) and must make checks against this skill to successfully implant the enhancement.

The big difference between spellware and other magic items, however, is that the spellcaster does not expend his own life energy (represented by XP) in its creation. Instead, the patient who is receiving the implant must pay the XP cost.

The spellware creator must have access to a special laboratory. These facilities often combine elements of a wizard's workshop and a medical clinic or biotech lab. Implanting spellware takes one hour per 1,000 credits in the enhancement's base price, with a minimum of one hour. Long, complicated procedures must be broken up into eight-hour operations. The creator can perform one such procedure each day, and he cannot rush the project by working longer. The creator can only implant one enhancement in a single patient at a time and can do nothing else while operating. The creator must work every day until the operation is complete—he cannot take a day off in the middle of the project. Any interruption that would ruin the creation of a conventional magic item also ruins the spellware operation, and all materials used and XP spent are lost.

The creator must make a Profession (surgeon) check each day during the project. The check's DC is determined by the complexity of the spellware enhancement the creator is implanting.

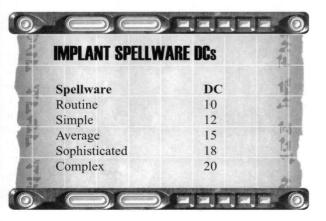

IMPLANT SPELLWARE DCs

Spellware	DC
Routine	10
Simple	12
Average	15
Sophisticated	18
Complex	20

If the check succeeds, the operation has gone as planned and the creator has made normal progress for that day. If the operation required eight hours or less to complete, the spellware has been successfully implanted. Otherwise, the creator must make another check on each subsequent day until the operation is complete.

If the creator fails a check, he has made no progress for that day. If he fails by 5 or more, supplies and materials are lost and the creator must pay one quarter of the spellware's market price to replace them.

Spellware typically costs one-half the market price in credits to create. This money is spent on a variety of arcane and medical supplies and equipment necessary for the procedure. The subject in whom the spellware is implanted must also pay the XP cost, which is 1/25 the market price of the enhancement.

For example, the *aura mask* enhancement has a market price of 12,000 credits. This is the amount your character will have to pay if he goes to a reputable clinic for the enhancement. The creator spends 6,000 credits on the supplies and equipment necessary to implant the spellware. The patient must also expend 480 XP when the enhancement is implanted. The operation takes three hours. If the creator fails his Profession (surgeon) check by 5 or more, he must pay 3,000 credits to replace lost materials and equipment before trying again.

SPELLWARE ENHANCEMENTS

Antitoxin: Runic surgery and arcane organ augmentation render the character immune to all natural poisons, toxins, and venoms. The spellware has no effect on magical or supernatural poisons. *Caster Level:* 7th; *Prerequisites:* Implant Spellware, *neutralize poison*; *Market Price:* 56,000 cr; *XP Cost*: 2,240; *Check DC:* 18.

Aquaform: This full-body modification is popular with sailors, divers, explorers and others who routinely operate in marine environments. The procedure involves extensive runic surgery and biomodification of the character's respiratory system and body. The character's lungs are imbued with the ability to extract oxygen from water as well as air. The ability operates continuously and the character can remain submerged indefinitely without fear of drowning. The character's hands and feet are lengthened, and webbing formed from cloned tissue is implanted between the digits. The character is considered an aquatic creature and is able to swim at a speed equal to his base speed. The character ordinarily need not make Swim checks, but gains a +8 circumstance bonus on any Swim check to perform special actions or maneuvers. The character can always choose to take 10 when swimming, even if rushed or threatened. The character can also use the run action

while swimming as long as he swims in a straight line. For practical purposes, a character with the aquaform enhancement is limited to an effective depth of about 500 feet: any deeper and the absence of light and extreme cold require further spellware enhancements, such as *darkvision* and *resist elements*. *Caster Level:* 5th; *Prerequisites:* Implant Spellware, *alter self, water breathing*; *Market Price:* 42,000 cr; *XP Cost*: 1,680; *Check DC:* 18.

Augmented Spellcasting: This spellware enhancement allows the user to cast spells of a single descriptor as if he were a spellcaster one level higher. The enhancement applies to all level-dependent effects, including range, duration, and damage, but does not allow the character to cast more or higher level spells than he can ordinarily cast. The character must choose a descriptor the enhancement will apply to before the procedure is performed. The spell descriptors are acid, chaotic, cold, darkness, death, electricity, evil, fear, fire, force, good, language-dependent, lawful, light, mind-affecting, sonic, and teleportation. Characters may purchase multiple enhancements that augment different descriptors, but each must be purchased separately. *Caster Level:* 9th; *Prerequisites:* Implant Spellware, Heighten Spell; *Market Price:* 20,000 cr; *XP Cost*: 800; *Check DC:* 20.

Aura Mask: For people in covert or criminal occupations, protection from alignment-divination magic is often crucial. This enhancement operates continuously, and its effect is identical to an *undetectable alignment* spell. The downside of the *aura mask*, of course, is that a concealed alignment can often be as revealing as one that isn't. Rumors suggest that select ISPD agents are given spellware that operates as a *misdirection* spell, allowing them to redirect and deceive divination spells at will. *Caster Level:* 3rd; *Prerequisites:* Implant Spellware, *undetectable alignment*; *Market Price:* 12,000 cr; *XP Cost*: 480; *Check DC:* 18.

Biosculpting: This enhancement involves cosmetic surgery, modification, and arcane biotherapy. The procedure offers a significant improvement in the character's physical appearance and personal appeal. The character gains a +2 circumstance bonus on all Charisma checks and Charisma-based skill checks. *Caster Level:* 3rd; *Prerequisites:* Implant Spellware, *change self*; *Market Price:* 2,000 cr; *XP Cost*: 80; *Check DC:* 15.

Boosted Reflexes: Pilots, soldiers, operatives, criminals, and others who rely on their reflexes to survive often favor the *boosted reflexes* enhancement. Runic surgery and tissue modification enhance major neural pathways, allowing nerve impulses to travel faster and with greater coordination. Boosted reflexes grant the

subject gains the ability to see 60 feet even in total darkness. Darkvision is black and white only but is otherwise like normal sight. This enhancement does not grant the character the ability to see in magical darkness. *Caster Level:* 3rd; *Prerequisites:* Implant Spellware, *darkvision*; *Market Price:* 8,000 cr; *XP Cost:* 320; *Check DC:* 15.

Doppelganger: This full-body modification requires extensive runic surgery and arcane tissue grafts. The character gains the ability to alter his appearance as if he were the target of a *change self* spell. Activating the spellware is a move-equivalent action. The magic affects not only the character's body but also his clothing, armor, weapons, and equipment. The character can alter his height by up to 1 foot, can look fatter or slimmer, and can manipulate other minor physical traits. The character cannot alter his apparent body type. The effect is an illusion (glamer) and does not alter the perceived tactile or audible properties of the character or his possessions. *Doppelganger* spellware will therefore not fool advanced security systems, such as voiceprint analyzers or thumbprint scanners. If the character uses the *doppelganger* modification in conjunction with a disguise, he gains a +10 bonus on the Disguise check. The effect lasts until the character deactivates it. The illusion can be maintained even while the character is asleep or unconscious, but it drops if the user dies. *Caster Level:* 5th; *Prerequisites:* Implant Spellware, *change self*; *Market Price:* 10,000 cr; *XP Cost:* 400; *Check DC:* 18.

Elemental Resistance: This enhancement is a must-have for soldiers, adventurers, and law enforcement officers who routinely come under fire from high-tech energy weapons. Runic surgery and biomodification imbue the character's body with the ability to disperse one type of harmful elemental energy. The basic enhancement protects the user from 5 points of energy damage per round, while the advanced enhancement allows the character to ignore the first 12 points of damage per round from the selected energy type. The character must select the energy type before the procedure is performed. Multiple enhancements that protect against different energy types can be implanted, but each must be purchased separately. *Caster Level:* 1st (basic), 3rd (advanced); *Prerequisites:* Implant Spellware, *endure elements* (basic), *resist elements* (advanced); *Market Price:* 2,000 cr (basic), 12,000 cr (advanced); *XP Cost:* 80 (basic), 480 (advanced); *Check DC:* 18 (basic), 20 (advanced).

Empath: This enhancement allows the user to sense and alter emotions in other living creatures. The ability to sense emotions is usable at will. The character can detect and identify the target creature's strongest current emotions or prevailing emotional state. The target creature can make a Will save (DC 11) to negate this effect.

character a +2 bonus on initiative checks and increase his speed by 10 feet. *Caster Level:* 5th; *Prerequisites:* Implant Spellware, *cat's grace*, *expeditious retreat*; *Market Price:* 10,000 cr; *XP Cost:* 250; *Check DC:* 20.

Danger Sense: This enhancement grants the user an uncanny ability to anticipate and react to danger. The character gains a +10 circumstance bonus on checks (Listen, Spot, etc.) to determine awareness and surprise at the beginning of combat. *Caster Level:* 5th; *Prerequisites:* Implant Spellware; *Market Price:* 2,000 cr; *XP Cost:* 80; *Check DC:* 18.

Darkvision: The character's eyes and optic nerves are modified and enchanted through runic surgery. The

The character also gains *calm emotions* and *emotion* as spell-like abilities, each usable 3 times per day. The target creature is allowed a Will save to negate each ability, and the DCs are 13 for *calm emotions* and 14 for *emotion*. *Caster Level:* 7th; *Prerequisites:* Implant Spellware, *calm emotions, emotion*; *Market Price:* 45,000 cr; *XP Cost:* 1,800; *Check DC:* 20.

Enhanced Ability: Genetically engineered tissue implants and arcane runic surgery significantly increase one of the character's physical ability scores. The character gains a +2 enhancement bonus to one physical ability score. Spellware that enhances mental abilities is also available at the listed prices. *Caster Level:* 5th; *Prerequisites:* Implant Spellware, *bull's strength, cat's grace, endurance*; *Market Price:* 4,000 cr (+2), 16,000 cr (+4), 36,000 cr (+6); *XP Cost:* 160 (+2), 640 (+4), 1,440 (+6); *Check DC:* 15 (+2), 18 (+4), 20 (+6).

Fast Healing: Runic surgery and arcane biotherapy vastly improve the character's ability to heal damage. A character with this spellware enhancement gains the fast healing ability. The character regains a number of hit points each round based on the sophistication of the enhancement (either 1 or 2 points). This enhancement does not restore hit points lost from starvation, thirst, or suffocation, and it does not allow the character to regrow or reattach lost body parts. *Caster Level:* 12th; *Prerequisites:* Implant Spellware, *heal*; *Market Price:* 20,000 cr (fast healing 1), 50,000 cr (fast healing 2); *XP Cost:* 800 (fast healing 1), 2,000 (fast healing 2); *Check DC:* 18.

Flight: This full-body spellware enhancement imbues the character with the ability of flight as if he were the subject of a *fly* spell. The character can fly with a speed of 90 feet (60 feet if the character wears medium or heavy armor). The character can ascend at half speed and descend at double speed. The flying subject's maneuverability rating is good. Using the fly spell requires as much concentration as walking, so the subject can attack or cast spells normally. The subject of a fly spell can charge but not run, and it cannot carry aloft more weight than its maximum load, plus any armor it wears. The ability to fly is based on magic rather than aerodynamics, so it is unaffected by environmental variables such as atmospheric pressure and gravity. A character with the *flight* enhancement can fly in the vacuum of deep space or in the gravity well of a gas giant. *Caster Level:* 5th; *Prerequisites:* Implant Spellware, *fly*; *Market Price:* 30,000 cr; *XP Cost:* 1,200; *Check DC:* 18.

Light Tolerance: Drow, orcs, and others who are hindered by bright light favor this enhancement. Runic surgery on the eyes and optic centers of the brain make the subject as tolerant to light as a normal human. This enhancement eliminates all penalties for light sensitivity without affecting the character's *darkvision* or other racial abilities. *Caster Level:* 5th; *Prerequisites:* Implant Spellware; *Market Price:* 12,000 cr; *XP Cost:* 480; *Check DC:* 18.

Low-Light Vision: This spellware enhancement allows the user to see twice as far as a normal human in starlight, moonlight, torchlight, and similar conditions of poor illumination. The character retains the ability to distinguish color and detail under these conditions. *Caster Level:* 3rd; *Prerequisites:* Implant Spellware; *Market Price:* 6,000 cr; *XP Cost:* 240; *Check DC:* 15.

Magic Sense: This enhancement involves arcane modification of specific regions of the character's brain, as well as the optic nerves and eyes. Magic sense allows the user to *detect magic* at will. *Caster Level:* 1st; *Prerequisites:* Implant Spellware, *detect magic*; *Market Price:* 2,000 cr; *XP Cost:* 80; *Check DC:* 18.

Phase Inducer: This sophisticated spellware enhancement imbues the character with the ability to phase in and out of the Ethereal Plane as if under the effects of a *blink* spell. This enhancement allows the user to *blink* a number of rounds each day equal to 5 plus his character level. These rounds may be split up into as many distinct periods as the user wishes as long as the total duration does not exceed the character's limit. *Caster Level:* 5th; *Prerequisites:* Implant Spellware, *blink*; *Market Price:* 15,000 cr; *XP Cost:* 600; *Check DC:* 20.

Retractable Claws: Razor-sharp talons are implanted into bioengineered and enchanted sheaths in the character's hands and forearms. These claws are typically crafted of high-tech materials such as carbon fiber or titanium. On a humanoid character, the claws extend from the backs of the hands between the wrist and the first row of knuckles. When fully extended, the claws are six to eight inches long. When the claws are retracted into the sheaths, the self-sealing openings on the hands are nearly invisible.

The character gains the benefits of the Improved Unarmed Attack feat—he is always considered armed when using the claws in melee. The character may take a full-attack action to attack with both claws in one round. The claws are considered light weapons. They are keenblades, and this effect is accounted for in their critical range. *Caster Level:* 3rd; *Prerequisites:* Implant Spellware, *alter self*; *Market Price:* 2,000 cr; *XP Cost:* 80; *Check DC:* 12.

Damage	Critical	Range Increment	Size	Weight	Type
1d6	17–20/x2	—	S	3 lb.	Slashing

Spell Resistance: Delicate and time-consuming arcane biotherapy renders the character resistant to

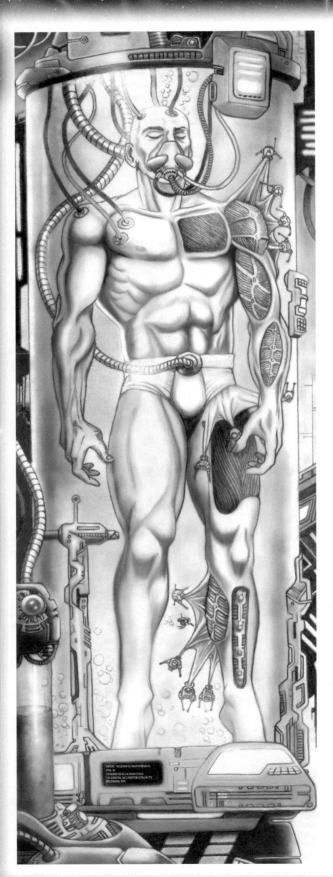

magic spells. The character gains variable SR depending on the sophistication (and expense) of the enhancement. In order to affect a character who has this enhancement with a spell, a spellcaster must roll the character's SR or higher on 1d20 + caster level. *Caster Level:* 9th; *Prerequisites:* Implant Spellware, *spell resistance*; *Market Price:* 10,000 cr (SR 13), 20,000 cr (SR 14), 30,000 cr (SR 15), 40,000 cr (SR 16), 50,000 cr (SR 17), 60,000 cr (SR 18), 70,000 cr (SR 19), 80,000 cr (SR 20); *XP Cost*: 400 (SR 13), 800 (SR 14), 1,200 (SR 15), 1,600 (SR 16), 2,000 (SR 17), 2,400 (SR 18), 2,800 (SR 19), 3,200 (SR 20); *Check DC:* 20.

Stealth: This spellware grants the character the ability to muffle his footfalls and blend with shadows. The enhancement grants a +4 competence bonus on Hide and Move Silently checks. An advanced upgrade is available that increases the competence bonus to +10. *Caster Level:* 5th; *Prerequisites:* Implant Spellware; *Market Price:* 640 cr (+4), 4,000 cr (+10); *XP Cost*: 25 (+4), 160; *Check DC:* 10.

Subdermal Armor: Runic surgery is used to modify and reinforce the character's skin and muscle tissues. The character gains damage reduction of variable effectiveness. The cost of the enhancement is based on the degree of protection it offers. *Caster Level:* 12th; *Prerequisites:* Implant Spellware, *stoneskin*; *Market Price:* 30,000 cr (5/+1), 40,000 cr (5/+2), 50,000 cr (5/+3, 10/+1), 60,000 cr (5/+4, 10/+2), 70,000 cr (5/+5, 10/+3), 80,000 cr (10/+4), 90,000 cr (10/+5); *XP Cost*: 1,200 (5/+1), 1,600 (5/+2), 2,000 (5/+3, 10/+1), 2,400 (5/+4, 10/+2), 2,800 (5/+5, 10/+3), 3,200 (10/+4), 3,600 (10/+5); *Check DC:* 18.

Telepath: It is believed that elite ISPD operatives commonly receive this multifunction spellware enhancement. The spellware allows the subject to communicate telepathically with any creature within 100 feet that has a language. The enhancement also grants the following spell-like abilities: *detect thoughts* (at will), *suggestion* (3/day), and *modify memory* (1/day). The subject uses these abilities as a 7th-level spellcaster. *Caster Level:* 7th; *Prerequisites:* Implant Spellware, *detect thoughts*, *modify memory*, *suggestion*; *Market Price:* 61,000; *XP Cost:* 2,440; *Check DC:* 20.

Translator: This enhancement involves extensive arcane modification of the speech centers of the character's brain. The spellware functions just as if the character were the subject of a *tongues* spell. It grants the character the ability to speak and understand the language of any intelligent creature, whether it is a racial tongue or a regional dialect. The character can speak only one language at a time, although he may be able to understand several languages. The *translator* enhancement does not enable the subject to speak with creatures that don't speak. The character can make himself understood as far as his voice carries. This spell does not predispose any creature addressed toward the subject in any way. *Caster Level:* 5th; *Prerequisites:* Implant Spellware, *tongues; Market Price:* 30,000 cr; *XP Cost:* 1,200; *Check DC:* 20.

Trauma Symbiote: A living organism implanted in the character's abdomen, the *trauma symbiote* imbues its host's body with its own life force. This magical energy protects the host's body from all forms of physical injury, providing the host with 20 extra hit points. Damage taken by the host is applied to the *symbiote* first. It protects the user until the *symbiote*'s hit points are reduced to 0 or less. When this occurs—after the damage is applied—the *symbiote* is automatically deactivated. A *trauma symbiote* reduced to –10 hit points is destroyed and no longer protects the host. Any damage left over from the attack that killed the *symbiote* is applied to the host.

For example, a character with a *trauma symbiote* is hit for 15 points of damage. The *trauma symbiote*'s hit points are reduced to 5 and the character takes no damage. On the following round, the character is hit for 7 points of damage. The *trauma symbiote* is at –2 hit points and the character takes no damage. The *symbiote* is now deactivated and does not protect the character from further damage until its damage is healed. However, if on the second round the character had been hit for 17 points of damage, the *trauma symbiote* would have been destroyed and the host would have taken 2 points of damage.

A wounded *sybmiote* is treated just like any living creature. When a *symbiote* drops below 0 hit points, it is dying. The player must roll each round to stabilize the *trauma symbiote*, otherwise it loses 1 hit point. If it reaches –10 hit points, it dies. The *symbiote* can be healed normally, including by natural and magical healing. The *trauma symbiote* heals 2 hit points per day regardless of the user's level of activity. *Trauma symbiotes* can be raised or resurrected. Voluntarily deactivating a *trauma symbiote* is a free action that does not provoke attacks of opportunity. *Caster Level:* 5th; *Prerequisites:* Implant Spellware; *Market Price:* 6,000 cr; *XP Cost:* 240; *Check DC:* 10.

DIVINE SPELLWARE

This is a special class of spellware that imbues paladins with the divine power of their gods. It is typically created by clerics of the paladin's order and is usually only offered to paladins in good standing as a reward for service. Paladins are not expected to pay for divine spellware, though they must pay an enhancement's XP cost.

Celestial Conversion: With the aid of allied outsiders, the paladin is imbued with celestial properties and gains the half-celestial template (MM 213). The paladin gains all of the listed abilities, including spell-like abilities based on level. Paladins with the celestial conversion never have wings, as they interfere with the paladin's ability to wear conventional armor and powered armor and often make it difficult to pilot vehicles effectively. Only the most favored and respected paladins of an order are granted this divine enhancement. A profane enhancement that grants blackguards the half-fiend template is also available. In all other respects, it is identical to the celestial conversion. *Caster Level:* 17th; *Prerequisites:* Implant Spellware, cleric of paladin's deity, *miracle, greater planar ally; Market Price:* 250,000 cr; *Check DC:* 20.

Enhanced Spellcasting: This divine enhancement grants the paladin the ability to prepare and cast one additional 1st-level spell each day. *Caster Level:* 7th; *Prerequisites:* Implant Spellware, cleric of paladin's deity; *Market Price:* 10,000 cr; *Check DC:* 18.

Enhanced Turning: This divine enhancement allows the paladin to turn undead as a paladin two levels higher than his class level. *Caster Level:* 5th; *Prerequisites:* Implant Spellware, cleric of paladin's deity; *Market Price:* 9,000 cr; *Check DC:* 15.

Extra Smite: This divine spellware grants the paladin the ability to use his smite evil ability an additional time per day. A profane version of this enhancement is also available to blackguards. *Caster Level:* 5th; *Prerequisites:* Implant Spellware, cleric of paladin's deity; *Market Price:* 6,000 cr; *Check DC:* 15.

Favored Enemy: This enhancement grants the paladin the ability to channel his deity's divine wrath against his enemy. When the paladin gains the enhancement, he chooses one type of outsider or undead, such as demons, devils, or vampires. Against this enemy, the paladin gains a +1 bonus to weapon damage rolls for every five class levels (+2 at 10th, +3 at 15th, +4 at 20th level). The paladin must be at least 5th level to gain this spellware enhancement. The paladin can apply this damage bonus to ranged attacks if he is within 30 ft. of his target. This ability can be used against creatures that are immune to critical hits. *Caster Level:* 12th; *Prerequisites:* Implant Spellware, cleric of paladin's deity; *Market Price:* 9,000 cr; *Check DC:* 18.

Holy Channeling: Once per day, the paladin with this enhancement can channel the power of his deity to smite evil foes. The paladin must be wielding an energy weapon, such as a laser or blaster weapon, to use this enhancement. As a free action, the paladin calls on the

power of his deity and sacred energy is channeled through the spellware to infuse the paladin's weapon. The paladin's next attack deals 4d6 points of bonus holy damage to any evil creature, in addition to the weapon's normal damage. This ability has no effect on a good or neutral target.

Caster Level: 9th; *Prerequisites:* Implant Spellware, cleric of paladin's deity, *searing light*; *Market Price:* 12,000 cr; *Check DC:* 18.

Improved Healing: A paladin with this enhancement gains a sacred bonus to Charisma only for the purposes of determining damage healed with the *lay on hands* ability. *Caster Level:* 5th; *Prerequisites:* Implant Spellware, cleric of paladin's deity; *Market Price:* 4,000 cr; *Check DC:* 15.

Improved Spellcasting: This powerful enhancement grants a paladin the ability to cast 5th-level spells. The paladin must be at least 17th level to gain this enhancement, and it allows him to cast a single 5th-level spell each day. These spells must be chosen from the following list: *break enchantment, commune, dispel evil, ethereal jaunt, greater command, raise dead, righteous might, spell resistance, total protection, true seeing.* *Caster Level:* 12th; *Prerequisites:* Implant Spellware,

cleric of paladin's deity; *Market Price:* 12,000 cr; *Check DC:* 18.

Ranged Smite: This enhancement allows the paladin to use his smite evil ability with a ranged attack. There are no special limitations on the range of the ability beyond those of the weapon the paladin is using. A profane version of this enhancement is also available to blackguards. *Caster Level:* 5th; *Prerequisites:* Implant Spellware, cleric of paladin's deity; *Market Price:* 15,000 cr; *Check DC:* 15.

Turn Outsiders: This powerful divine enhancement grants the paladin the ability to turn outsiders as he would undead. When the paladin is given the enhancement, he chooses one type of outsider, usually demons or devils. The paladin can turn outsiders of this type as undead with twice their Hit Dice. In all other respects, the ability is identical to the paladin's ability to turn undead, and turning outsiders counts as one of the paladin's turn attempts for the day. *Caster Level:* 15th; *Prerequisites:* Implant Spellware, *dismissal*; *Market Price:* 18,000 cr; *Check DC:* 20.

CHAPTER SEVEN

MONSTERS

The known galaxy is populated with millions upon millions of species, from single-celled organisms to the magnificent Dragon Emperor himself. As they did with the civilized races, the gods seeded countless worlds with the same plants, animals, and monsters, and you can find complete descriptions of hundreds of these creatures in the core rules and other d20 System sources.

From one planet to another—or even from one region on a planet to another—there are often slight variations in the same species. In most cases, these are simple differences, such as variant colorations or minor variations in physiology. Occasionally, however, the differences are more profound and some planets may boast whole subspecies that are unlike any of their cousins found elsewhere in the known galaxy. For example, the trolls indigenous to the largest continent on Duravon are known to be immune to acid and in fact to have acidic blood that can burn right through high-tech composite armor.

There are even some creatures that are unique among the stars. Whether they are the product of some strange experiment of the gods or the creation of some unknown alien intelligence is impossible to say. Moreover, as the sentient races expanded across the stars, they encountered numerous new species that were well adapted to space or other hostile environments.

Several of these creatures are described in this chapter. Further, the infinite variety and variation of species in the known galaxy offers the DM an unlimited canvas on which to exercise his creativity. The monsters of the **Dragonstar** universe are truly limited only by your imagination.

CHARACTERISTICS

There are a few new characteristics of creatures in **Dragonstar** that you need to be familiar with to understand their descriptions. These are discussed below.

NEW SUBTYPES

Two new creature subtypes are used in **Dragonstar**.

Radiation: The creature is immune to the effects of radiation.

Space: The creature is immune to the effects of vacuum. It does not need to breathe, and it is unaffected by radiation.

NEW CLIMATE/TERRAIN

There are three new climate/terrain types.

Aerial: This terrain represents a planetary atmosphere within the troposphere or stratosphere, to a maximum altitude of about 30 miles.

Near Orbit: This is anywhere in the mesosphere or thermosphere, from 30 miles to 400 miles in atmosphere.

Space: This refers to outer space or any region where hard vacuum prevails.

ASTERWRATH

Colossal Aberration (Space)

Hit Dice:	50d8+450 (675 hp)
Initiative:	+1 (Dex)
Speed:	Fly 5,000 ft. (perfect)
AC:	21 (–8 size, +1 Dex, +18 natural)
Attacks:	Slam +51 melee
Damage:	Slam 2d6+33
Face/Reach:	100 ft. by 100 ft./25 ft.
Special Attacks:	Spell-like abilities
Special Qualities:	Darkvision 1,000 ft., space subtype
Saves:	Fort +25, Ref +17, Will +29
Abilities:	Str 55, Dex 13, Con 29, Int 2, Wis 12, Cha 2
Skills:	Hide +16, Intuit Direction +11, Spot +16
Feats:	Endurance, Power Attack, Low-G Tolerance, Zero-G Tolerance
Climate/Terrain:	Space
Organization:	Solitary, pair, or cluster (3–6)
Challenge Rating:	17
Treasure:	Double standard
Alignment:	Always neutral
Advancement:	51–100 HD (Colossal)

The asterwrath is the terror of any star system. As massive as an asteroid and similar in size and appearance, the creature prefers to hide in asteroid belts, attacking unwary spacecraft that wander near.

Asterwraths feed on metals. Normally they roam through asteroid belts looking for ore they can digest by absorbing it through their rocky skin over a period of days. However, some have developed a taste for refined metals, and they consider spacecraft hulls to be a real treat.

Once it finds a food source—and, if necessary, defeats it—the asterwrath presses up against it, deforming a side of itself against its meal. In the course of a single day, the asterwrath's digestive microbes can eat a Colossal hole through six inches of steel or other substance with a similar hardness. It takes an asterwrath a full day to devour a Huge ship, two for a Gargantuan ship, and three for a Colossal ship. Smaller ships usually aren't worth an asterwrath's trouble, and it normally doesn't bother to attack these unless it is injured or starving.

When the asterwrath is finished with its meal, all that remains is any organic material that may have been part of the structure. The asterwrath is incapable of digesting such material.

COMBAT

When an asterwrath spots a starcraft nearby, it sets off on a near-miss intercept course, hoping that the occupants of the starcraft do not notice it or, if they do, assume the "asteroid" is bound to pass them safely by. When it gets close enough, it suddenly changes courses and slams into the ship.

Once it begins attacking, an asterwrath continues to batter a ship until it is entirely destroyed or loses power. The asterwrath ignores escape pods and the like, as these aren't large enough to distract it from the "meal" from which the pods were launched.

Space Subtype (Ex): Immune to radiation and vacuum.

Envelop (Ex): An asterwrath can try to envelop a Colossal or smaller object or creature as a standard action. The creature makes a grapple attempt that does not provoke attacks of opportunity. If the asterwrath is enveloping a spacecraft, the pilot makes the opposed check using his Pilot skill modified by his ship's special size modifier (PHB 137). Simply extend the modifiers for ships larger than Colossal (+20 for Colossal II, +24 for Colossal III, etc.). Once it has been enveloped, it is very difficult for a ship to escape the asterwrath's clutches. The creature will remain wrapped around its prey and continue feeding on its hull, as described above.

Skills: An asterwrath looks very much like the asteroids among which it normally makes its home. The only obvious difference is that it can move independently. When alone, an asterwrath gains a +8 racial bonus on Hide checks. When in an asteroid belt, it gains an additional +4 circumstance bonus. These bonuses apply only for the purposes of visual searches and not sweeps by electronic sensors such as radar.

BURSTBEAST

Small Aberration (Space)

Hit Dice:	1/4d8 (1 hp)
Initiative:	+3 (+3 Dex)
Speed:	Fly 20 ft.
AC:	14 (+1 size, +3 Dex)
Attacks:	Touch –4 melee
Damage:	1 and poison
Face/Reach:	5 ft. by 5 ft./5 ft.
Special Attacks:	Explode
Special Qualities:	Blindsight 60 ft., plantlike, space subtype, spherical
Saves:	Fort +0, Ref +3, Will +2
Abilities:	Str 1, Dex 16, Con 10, Int 2, Wis 10, Cha 1
Skills:	Hide +7
Feats:	—
Climate/Terrain:	Any aerial
Organization:	Bunch (2–5), colony (11–20), or school (41–60)
Challenge Rating:	1/8
Treasure:	None
Alignment:	Always neutral
Advancement:	1–2 HD (Medium-size)

Burstbeasts are strange creatures that were first discovered floating in schools in the upper atmosphere of a gas giant. They have since spread to countless planets throughout the known galaxy.

Burstbeasts are small, spherical creatures that float in the air until they approach a possible victim. A school of burstbeasts seems entirely innocent at first glance, almost like a flock of pale balloons floating in formation. However, when they get close enough to sense a victim, they become aggressive and dangerous. When they make contact with their victims, a volatile chemical reaction inside their gaseous bodies causes them to explode violently.

A burstbeast explodes upon taking or inflicting a single hit point of damage. When this occurs, the ripe spores on the interior of its balloonlike skin are flung far and wide, ready to grow into burstbeasts themselves.

Under the right conditions, a burstbeast grows to maturity within a week. Immature burstbeasts stay with any school they can find, but they do not attack until they are at least Small in size.

Burstbeast spores can live indefinitely in space, although they cannot grow and mature in these conditions. Spores attached to the hulls of spacecraft or the hides of space-going creatures have distributed this species throughout the Dragon Empire.

Characters familiar with burstbeasts can identify the spores with a Spot check (DC 10). Burstbeasts shrivel and die in water, and a simple scrubbing removes them from anything to which they are attached.

A mature burstbeast hit by even a few drops of water bursts immediately. For this reason, burstbeasts are only found near the ground on clear days. If there is any chance of rain, the creatures immediately soar up into the sky at top speed, hoping to make it above the clouds before they are caught in a fatal shower.

COMBAT

Upon finding a potential victim, a mature (Small or larger) burstbeast flies directly toward it and attacks.

Explode (Ex): Once a burstbeast takes or inflicts a single point of damage, it explodes. This deals 1d6 points of fire damage to anyone within 10 feet. Characters caught in this area can make a Reflex save (DC 15) for half damage.

Plantlike (Ex): Burstbeasts are immune to poison, sleep, paralysis, stunning, and mind-influencing effects. They can be polymorphed, however.

Space Subtype (Ex): Immune to radiation and vacuum.

DRAGONS

SPACE DRAGON

Dragon (Space)
Climate/Terrain: Any, including aerial, near orbit, and space
Organization: Wyrmling, very young, young, juvenile, and young adult: solitary or clutch (2–5); adult, mature adult, old, very old, ancient, wyrm, or great wyrm: solitary, pair, or family (1–2 and 2–5 offspring)
Challenge Ratings: Wyrmling 3; very young 4; young 6; juvenile 9; young adult 12; adult 14; mature adult 17; old 19; very old 20; ancient 22; wyrm 23; great wyrm 25
Treasure: Double standard
Alignment: Always lawful neutral
Advancement: Wyrmling 8–9 HD (Medium-size); very young 11–12 HD (Large); young 14–15 HD (Large); juvenile 17–18 HD (Large); young adult 20–21 HD (Huge); adult 23–24 HD (Huge); mature adult 26–27 HD (Huge); old 29–30 HD (Gargantuan); very old 32–33 (Gargantuan); ancient 35–36 HD (Gargantuan); wyrm 38–39 HD (Colossal); great wyrm 41+ HD (Colossal)

Space dragons are muscular black creatures who make their home in the vast void of space. They are most comfortable in the blackness between the stars, and there are some who have never touched the surface of a planet.

Throughout a space dragon's life, its scales are an inky black. As the creature gets older, glowing spots appear scattered across its hide, making it look like the dragon is clothed in the night sky.

Many space dragons spend most of their time sailing among the stars. They are often seen in the company of space kraken, especially when a dragon wishes to hitch a *teleport* to a new part of the galaxy. When such creatures do settle down and lair, however, they usually do so on a remote moon, asteroid, or comet.

Space dragons are rarely encountered within a planetary atmosphere. When they do approach a planet's surface, they prefer to do so at night.

In outer space, space dragons usually communicate with each other—and sometimes star dragons as well—by means of a complex series of gestures and body movements that requires the use of talon, tail, and wing. Space dragons sometimes find themselves jockeying for territory against their cousins, the star dragons. Over the millennia, though, the stand-offish space dragons have

SPACE DRAGONS BY AGE

Age	Size	Hit Dice (hp)	AC	Attack Bonus	Fort Save	Ref Save	Will Save	Breath Weapon (DC)	Fear DC	SR
Wyrmling	M	7d12+14 (59)	17 (+7 natural)	+10	+7	+5	+5	2d10 (16)	—	—
Very young	L	10d12+30 (95)	18 (−1 size, +9 natural)	+14	+10	+7	+8	4d10 (18)	—	—
Young	L	13d12+39 (123)	21 (−1 size, +13 natural)	+19	+11	+8	+9	6d10 (19)	—	—
Juvenile	L	16d12+64 (168)	24 (−1 size, +15 natural)	+24	+14	+10	+12	8d10 (22)	—	—
Young adult	H	19d12+95 (218)	26 (−2 size, +18 natural)	+27	+16	+11	+13	10d10 (24)	21	19
Adult	H	22d12+110 (253)	29 (−2 size, +21 natural)	+31	+18	+13	+17	12d10 (25)	24	21
Mature Adult	H	25d12+150 (312)	32 (−2 size, +24 natural)	+34	+20	+14	+18	14d10 (28)	26	23
Old	G	28d12+196 (378)	33 (−4 size, +27 natural)	+36	+23	+16	+21	16d10 (30)	29	24
Very old	G	31d12+248 (449)	36 (−4 size, +30 natural)	+40	+25	+17	+23	18d10 (33)	31	26
Ancient	G	34d12+306 (527)	39 (−4 size, +33 natural)	+44	+28	+19	+26	20d10 (34)	34	28
Wyrm	G	37d12+370 (610)	42 (−4 size, +36 natural)	+48	+30	+20	+27	22d10 (38)	35	30
Great Wyrm	C	40d12+400 (660)	41 (−8 size, +39 natural)	+49	+32	+22	+30	24d10 (40)	38	32

Age	Speed	Str	Dex	Con	Int	Wis	Cha	Special Abilities	Caster Level*
Wyrmling	60 ft., fly 200 ft. (poor)	17	10	15	10	11	10	Darkvision 100 ft., *fly*, space subtype	—
Very young	60 ft., fly 200 ft. (poor)	21	10	17	12	13	12		—
Young	60 ft., fly 200 ft. (poor)	25	10	17	12	13	12		1st
Juvenile	60 ft., fly 200 ft. (poor)	29	10	19	14	15	14		3rd
Young adult	60 ft., fly 200 ft. (poor)	31	10	21	14	15	14	Damage reduction 5/+1	5th
Adult	60 ft., fly 200 ft. (poor)	33	10	21	16	19	16	Darkvision 1,000 ft.	7th
Mature Adult	60 ft., fly 200 ft. (poor)	33	10	23	18	19	18	Damage reduction 10/+1	9th
Old	60 ft., fly 250 ft. (clumsy)	35	10	25	20	21	20	*Total protection*	11th
Very old	60 ft., fly 250 ft. (clumsy)	37	10	27	22	23	22	Damage reduction 15/+2	13th
Ancient	60 ft., fly 250 ft. (clumsy)	39	10	29	24	25	24	*Tractor beam*	15th
Wyrm	60 ft., fly 250 ft. (clumsy)	41	10	31	24	25	24	Damage reduction 20/+3	17th
Great Wyrm	60 ft., fly 250 ft. (clumsy)	45	10	31	26	27	26	*Implosion*	19th

* Can also cast cleric spells from the Law and Destruction domains as arcane spells.

realized that they prefer the company of star dragons to that of nearly any air breather.

Space dragons occasionally consume ice and other elements from comets, but it is believed that they can live for centuries with no sustenance at all.

The space dragons do not comprise one of the 10 major dragon clans. They are unconcerned with politics and prefer to avoid contact with the races of the Dragon Empire.

COMBAT

Space dragons are not violent by nature, and they rarely have any fixed territory to defend. They will defend themselves if pressed, however. If seriously threatened, a space dragon will flee into the darkness of space, hoping to lose any pursuer in the void the dragon knows so well. When cornered, space dragons fight ferociously. They do not toy with their victims, always using the deadliest attack available to them. Older space dragons rely on their spellcasting abilities to avoid dangerous conflicts.

Standard Dragon Abilities: Space dragons have all of the standard size-related statistics of dragons: face and reach, number and damage of attacks, and breath weapon areas.

Exceptional Abilities: Space dragons have all of the standard exceptional abilities of dragons. These include frightful presence, immunity to sleep and paralysis effects, spell resistance, blindsight, and keen senses.

Breath Weapon (Su): A space dragon's breath weapon follows the standard rules for dragon breath

STAR DRAGON

Dragon (Radiation)

Climate/Terrain: Any, including aerial, near orbit, and space

Organization: Wyrmling, very young, young, juvenile, and young adult: solitary or clutch (2–5); adult, mature adult, old, very old, ancient, wyrm, or great wyrm: solitary, pair, or family (1–2 and 2–5 offspring)

Challenge Ratings: Wyrmling 4; very young 6; young 8; juvenile 10; young adult 13; adult 15; mature adult 18; old 20; very old 21; ancient 23; wyrm 24; great wyrm 26

Treasure: Double standard

Alignment: Always chaotic neutral

Advancement: Wyrmling 9–10 HD (Medium-size); very young 12–13 HD (Large); young 15–16 HD (Large); juvenile 18–19 HD (Large); young adult 21–22 HD (Huge); adult 24–25 HD (Huge); mature adult 27–28 HD (Huge); old 30–31 HD (Gargantuan); very old 33–34 (Gargantuan); ancient 36–37 HD (Gargantuan); wyrm 39–40 HD (Colossal); great wyrm 42+ HD (Colossal)

weapons. The space dragon's breath weapon is a cone of pure void. Creatures struck by it take the listed amount of damage from effects similar to vacuum exposure.

Space Subtype: A space dragon is immune to the effects of vacuum. It does not need to breathe, and it is unaffected by radiation.

Skills: Space dragons have the same access to skills and the same number of skill points as other dragons. Additionally, they gain a +8 racial bonus on Freefall checks.

Feats: Space dragons get the standard number of feats for dragons and have access to all of the normal dragon feats. All space dragons have the Zero-G Tolerance feat.

Fly (Sp): Space dragons are hatched with the power of magical flight. This ability works like the spell, but it has a permanent duration and it allows the dragon to fly at its winged flying speed, even in space. The creature's maneuverability is good. However, this ability only works in outer space. In an atmosphere, the dragon relies on winged flight.

Spell-Like Abilities (Sp): 3/day—*total protection*, *tractor beam*, and *implosion*.

Star dragons are long and sinewy, full of a true passion for life. They are wild and free, reveling in the energy and boundless possibilities of the universe.

A star dragon wyrmling's scales are bright yellow, like those of a healthy main-sequence star. As the creature ages, the scales darken in hue, eventually becoming the color of a red giant as the dragon reaches adulthood. When the creature reaches old age, its scales begin to brighten again. Great wyrms are almost too bright to view directly, radiating light with the brilliance of a white dwarf.

Star dragons can live just about anywhere, though they rarely bother entering an atmosphere. Instead, they prefer to soar among the stars. Many star dragons make their lairs in the hollowed-out centers of large asteroids, protected from most hazards by the sheer remoteness of their homes. They often attract entire clusters of asterwraths and train them to protect their lairs from would-be trespassers.

The only time many star dragons enter a planetary atmosphere is when they lay their eggs. Hatchling star dragons are not born with the ability to survive the rigors of space. When they become juveniles, they are able to leave the planet of their hatching under their own power.

Once in outer space, star dragons usually communicate with each other by means of the same sign language used by space dragons. Star dragons often find them-

STAR DRAGONS BY AGE

Age	Size	Hit Dice (hp)	AC	Attack Bonus	Fort Save	Ref Save	Will Save	Breath Weapon (DC)	Fear DC	SR
Wyrmling	M	8d12+16 (68)	17 (+7 natural)	+11	+8	+6	+8	2d10 (16)	—	—
Very young	L	11d12+33 (104)	19 (−1 size, +10 natural)	+15	+10	+7	+10	4d10 (18)	—	—
Young	L	14d12+42 (133)	22 (−1 size, +13 natural)	+20	+12	+9	+12	6d10 (20)	—	—
Juvenile	L	17d12+68 (178)	25 (−1 size, +16 natural)	+25	+14	+10	+14	8d10 (22)	—	—
Young adult	H	20d12+100 (230)	27 (−2 size, +19 natural)	+28	+17	+12	+16	10d10 (25)	24	21
Adult	H	23d12+115 (264)	30 (−2 size, +22 natural)	+32	+18	+13	+18	12d10 (26)	26	23
Mature Adult	H	26d12+156 (325)	33 (−2 size, +25 natural)	+36	+21	+15	+20	14d10 (29)	28	25
Old	G	29d12+203 (391)	34 (−4 size, +28 natural)	+39	+23	+16	+23	16d10 (31)	31	27
Very old	G	32d12+256 (464)	37 (−4 size, +31 natural)	+43	+26	+18	+26	18d10 (34)	34	28
Ancient	G	35d12+315 (542)	40 (−4 size, +34 natural)	+47	+28	+19	+28	20d10 (36)	36	30
Wyrm	C	38d12+380 (672)	39 (−8 size, +37 natural)	+47	+31	+21	+31	22d10 (39)	39	31
Great Wyrm	C	41d12+451 (717)	42 (−8 size, +40 natural)	+51	+33	+22	+33	24d10 (41)	41	33

Age	Speed	Str	Dex	Con	Int	Wis	Cha	Special Abilities	Caster Level*
Wyrmling	60 ft., fly 200 ft. (poor)	17	10	15	14	15	14	Radiation subtype	—
Very young	60 ft., fly 200 ft. (poor)	21	10	17	16	17	16		—
Young	60 ft., fly 200 ft. (poor)	25	10	17	16	17	16	*Fly*	—
Juvenile	60 ft., fly 200 ft. (poor)	29	10	19	18	19	18	Darkvision 1,000 ft., immune to vacuum	1st
Young adult	60 ft., fly 200 ft. (poor).	31	10	21	18	19	18	Damage reduction 5/+1	3rd
Adult	60 ft., fly 200 ft. (poor).	33	10	21	20	21	20		5th
Mature Adult	60 ft., fly 200 ft. (poor)	35	10	23	20	21	20	Damage reduction 10/+1	7th
Old	60 ft., fly 250 ft. (clumsy)	39	10	25	24	25	24	*Total protection*	9th
Very old	60 ft., fly 250 ft. (clumsy)	41	10	27	26	27	26	Damage reduction 15/+2	11th
Ancient	60 ft., fly 250 ft. (clumsy)	43	10	29	28	29	28	*Tractor beam*	13th
Wyrm	60 ft., fly 250 ft. (clumsy)	45	10	31	30	31	30	Damage reduction 20/+3	15th
Great Wyrm	60 ft., fly 250 ft. (clumsy)	47	10	33	32	33	32	*Sunburst*	17th

* Can also cast cleric spells from the Chaos and Sun domains as arcane spells.

selves in conflict with the space dragons, but relations between the two subspecies are generally good. Legends tell of ancient wars between the two, but they have become closer allies with the rise to preeminence of the terrestrial dragons.

Star dragons absorb solar radiation, collecting it in the huge wings that act as organic solar panels. Because they rely on solar energy for sustenance, star dragons are rarely found far from the light of a sun. It is believed that star dragons can survive without sunlight for extended periods at a low level of activity.

The star dragons are not represented by the 10 major dragon clans. Like the space dragons, they prefer to stay out of political affairs. To the star dragons, there is plenty of room in the universe, and unlike their terrestrial cousins, they have no need to cluster around the few oxygen-soaked planets scattered across the galaxy.

COMBAT

Unless they are protecting a planet-bound clutch of eggs or a nest full of hatchlings, star dragons rarely become involved in physical combat. Encounters with other beings in the wide-open reaches of space are extremely uncommon, and most star dragons simply wish to be left to themselves. If confronted by a dangerous foe, star dragons will usually attempt to flee.

When forced to fight, star dragons can be terrifying enemies. They often rely on treachery and trickery to carry the day. All but the most powerful star dragons will be completely overmatched by armed starships, and they avoid them as a rule.

Older star dragons use their spellcasting abilities in self-defense when necessary, and their breath weapons are deadly to unprotected victims.

Standard Dragon Abilities: Star dragons have all of the standard size-related statistics of dragons: face and reach, number and damage of attacks, and breath weapon areas.

Exceptional Abilities: Star dragons have all of the standard exceptional abilities of dragons. These include frightful presence, immunity to sleep and paralysis effects, spell resistance, blindsight, and keen senses.

Breath Weapon (Su): A star dragon's breath weapon follows the standard rules for dragon breath weapons. Star dragons breathe a line of high-energy radiation. Any creature struck by it absorbs a number of doses of radiation as listed in the table below.

Size	Length	Doses
Medium-size	60 ft.	1
Large	80 ft.	2
Huge	100 ft.	3
Gargantuan	120 ft.	4
Colossal	140 ft.	5

Radiation Subtype: A star dragon is immune to the effects of radiation.

Skills: Star dragons have the standard access to skills and number of skill points. They gain a +8 racial bonus to Freefall checks.

Feats: Star dragons get the standard number of feats for dragons and have access to all of the normal dragon feats. All space dragons have the Zero-G Tolerance feat.

Fly (Sp): All young and older star dragons have the power of magical flight. This ability works like the spell, but it has a permanent duration and it allows the dragon to fly at its winged flying speed, even in space. The creature's maneuverability is good. However, this ability only works in outer space. In an atmosphere, the dragon relies on winged flight.

Vacuum Immunity (Su): As a juvenile or older, the star dragon is immune to the effects of vacuum and no longer needs to breathe.

Spell-Like Abilities (Sp): 3/day—*total protection*, *tractor beam*, and *sunburst*.

Electric Ooze

Medium-size Ooze

Hit Dice:	3d10+10 (26 hp)
Initiative:	–5 (Dex)
Speed:	10 ft.
AC:	5 (–5 Dex)
Attacks:	Slam +3 melee
Damage:	Slam 1d6+1 and 1d6 electricity
Face/Reach:	5 ft. by 5 ft./5 ft.
Special Attacks:	Improved grab, shock, constrict 1d6+1 and 1d6 electricity
Special Qualities:	Blindsight, immunity to cold, fire, and electricity, ooze, camouflage
Saves:	Fort +1, Ref –4, Will –4
Abilities:	Str 12, Dex 1, Con 11, Int —, Wis 1, Cha 1
Skills:	—
Feats:	—
Climate/Terrain:	Any
Organization:	Solitary
Challenge Rating:	4
Treasure:	None
Alignment:	Always neutral
Advancement:	4–6 HD (Medium-size); 7–9 HD (Large)

The electric ooze is a translucent ooze that crackles with tiny arcs of electricity in combat. It is attracted to and feeds on electrical currents.

An electric ooze appears to be a pool of clear water until it is aroused to action. It often spreads itself out thinly over an area so as to blend in with the surface it clings to. The first sign of an electric ooze's presence is often a temporary power drain that dims lights and shuts down sensitive devices. The ooze only feeds for a minute every four hours or so. Eventually, this pattern of disturbances usually leads the curious to investigate.

COMBAT

When the ooze senses someone approaching, it freezes in place until the intruder comes close enough to be attacked. Then the ooze rears up and lashes out wildly. As the ooze battles, blue arcs of electricity crawl along its surface. If the ooze lands an attack, it delivers a nasty shock by discharging this stored energy.

Blindsight (Ex): An electric ooze's entire body is a primitive sensory organ that can ascertain prey by scent and vibration within 60 feet.

Ooze: Immune to mind-influencing effects, poison, sleep, paralysis, stunning, and polymorphing. Not subject to critical hits.

Camouflage (Ex): A character can only idenfity an electric ooze with a successful Spot check (DC 15).

Constrict (Ex): Once an electric ooze has grabbed a victim, it can automatically deal constriction and electricity damage with a successful grapple check.

Immunity to Electricty (Ex): In addition to the standard immunities of an ooze, the electric ooze is immune to electricity.

Improved Grab (Ex): If the electric ooze manages to strike a target with its slam attack, it can then constrict the victim.

Shock (Ex): High-voltage electrical current passes through the electric ooze. When the ooze hits someone with a melee attack, it deals electrical damage as well.

Elementals

Radiation Elemental

Radiation Elemental, Small
Small Elemental (Radiation)

Hit Dice:	2d8 (9 hp)
Initiative:	+5 (+1 Dex, +4 Improved Initiative)
Speed:	Fly 100 ft. (perfect)
AC:	13 (+1 size, +1 Dex, +1 natural)
Attacks:	Slam +3 melee
Damage:	Slam 1d4 plus 1 dose of radiation
Face/Reach:	5 ft. by 5 ft./5 ft.
Special Attacks:	Irradiate
Special Qualities:	Elemental, radiation subtype
Saves:	Fort +0, Ref +4, Will +0
Abilities:	Str 10, Dex 13, Con 10, Int 4, Wis 11, Cha 11
Skills:	Listen +5, Spot +5
Feats:	Improved Initiative, Weapon Finesse (slam)

Radiation Elemental, Medium
Medium-Size Elemental (Radiation)

Hit Dice:	4d8+8 (26 hp)
Initiative:	+7 (+3 Dex, +4 Improved Initiative)
Speed:	Fly 100 ft. (perfect)
AC:	14 (+3 Dex, +1 natural)
Attacks:	Slam +6 melee
Damage:	Slam 1d6 and 1 dose of radiation
Face/Reach:	5 ft. by 5 ft./5 ft.
Special Attacks:	Irradiate

Special Qualities: Elemental, radiation subtype
Saves: Fort +3, Ref +7, Will +1
Abilities: Str 12, Dex 17, Con 14, Int 4, Wis 11, Cha 11
Skills: Listen +7, Spot +7
Feats: Improved Initiative, Weapon Finesse (slam)

Radiation Elemental, Large
Large Elemental (Radiation)

Hit Dice: 8d8+24 (60 hp)
Initiative: +9 (+5 Dex, +4 Improved Initiative)
Speed: Fly 100 ft. (perfect)
AC: 16 (–1 size, +5 Dex, +2 natural)
Attacks: Slam +10/+5 melee
Damage: Slam 2d6+3 and 2 doses of radiation
Face/Reach: 5 ft. by 5 ft./10 ft.
Special Attacks: Irradiate
Special Qualities: Damage reduction 10/+1, elemental, radiation subtype
Saves: Fort +5, Ref +11, Will +2
Abilities: Str 14, Dex 21, Con 16, Int 6, Wis 11, Cha 11
Skills: Listen +11, Spot +11
Feats: Improved Initiative, Weapon Finesse (slam), Zero-G Tolerance

Radiation Elemental, Huge
Huge Elemental (Radiation)

Hit Dice: 16d8+64 (136 hp)
Initiative: +11 (+7 Dex, +4 Improved Initiative)
Speed: Fly 100 ft. (perfect)
AC: 17 (–2 size, +7 Dex, +2 natural)
Attacks: Slam +17/+12/+7 melee
Damage: Slam 2d8+6 and 3 doses of radiation
Face/Reach: 10 ft. by 5 ft./15 ft.
Special Attacks: Irradiate
Special Qualities: Damage reduction 10/+2, elemental, radiation subtype
Saves: Fort +9, Ref +17, Will +5
Abilities: Str 18, Dex 25, Con 18, Int 6, Wis 11, Cha 11
Skills: Listen +18, Spot +18
Feats: Improved Initiative, Mobility, Weapon Finesse (slam), Zero-G Tolerance

Radiation Elemental, Greater
Huge Elemental (Radiation)

Hit Dice: 21d8+84 (178 hp)
Initiative: +12 (+8 Dex, +4 Improved Initiative)
Speed: Fly 100 ft. (perfect)
AC: 22 (–2 size, +8 Dex, +6 natural)
Attacks: Slam +21/+16/+11 melee
Damage: Slam 2d8+7 and 3 doses of radiation
Face/Reach: 10 ft. by 5 ft./15 ft.
Special Attacks: Irradiate
Special Qualities: Damage reduction 10/+2, elemental, radiation subtype
Saves: Fort +11, Ref +20, Will +7
Abilities: Str 20, Dex 27, Con 18, Int 6, Wis 11, Cha 11
Skills: Listen +23, Spot +23
Feats: Improved Initiative, Mobility, Spring Attack, Weapon Finesse (slam), Zero-G Tolerance

Radiation Elemental, Elder
Huge Elemental (Radiation)

Hit Dice: 24d8+84 (204 hp)
Initiative: +13 (+9 Dex, +4 Improved Initiative)
Speed: Fly 100 ft. (perfect)
AC: 23 (–2 size, +9 Dex, +6 natural)
Attacks: Slam +25/+20/+15/+10 melee
Damage: Slam 2d8+9 and 3 doses of radiation
Face/Reach: 10 ft. by 5 ft./15 ft.
Special Attacks: Irradiate
Special Qualities: Damage reduction 15/+3, elemental, radiation subtype
Saves: Fort +12, Ref +23, Will +8
Abilities: Str 22, Dex 29, Con 18, Int 6, Wis 11, Cha 11
Skills: Listen +26, Spot +26
Feats: Improved Initiative, Mobility, Spring Attack, Weapon Finesse (slam), Zero-G Tolerance

Climate/Terrain: Any
Organization: Solitary
Challenge Rating: Small 1; medium 3; large 5; huge 7; greater 9; elder 11
Treasure: None
Alignment: Usually neutral
Advancement: Small 3 HD (Small); medium 5–7 HD (Medium-size); large 9–15 (Large); huge 17–20 HD (Huge); greater 22–23 HD

(Huge); elder 25+ HD (Huge)

A radiation elemental is a living incarnation of high-energy radiation. It glows with the hellish fires of a nuclear reactor. Radiation elementals are fast and silent, though their radiance always betrays their presence. Their touch causes a creature's skin to burn and blister as its body is poisoned by the invisible particles streaming from the elemental.

A radiation elemental appears as a pillar of glowing energy. Twin, whiplike rays occasionally shoot out from the elemental's body long enough to attack a foe, then fade out as if they never existed. The creature glows with a ghastly green light. Spots of bright yellow light seem to move across its body, giving the appearance of flickering eyes.

Radiation elementals can exist just about anywhere: under the sea, on the land, in the air, or in space. Radiation elementals use the languages favored by other elementals: Auran, Teran, Ignan, or Aquan.

COMBAT

Radiation elementals attack methodically and without emotion. They often flee from combat once they have irradiated their opponent, knowing their high-energy poison will eventually doom their enemy.

Elemental: Immune to poison, sleep, paralysis, and stunning. Not affected by critical hits.

Irradiate (Ex): When a radiation elemental hits a target in melee, it exposes the victim to one or more doses of radiation.

Radiation Subtype (Ex): Immune to the effects of radiation.

SPACE ELEMENTAL

Space Elemental, Small
Small Elemental (Space)

Hit Dice:	2d8 (9 hp)
Initiative:	+7 (+3 Dex, +4 Improved Initiative)
Speed:	Fly 100 ft. (perfect)
AC:	15 (+1 size, +3 Dex, +1 natural)
Attacks:	Slam +5 melee
Damage:	Slam 1d4 and suffocation
Face/Reach:	5 ft. by 5 ft./5 ft.
Special Attacks:	Suffocation
Special Qualities:	Elemental, space subtype
Saves:	Fort +0, Ref +6, Will +0
Abilities:	Str 10, Dex 17, Con 10, Int 4, Wis 11, Cha 11
Skills:	Listen +5, Spot +5
Feats:	Improved Initiative, Weapon Finesse (slam), Zero-G Tolerance

Space Elemental, Medium
Medium-size Elemental (Space)

Hit Dice:	4d8+8 (26 hp)
Initiative:	+9 (+5 Dex, +4 Improved Initiative)
Speed:	Fly 100 ft. (perfect)
AC:	16 (+5 Dex, +1 natural)
Attacks:	Slam +8 melee
Damage:	Slam 1d6+1 and suffocation
Face/Reach:	5 ft. by 5 ft./5 ft.
Special Attacks:	Suffocation
Special Qualities:	Elemental, space subtype
Saves:	Fort +3, Ref +9, Will +1
Abilities:	Str 12, Dex 21, Con 14, Int 4, Wis 11, Cha 11
Skills:	Listen +7, Spot +7
Feats:	Improved Initiative, Weapon Finesse (slam), Zero-G Tolerance

Space Elemental, Large
Large Elemental (Space)

Hit Dice:	8d8+24 (60 hp)
Initiative:	+11 (+7 Dex, +4 Improved Initiative)
Speed:	Fly 100 ft. (perfect)
AC:	18 (−1 size, +7 Dex, +2 natural)
Attacks:	Slam +12/+7 melee
Damage:	Slam 2d6+3 and suffocation
Face/Reach:	5 ft. by 5 ft./10 ft.
Special Attacks:	Suffocation
Special Qualities:	Damage reduction 10/+1, elemental, space subtype
Saves:	Fort +5, Ref +13, Will +2
Abilities:	Str 14, Dex 25, Con 16, Int 6, Wis 11, Cha 11
Skills:	Listen +11, Spot +11
Feats:	Flyby Attack, Improved Initiative, Weapon Finesse (slam), Zero-G Tolerance

Space Elemental, Huge
Huge Elemental (Space)

Hit Dice:	16d8+64 (136 hp)
Initiative:	+13 (+9 Dex, +4 Improved Initiative)
Speed:	Fly 100 ft. (perfect)
AC:	19 (−2 size, +9 Dex, +2 natural)
Attacks:	Slam +19/+14/+9 melee
Damage:	Slam 2d8+6 and suffocation
Face/Reach:	10 ft. by 5 ft./15 ft.
Special Attacks:	Suffocation
Special Qualities:	Damage reduction 10/+2, elem-

	ental, space subtype
Saves:	Fort +9, Ref +19, Will +5
Abilities:	Str 18, Dex 29, Con 18, Int 6, Wis 11, Cha 11
Skills:	Listen +18, Spot +18
Feats:	Flyby Attack, Improved Initiative, Weapon Finesse (slam), Zero-G Tolerance

Space Elemental, Greater
Huge Elemental (Space)

Hit Dice:	21d8+84 (178 hp)
Initiative:	+14 (+10 Dex, +4 Improved Initiative)
Speed:	Fly 100 ft. (perfect)
AC:	24 (–2 size, +10 Dex, +6 natural)
Attacks:	Slam +23/+18/+13 melee
Damage:	Slam 2d8+7 and suffocation
Face/Reach:	10 ft. by 5 ft./15 ft.
Special Attacks:	Suffocation
Special Qualities:	Damage reduction 10/+2, elemental, space subtype
Saves:	Fort +11, Ref +22, Will +7
Abilities:	Str 20, Dex 31, Con 18, Int 6, Wis 11, Cha 11
Skills:	Listen +23, Spot +23
Feats:	Dodge, Flyby Attack, Improved Initiative, Weapon Finesse (slam), Zero-G Tolerance

Space Elemental, Elder
Huge Elemental (Space)

Hit Dice:	24d8+84 (204 hp)
Initiative:	+15 (+11 Dex, +4 Improved Initiative)
Speed:	Fly 100 ft. (perfect)
AC:	25 (–2 size, +11 Dex, +6 natural)
Attacks:	Slam +27/+22/+17/+12 melee
Damage:	Slam 2d8+9 and suffocation
Face/Reach:	10 ft. by 5 ft./15 ft.
Special Attacks:	Suffocation
Special Qualities:	Damage reduction 15/+3, elemental, space subtype
Saves:	Fort +12, Ref +25, Will +8
Abilities:	Str 22, Dex 33, Con 18, Int 6, Wis 11, Cha 11
Skills:	Listen +26, Spot +26
Feats:	Dodge, Flyby Attack, Improved Initiative, Weapon Finesse (slam), Zero-G Tolerance
Climate/Terrain:	Any
Organization:	Solitary
Challenge Rating:	Small 1; medium 3; large 5; huge 7; greater 9; elder 11

Treasure:	None
Alignment:	Usually neutral
Advancement:	Small 3 HD (Small); medium 5–7 HD (Medium-size); large 9–15 (Large); huge 17–20 HD (Huge); greater 22–23 HD (Huge); elder 25+ HD (Huge)

Unlike other elementals, the space elemental is not an embodiment of a specific form of physical matter. Rather, it is the embodiment of the void between the stars.

Space elementals are fast and silent. Their spherical bodies are pitch black, insubstantial, and do not reflect light. Spots of illumination that look like constellations of tiny stars form where one might expect eyes to be. In combat, the touch of a space elemental can suck the breath from a victim's lungs.

A space elemental can exist just about anywhere, though it prefers the emptiness of space. If it spends more than three days in contact with dense matter—including even a standard planetary atmosphere—the elemental dies. The resulting implosion can be lethal to anyone in the elemental's vicinity.

Space elementals can understand the languages of the other elementals: Auran, Teran, Ignan, or Aquan. However, they cannot speak, as the hard vacuum that forms their bodies does not allow the transmission of sound.

COMBAT

A space elemental attacks by slamming into a target, attempting to envelop its foe with its body. This close contact exposes the victim to hard vacuum and can cause rapid suffocation.

Elemental: Immune to poison, sleep, paralysis, and stunning. Not affected by critical hits.

Death Implosion (Ex): When a space elemental is killed, it loses its physical coherence. Surrounding matter rushes violently to fill the void left by the elemental. This causes a concussive effect that deals 1d6 points of damage for every two Hit Dice the creature has. Creatures within 10 feet of the elemental when it implodes are affected and can make a Reflex save (DC 15) for half damage.

Space Subtype (Ex): Immune to the effects of vacuum. A space elemental does not need to breathe, and it is unaffected by radiation.

Suffocation (Ex): When a space elemental hits a target in melee, the target must make a Fortitude save or begin to suffocate. The first time this save is failed, the victim falls unconscious. The second time, the victim falls to –1 hit points and is dying. The third time, the victim suffocates.

If the space elemental manages to grapple a victim and the victim fails the Fortitude save, the victim does not get to save again until the elemental releases the hold.

The DC for the Fortitude save is based on the elemental's size. This is shown on the table below.

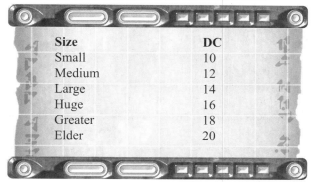

Size	DC
Small	10
Medium	12
Large	14
Huge	16
Greater	18
Elder	20

LASERBALL

Fine Construct

Hit Dice:	1/8d10 (1 hp)
Initiative:	+0
Speed:	Fly 30 ft. (perfect)
AC:	22 (+4 Dex, +8 size)
Attacks:	Holdout laser +12 ranged
Damage:	1d10
Face/Reach:	1/2 ft. by 1/2 ft./0 ft.
Special Attacks:	—
Special Qualities:	Construct, darkvision 60 ft., fly
Saves:	Fort +0, Ref +4, Will +0
Abilities:	Str 4, Dex 19, Con —, Int —, Wis 11, Cha 1
Skills:	—
Feats:	—
Climate/Terrain:	Any aerial
Organization:	Solitary, string (2–5)
Challenge Rating:	1
Treasure:	None
Alignment:	Always neutral
Advancement:	1/4 HD (Diminutive)

A laserball is a spherical construct about six inches in diameter. It flits around in the air and zaps targets with its laser, darting about like a *hasted* butterfly.

Laserballs were originally designed as training devices, but it was immediately obvious how useful they could be for security as well. They are expensive but wonderfully effective. They also make great conversation pieces for their owners. Robotic, non-magical versions have been manufactured, but the extreme maneuverability allowed by magical flight has proven impos-

sible to match in a small mechanical device.

A laserball's owner can direct it verbally in combat or let it act independently. The laserball recognizes its owner's voice and only takes orders from him or another person the owner has authorized. If the laserball gets conflicting orders from two or more people, it stops and hovers, waiting for clarification. It still defends itself if attacked while operating in this standby mode.

A laserball can be ordered to patrol an area or guard an object or entrance. Any time someone it does not recognize enters the patrolled or guarded area, the laserball attacks. It can be programmed to accept a password as well.

COMBAT

When a laserball spots an intruder, it zips around the target, looking for an open shot. If coordinating with others, it tries to flank the target. It can move in extremely close to a target and still fire its tiny laser.

Construct: Immune to mind-influencing effects, poison, disease, and similar effects. Not subject to critical hits, subdual damage, ability damage, energy drain, or death from massive damage.

Flight (Sp): The laserball's magical construction allows it to fly as the spell as a free action.

SOULMECH

Medium-Size Construct

Hit Dice:	2d10 (11 hp)
Initiative:	+0
Speed:	40 ft.
AC:	10
Attacks:	Dagger +2 melee; or light autopistol pistol +0 ranged
Damage:	Dagger 1d4+1; light autopistol 1d10
Face/Reach:	5 ft. by 5 ft./5 ft.
Special Qualities:	Soulmech traits
Saves:	Fort +0, Ref −1, Will +3
Abilities:	Str 13, Dex 9, Con —, Int 13, Wis 10, Cha 8
Skills:	Repair +10, Use Device +7
Feats:	Ambidexterity, Skill Focus (Repair), Technical Proficiency
Climate/Terrain:	Any
Organization:	Solitary or team (2–4)
Challenge Rating:	2
Treasure:	Standard
Alignment:	Any
Advancement:	By character class

Soulmechs are robotic constructs animated with a sentient soul. They are created by transferring a living soul into a complex neural net that is then installed in a robotic body. Soulmechs are encountered in many different shapes and forms. The most common are humanoid, for a couple of reasons. First, the souls that animate most soulmechs once possessed humanoid bodies and familiar forms are the most comfortable for them. Second, a humanoid body is an extremely versatile construction for which all sorts of equipment, replacement parts, and upgrades can be readily obtained. However, a soulmech's neural net can be installed in just about any kind of sophisticated machine.

Many soulmechs owe their robotic bodies to the people who created them. These soulmechs frequently work for years to pay off this debt. Because soulmechs can labor tirelessly and are effectively immortal, most find these obligations are a small and short-term price to pay for a second chance at life.

Free soulmechs often wander the galaxy looking for new experiences. Some pursue a means to be returned to organic life, but others revel in their theoretical immortality. Some soulmechs react against their mechanical existence and devote their lives to the study of living things, but most embrace it, becoming mechanists, technicians, and pilots. Their robotic bodies do not prevent them from working magic, and a few soulmechs become sorcerers, wizards, and even clerics.

COMBAT

Many soulmechs prefer to avoid physical confrontation with their foes. While they are hardy warriors, they are all too aware that life is fragile enough in any form that it should not be needlessly risked. When possible, soulmechs often prefer to avoid combat, or failing that, to resolve violent conflicts as quickly as possible.

Soulmech Traits (Ex): Soulmechs have a number of racial traits.

- Like magical constructs, soulmechs do not have Constitution scores.
- Low-light Vision: Soulmechs can see twice as far as a human in starlight, moonlight, torchlight, and similar conditions of poor illumination. They retain the ability to distinguish color and detail under these conditions.
- Ambidexterity: Due to their artificial brains and robotic bodies, soulmechs do not favor one hand like organic beings. Soulmechs receive the Ambidexterity feat for free.
- +2 racial bonus on Disable Device, Repair, and Use Device checks: Soulmechs have an innate understanding of machines.

- +4 racial bonus on Knowledge (mathematics) checks: A soulmech's computerized mind can make calculations much more quickly and easily than an organic being's.
- −4 racial penalty on Swim checks: Soulmechs do not have significant air pockets in their robotic bodies, and they lack buoyancy as a result.
- Soulmechs have no sense of smell or taste, and they do not eat or drink.
- Soulmechs do not breathe.
- Immunity to necromantic or death effects that require or target a living body. Soulmechs are subject to effects that target a living creature's spirit or soul, including energy drain.
- Immunity to poison, sleep, paralysis, stunning, disease, subdual damage, and damage or drain to physical ability scores. Soulmechs are subject to critical hits. They have minds and can suffer damage to their mental abilities.
- Immunity to any effect that requires a Fortitude save, unless it also works on objects.
- Soulmechs are unaffected by *dispel magic* or any antimagic field. In effect, the spell that created the soulmech has run its course.
- Unlike true constructs, soulmechs have minds and are therefore vulnerable to mind-affecting spells and effects.
- Soulmechs cannot heal damage on their own and cannot be healed by divine magic. They cannot be healed by psionic powers that require a living body. They can be repaired and healed by arcane magic.
- Cannot be *raised* or *resurrected*. A new *soul bind* spell cast immediately after the character's death will allow it to be transferred to a new neural net.
- Cannot increase physical ability scores (Strength, Dexterity) as the character advances in level. The character may still increase mental ability scores (Intelligence, Wisdom, Charisma).
- Cannot benefit from magic (spells or items) that enhances physical ability scores (e.g., *bull's strength* or *gauntlets of ogre power*).
- Cannot ingest potions, drugs, or spell components that must be consumed.
- Cannot use spellware.
- Soulmechs can learn, prepare, and cast spells normally, except for the prohibition on ingested spell components.
- Soulmechs are living creatures, not undead. They cannot be turned or rebuked.
- Soulmechs are internally powered and do not require recharging.
- Soulmechs are effectively immortal. They do not age and cannot die of old age.
- No matter the soulmech's original race, he doesn't

get any of the standard racial traits not specifically listed here. For instance, a dwarf soulmech loses his stonecunning ability.

SOCIETY

Soulmechs have no real society of their own. They often prefer the company of the people they knew in their former lives, but just as often they start afresh. In some large cities, soulmechs have been known to form loose-knit social groups that meet regularly so members can discuss social issues, offer mutual support, and exchange information.

Many soulmechs were victims of lethal accidents or incidents. Upon their untimely deaths, their souls were captured and placed into their new bodies. In some cases, this was done without the soul's consent: The new soulmech finds himself indebted to a stranger…or even an enemy from his former life.

Some soulmechs are as friendly and approachable as they were in life—possibly even more so. Relieved of the limitations of organic bodies, they revel in their new freedoms and expanded capabilities. The opportunities and the long life that lies before them can be exhilarating.

Other soulmechs are not nearly as content with their lot. These melancholy souls are trapped between their dissatisfaction with their new forms and their desire to live. Many of these bitter soulmechs live solitary lives, seeing as few people as possible and spending most of their time with the machines whose forms they now share.

CHARACTERS

A soulmech's favored class is mechanist. Those who are considered leaders in their loose communities are often mechanists or mechanist/wizards.

SPACE KRAKEN

Gargantuan Magical Beast (Space)

Hit Dice:	20d10+180 (290 hp)
Initiative:	+4 (Improved Initiative)
Speed:	Fly 1,000 ft. (good)
AC:	16 (–4 size, +10 natural)
Attacks:	2 tentacle rakes +28 melee, 6 arms +23 melee, bite +23 melee
Damage:	Tentacle rake 2d8+12, arm 1d6+6, bite 4d6+6
Face/Reach:	20 ft. by 40 ft./10 ft. (100 ft. with tentacles)
Special Attacks:	Darkvision 1,000 ft., improved grab, constrict 2d8+12 or

	1d6+6
Special Qualities:	Space subtype, teleport hitcher
Saves:	Fort +21, Ref +12, Will +13
Abilities:	Str 34, Dex 10, Con 29, Int 21, Wis 20, Cha 10
Skills:	Concentration +14, Freefall +15, Intuit Direction +15, Knowledge (astronomy) +10, Navigate +10, Search +10, Spot +10
Feats:	Alertness, Blind-Fight, Improved Critical (tentacle), Improved Initiative, Improved Trip, Iron Will, Zero-G Tolerance
Climate/Terrain:	Space
Organization:	Solitary or pod (2–4)
Challenge Rating:	12
Treasure:	Triple standard
Alignment:	Always neutral
Advancement:	21–32 HD (Gargantuan); 33–60 HD (Colossal)

The space kraken is a close cousin to the king under the waves, the kraken. It plies the spacelanes instead of the sealanes, feeding off of asterwraths and the occasional small ship or shuttle. The space kraken roams star systems throughout the known galaxy, often soaring in and out of asteroid belts in search of food.

When a space kraken encounters a ship, it's rarely looking for a fight. Frequently, however, the creature will try to hitch a ride on the much faster vessel. Unless a space kraken can catch a ride on a ship equipped with a starcaster, it will be confined to a single star system for the duration of its life. While they are long-lived, these creatures move far too slowly to travel between the stars.

Of course, many a starship captain has panicked when a space kraken grappled his ship. Fearful crews often make the mistake of attacking the creatures. If attacked, a space kraken retaliates mercilessly. On the other hand, if the ship teleports away, taking the kraken with it, the creature will almost always go its own way and leave its benefactor alone. If the ship cuts power and doesn't move, the space kraken will move on after a brief time.

More than one deep-space mission has reported finding a well-preserved space kraken's corpse floating out in the blackness. Sometimes the crews of these ships received a rude surprise when they probed the creature, as a massive eye opened and fixed the craft with a baleful glare. Apparently, space krakens put themselves into extended hibernation for years or even decades at a time.

Many veteran pilots and spacers speak in awe of wit-

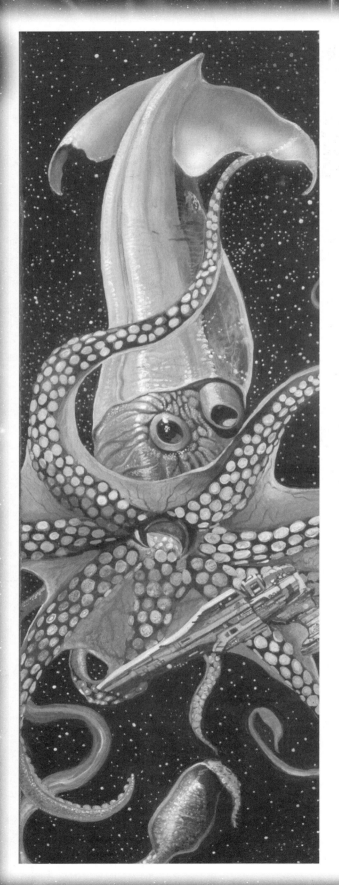

nessing a battle between a space kraken and an aster-wrath. The mighty battles between these massive foes seem to shake the heavens and can be dangerous indeed for ships that stray too close.

Legends of space krakens large enough to endanger even imperial dreadnoughts persist but have never been substantiated.

COMBAT

Space krakens lash out at victims with their tentacles, then drag the victims into range of their six arms. Once the life has been squeezed out of the victim, the space kraken drags it into its gaping maw. Space krakens cannot feed on inorganic matter. If they attack spacecraft, it is usually in self-defense.

Improved Grab (Ex): To use this ability, the space kraken must hit an opponent of up to Huge size with an arm or tentacle attack. If it gets a hold, it can constrict.

Constrict (Ex): A space kraken deals automatic arm or tentacle damage with a successful grapple check against Huge or smaller creatures.

Space Subtype (Ex): Immune to radiation and vacuum.

Spell-Like Abilities: 2/day—*tractor beam*. Treat as if cast by a 13th-level wizard (save DC 22).

Teleport Hitcher (Ex): If the space kraken gets a hold of a Colossal or larger starship, the ship will take the creature with it if it teleports to another location. The kraken is unharmed by this unorthodox method of travel.

CHAPTER EIGHT

RUNNING DRAGONSTAR

Running a **Dragonstar** game is pretty similar to running a traditional fantasy campaign using the d20 System. There are relatively few new rules to learn, and if you're already familiar with the system, you shouldn't have any trouble adapting to **Dragonstar**.

Most of the new rules you'll need to run a **Dragonstar** campaign are presented in the *Starfarer's Handbook*. This chapter expands on them, providing rules and guidelines for use in special situations and unique environments.

MONEY

As discussed in the *Starfarer's Handbook*, the standard unit of currency in the Dragon Empire is the imperial credit. The credit (cr) is equivalent to a gold piece in traditional fantasy games. Credits can be broken down into deks (0.1 cr) and cents (0.01 cr), which are equivalent to silver and copper pieces, respectively.

BANKS

There are millions of banks scattered across the Dragon Empire, from local branches to vast interstellar financial institutions that buy and sell whole corporations. If you have a bank account, you can deposit money directly into the account, withdraw funds from it as needed, or transfer money between accounts. On developed worlds, the vast majority of legitimate transactions are electronic: Numbers are added and subtracted from the appropriate accounts and nothing tangible ever changes hands.

Most payments are made by direct electronic transfer from one account to another. For example, when an employee is paid by his corporation, the amount of his salary is deposited directly into his designated account. When he pays his taxes, money is transferred electronically from his account to a limited-access account maintained by the Ministry of the Treasury.

You can access your bank account with a datapad if the area you're in has a developed communications network. You can even make transactions from one throneworld to another over the InfoNet. Even if you don't have a datapad or access to a network, you can access your account from electronic terminals located throughout the developed worlds of the Empire.

CREDIT CHIPS

While datapads give you access to your accounts and allow you to make a variety of transactions, credit chips are essentially "virtual wallets" that store credits electronically. Credit chips are thumbprint and pheromone activated and respond to both voice commands and coded electronic signals. Credit chips can be slotted into automated processor terminals or datapads to transfer credits from an account to the chip or vice versa. You can also transfer credits from one credit chip to another via wireless electronic link.

Credit chips were designed for the convenience of the user. They allow you to make quick and easy purchases from any properly equipped vendor, automated terminal, or even individuals with their own credit chip. These simple devices are much more portable and convenient and still provide all the versatility of hard currency.

Transactions made with credit chips, however, are much easier to trace than those using hard currency. The chip's onboard computer maintains a log of all transactions and the identification code of all accounts and credit chips involved in the transactions. Every time a credit chip is slotted into a networked terminal—such as those maintained by banks and other financial institutions—these records are automatically transferred to permanent storage. If you want to cover the electronic trail, you can discard a credit chip after making a payment. However, this leaves an "open transfer" on the records of the bank that maintains your account, and this can raise flags that alert both bank employees and government investigators.

EXAMPLE

Justica Eagle has an account at a major bank in Betherian on Galador. At one of the electronic terminals in the city, she transfers 3,000 cr from her account to a credit chip. She then gets in an autocab, makes the short trip down the Long Road, and crosses over to Rilion. Justica stops in one of the small bordertowns near the gate and meets some underworld contacts. She buys an assault blaster from a local arms dealer, transferring 2,500 cr from her credit chip to the dealer's. She has 500 cr left on the chip to pay the autocab and make a few purchases before she attempts to smuggle the restricted weapon back into Betherian.

CASH

While the Empire's developed worlds operate almost entirely on electronic currency, there are many places in the known galaxy that lack the communications infrastructure to support such an advanced economy. On many Outlands worlds—even those that have recently been colonized—the computer networks necessary for an electronic economy simply do not exist. If you want to buy or sell something on these worlds, you must either operate on the barter system or have access to a currency the locals will honor.

Those operating on the margins of the law—or beyond them—often do not want their transactions and exchanges to be monitored or traced back to them. They hide illicit or questionable commercial activity from financial institutions, employers, law enforcement, and a variety of government agencies.

In the Outlands and the underworlds of the developed planets, cash is still king. Cash versions of the imperial credit are circulated by the Ministry of the Treasury through major financial institutions. This currency is available in denominations of 0.01 (one cent), 0.1 (one dek), 1, 10, 100, and 1,000 cr. Most of this currency is used in legitimate business—often in trade with underdeveloped Outlands colonies—but a lot of it finds its way into the gray and black markets of the Empire's semi-legitimate and criminal underworlds and invisible economies.

Coins minted from precious metals are common throughout the Outlands and usually honored on imperial worlds as well. These coins are often melted down and reminted as they circulate from planet to planet, losing little if any of their original value. Molecular analysis can reveal the composition of coins, but they are otherwise effectively impossible to trace. Their principle drawback, of course, is that they are bulky and heavy, making them inconvenient and often expensive to transport in large quantities.

Travelers and Outlanders do plenty of trade in gems and jewelry as well. While it may be possible to trace such valuables back to their point of origin, this cannot usually establish a record of possession and exchange and is therefore rarely effective in identifying and tracing illegal activity.

BARTER

On some worlds, even physical currency is uncommon. Instead, the economy is dominated by personal exchanges of goods and services: barter. On somewhat developed worlds, the value of traded goods and services may be measured in terms of credits or gold pieces; on more primitive worlds, the locals may have no experience with or understanding of currency. On worlds where the barter system figures prominently in the local economy, there is an art to even the simplest trades. With no fixed prices for anything, the Diplomacy skill is crucial for haggling a favorable deal and Appraise is required to accurately judge the value of trade goods.

TRANSPORTATION

During the course of their adventures in the Dragon Empire, the characters will do a lot of traveling. A single adventure can take the characters from one side of a city to another or even across the known galaxy and back. Many times, the characters won't have their own vehicle—or perhaps not an appropriate one—and will have to either hire a charter or rely on public transportation.

For full details on many of the vehicles available in **Dragonstar**, consult the *Starfarer's Handbook*. This section discusses how to arrange for transportation and details the various costs involved.

PUBLIC TRANSPORTATION

The developed worlds of the Dragon Empire have excellent public transportation systems. In the largest cities, parking for private vehicles is often at a premium, and the costs for purchasing, maintaining, and insuring such a vehicle are prohibitive for many common folk. Travel between cities is usually accomplished by bullet trains or aircraft. Nothing beats a *teleport* for sheer speed and convenience, of course, but it is expensive and sometimes dangerous.

BUSES AND TRAINS

Many different kinds of buses are common in the Dragon Empire, from conventional ground vehicles, to hovercraft, to air transports. Most trains operate on magnetic levitation technology and are capable of reaching truly amazing speeds. These bullet trains can cross entire continents in a matter of a few hours.

Buses and trains run on regular schedules, and these will not always be convenient for the characters. These common public conveyances do run more frequently during peak hours, sometimes every few minutes along major routes. Of course, seating can be precious at these times as well. Buses and trains see the least use during the late nighttime and early morning hours.

Along with fixed schedules, the other major drawback of buses and trains are their fixed routes. They are often poor choices for transportation to out of the way locations.

SLIDEWALKS

Slidewalks are popular methods of transportation in major cities because they avoid the scheduling limitations of buses and trains. Slidewalks are networks of pedestrian conveyors that crisscross a city. You enter the network by stepping onto a slow-moving access walk and can then move on to progressively faster lines that cover more ground. The fastest lines reach speeds of up to 100 miles per hour.

Slidewalks are normally only found in the most densely populated regions of the Dragon Empire. The largest and most heavily trafficked network is built in tunnels running below the Long Road.

SPACECRAFT AND AIRCRAFT

Spacecraft equipped with starcasters are the fastest method of large-scale transportation between planets and star systems. A variety of aircraft, most equipped with Vertical Take-Off and Landing capability, are the most common method of rapid atmospheric travel.

Starports and airports are notorious for their extraordinary security measures. Typically, weapons and offensive magic items are prohibited in these facilities and onboard commercial flights. Exceptions are typically made for characters with licensed spellware, as it cannot be removed, but there are some high-security air- and spaceports that are completely off limits to characters with potentially dangerous enhancements. In rare cases, commercial flights may offer service to such characters but require them to travel in specially designed cabins affected by antimagic fields.

WATERCRAFT

On planets with extensive oceans, sea travel is common even in the most developed parts of the Empire. Ships are a very cost-effective means of transporting large cargoes on a planetary surface, and submersibles are often used on planets with surface conditions that make travel hazardous. Cruise ships and charter craft remain a popular form of vacation travel.

TELEPORTATION

Some major planets, large cities, and important locations are linked by permanent teleportation circles. The portals connecting the Long Road are just one example of the application of teleportation technology in the Dragon Empire. Due to their expense and built-in limitations, these facilities remain somewhat uncommon. In many cases, they are accessible only to a privileged few—such as the aristocracy—or only for specific, high-priority missions.

HIRING A RIDE

Transportation	Cost
Public	
Bus (local)	1 cr/trip
Bus (long distance)	0.1 cr/mile
Train (local)	2 cr/trip
Train (long distance)	0.2 cr/mile
Slidewalk (local)	1 cr/trip
Ferry (local)	0.25 cr/trip
Cruise ship (long distance)	0.2 cr/mile
Passenger submarine (local)	1 cr/trip
Aircraft (planetary)	0.1 cr/mile
Spacecraft (planetary)	0.2 cr/mile
Spacecraft (interplanetary)	0.02 cr/mile
Spacecraft (interstellar)	200 cr/day
Teleport	500 cr
Antimagic field premium	+50%
Private	
Taxicab (local or long distance)	0.5 cr/mile
Hovertaxi (local or long distance)	1 cr/mile
Helicopter (local or long distance)	1 cr/mile
Taxiboat (local or long distance)	0.5 cr/mile
Taxisub (local or long distance)	1 cr/mile
Aircraft (planetary)	0.2 cr/mile
Spacecraft (planetary)	0.4 cr/mile
Spacecraft (interplanetary)	0.04 cr/mile
Spacecraft (interstellar)	1,000 cr/day plus 10,000 cr per *teleport*

HIRING A RIDE

When public transportation just won't do, a character may need to arrange for private transportation. In major cities, there are many different options, from taxis to chartered boats and aircraft. In the Outlands or in less developed areas of imperial worlds, options may be much more limited.

Average costs for various forms of transportation are listed below. These can vary greatly from place to place. The prices listed below are all for one-way trips. The fees for private transportation vary the most and are a matter of negotiation between the passengers and their pilot. See the table on the previous page for details.

SPECIAL ABILITIES

The d20 System core rules describe many different special abilities and conditions. Most of these work the same in **Dragonstar** as they do in a traditional fantasy campaign. This section provides additional rules and expanded discussions covering the use of special abilities and conditions in the **Dragonstar** universe. If a special ability is not listed here, you can assume that it is unchanged.

ABILITY SCORE LOSS

Soulmechs can be affected normally by attacks that cause ability score damage to Intelligence, Wisdom, and Charisma. They cannot be affected by attacks that cause damage to Strength and Dexterity. Soulmechs are immune to attacks that affect Constitution because they have no Constitution score.

BLINDSIGHT

This special ability does not function in outer space. Since there is no air to transmit sounds, smells, vibrations, or variations in temperature, a creature cannot rely on secondary senses to replace sight.

BURROW

Creatures that can burrow cannot tunnel through many modern materials. If a creature's description states that it can burrow through rock, the creature can penetrate anything of hardness 8 or less. This includes plastic and aluminum but not metals and composites.

BREATH WEAPON

Breath weapons work normally in vacuum, even in outer space.

CONSTRUCT

Constructs, including robots and soulmechs, function normally in vacuum. Magically created constructs, such as golems, can be affected by the *repair damage* spells described in the *Starfarer's Handbook*. The magic immunity ability of golems and similar constructs does not apply to these spells.

Constructs are immune to all forms of radiation.

DISEASES

There are many different kinds of diseases in **Dragonstar**, ranging from the common cold to bioengineered, military-grade retroviruses. Some sample diseases are listed in the table below.

Common Cold: This is a group of viruses that attack the respiratory system and cause congestion, aches and pains, and other symptoms.

Influenza: Also known as "the flu," this is a more tenacious virus than the cold, with similar but more severe effects. It manifests in many different strains.

Malaria: A parasitical disease of the blood transmitted by insect bites. The disease causes severe chills and fever.

Meningitis: This inflammation of the membranes around the spine and brain causes severe headaches,

Disease	Infection	DC	Incubation	Damage
Common cold	Contact/Inhaled	10	1d3 days	1d4 Str
Influenza	Inhaled	14	1d4 days	1d6 Str
Malaria	Injury	10	1d3 days	1d3 Con, 1d3 Dex
Meningitis	Contact	14	1d6 days	1d6 Dex, 1d4 Con
Pneumonia	Inhaled	14	1d6 days	1d6 Con
Retrovirus	Contact	10	2d6 days	2d4 Con

vomiting, and possible paralysis.

Pneumonia: A form of severe respiratory infection that can cause death if untreated.

Retrovirus: These insidious viruses reproduce by infecting and rewriting the victim's DNA, causing a wide variety of debilitating and potentially lethal complications, symptoms, and diseases.

HEALING DISEASES

Advanced medicine has developed cures or effective treatments for all but a few nonmagical diseases. The trick is getting treatment before the disease does too much damage. In the Outlands, this can be difficult, but it's not impossible.

Standard medkits give skilled medical professionals a +10 circumstance bonus on their Heal checks to treat any of the nonmagical diseases listed here or in the core rules. While in the care of a healer with access to advanced medicine, characters recover 2 points of ability score damage per day. The diseased character must be in the healer's care and spend most of each day resting to gain these benefits.

A character placed in a functional and fully supplied autodoc completely recovers from any of the listed diseases within one day.

ETHEREALNESS

Ethereal creatures are unaffected by changes in gravity. There is no gravity on the Ethereal Plane. This does not require creatures traveling on the Ethereal Plane to make Freefall checks, however. Ethereal creatures can move wherever and however they like without being affected by physical forces such as gravity or friction.

FLYING

If a creature uses wings to fly, it cannot fly in a vacuum. It requires air to provide lift and thrust. Within the troposphere—up to about 10 miles in altitude on a 1g planet—a winged creature can fly normally. Within the stratosphere—from 10 to 30 miles up on a 1g planet—the creature loses two steps in maneuverability. If the creature's maneuverability is poor or clumsy to begin with, it cannot fly in the stratosphere at all. No winged creatures can fly above the stratosphere. The air is simply too thin to support winged flight. Creatures that fly purely by magical means ignore these restrictions.

FIRE

Normal fires need oxygen to burn, and there is no oxygen in space. Any normal fire exposed to vacuum is instantly snuffed. Magical fires burn just fine without oxygen. However, they cannot ignite normal fires. For example, a *fireball* would discharge normally in vacuum, but it could not set flammable materials alight.

GASEOUS FORM

Even when exposed to vacuum, a creature in gaseous form is not dispersed. The creature is unaffected by extremes in atmospheric pressure.

The gas the creature changes into is not flammable and cannot sustain a fire. However, the creature can be damaged normally by fire.

The gas is not breathable and cannot be used as an air supply.

Most hatches and all airlocks are sealed. A creature in gaseous form cannot pass through them when they are closed and secured.

Gaseous creatures are unaffected by alterations in gravity. Their mass is too negligible for variant gravity to have a noticeable effect on them.

GAZE ATTACKS

Gaze attacks do not work through any form of broadcast media. Recorded images of a gaze attack—whether still or full motion—have no effect on anyone looking at them. As a result, a character viewing a creature with a gaze attack through some form of imaging device does

Poison	Type	DC	Initial Damage	Secondary Damage	Price
Arsenic	Ingested	15	2d6 Str	1d6 Str	100 cr
Cyanide	Ingested	17	3d6 Str	0	200 cr
Mustard gas	Contact	20	3d10 hp	1d6 Con	300 cr
Nerve gas	Inhaled	20	Paralysis	3d6 Con	500 cr
Rat poison	Ingested	12	1d6 Con	1d4 Con	5 cr

not have to make a saving throw to resist the attack. Devices that transmit light directly, such as optical telescopes or gun scopes, do not protect against gaze attacks.

The eyes of robots and soulmechs are electronic, but they do not create recorded images. They feed visual stimuli directly to the soulmech's visual processors. In this respect, they are similar in design to the eyes of organic beings. As a result, soulmechs and robots are not immune to gaze attacks unless they are otherwise immune to the effect of the attack. This typically includes any gaze attack that is resisted with a Fortitude save.

INCORPOREALITY

Incorporeal creatures are unaffected by changes in gravity. As incorporeal beings, they have no mass. A ghost or similar creature that manifests physically still remains weightless and insubstantial.

INVISIBILITY

Characters using active sonar imaging devices can see invisible creatures. The vision is in black and white, similar to darkvision.

In vacuum, a creature cannot use its hearing or sense of smell to detect or locate an invisible creature.

PARALYSIS AND HOLD

Robots and soulmechs are immune to paralysis. They are not immune to *hold* spells that affect the mind.

PLANTS

Plants exposed to vacuum can suffer damage from suffocation. Even underwater, most plants are able to gather the carbon dioxide they need to live, but they cannot survive true vacuum. Of course, plants are very different from animals physiologically and they react to the effects of vacuum differently as well. After each hour of exposure to vacuum, a planet takes 1d6 points of damage.

POISON

There are many different poisons available in **Dragonstar**. In addition to those described in the core rules, some of the more common ones are listed in the table on the previous page.

ANTIDOTES

Advanced medical technology makes it relatively simple to treat most exposures to poison. It's impossible to prevent the initial damage a poison inflicts, simply because of a lack of time before the effects set in. However, the timely administration of an antidote—which can be found in any standard medkit or in the supplies of any autodoc—grants the victim a +10 circumstance bonus to the Fortitude save to avoid secondary damage. Broad-spectrum antidotes are available that are effective against many common poisons. There may be no effective antidotes for certain rare poisons, at the DM's discretion.

PSIONICS

The same rules governing magic determine the effects of psionic abilities on soulmechs. A soulmech's physical ability scores cannot be affected by psionics. Soulmechs cannot be healed by psionic abilities that require a living body, such as *biofeedback* and *body adjustment*.

Subject to these limitations, soulmechs can gain levels in psionic classes and can use psionic powers.

SCENT

Scent does not work in vacuum, as there is no medium to transmit smells.

Soulmechs and other machines do have a scent. However, their scent is faint relative to organic creatures, and they can only be detected within 15 feet or 7 feet if downwind.

The standard DC for tracking a soulmech or other high-tech machine by scent is 15. For purposes of being detected or tracked by this ability, creatures in sealed environment suits (HEV suits, powered armor, and so on) are treated as machines.

SONIC ATTACKS

As with gaze attacks, sonic attacks are supernatural abilities and their effects cannot be recorded or transmitted electronically. Soulmechs are affected normally by sonic attacks, subject to their other immunities.

TREMORSENSE

This ability can be used wherever there are solid surfaces to transmit vibrations, including buildings, vehicles, starships, and space stations. Creatures with this ability can sense vibrations from other floors or levels of an enclosed structure as long as they are within range.

THE ENVIRONMENT

There are many unique environments that characters are bound to encounter in their travels throughout the Dragon Empire. Many environmental effects are discussed in the core rules. This section covers several environments and their effects that figure prominently in a **Dragonstar** campaign.

VACUUM

Exposure to vacuum doesn't directly harm a creature. Your head or lungs don't explode from your body's internal pressures, and you aren't instantly frozen by the coldness of space. You might suffer a bit from overexposure to unfiltered UV radiation, but that's likely going to be your least concern should you survive.

The most immediate problem for an unprotected creature in outer space is the complete lack of air. If you have air in your lungs when you're exposed to vacuum, it is instantly expelled. If you try to hold your breath, you take 1d6 points of damage as the air is forced out and your lungs are damaged. Holding your breath is an instinctive reaction; unless you're prepared, there's a chance you'll do it even if you know better. When initially exposed to vacuum, you must succeed at a Will save (DC 15) to avoid instinctively holding your breath. Those with significant training and experience can substitute a Profession (spacer) check for the saving throw.

With no air in your lungs, you must immediately make a Constitution check (DC 10) or pass out. Every subsequent round, you must make the check again and the DC increases by +2. Once you fail the check, you immediately fall unconscious (0 hp) and are dying. On the following round, you drop to –1 hp. On the third round, you suffocate.

If you don't need to breathe or have some source of air, suffocation isn't a problem. In this case, all you have to worry about is radiation and temperature extremes.

If your skin is exposed to unfiltered sunlight, you take 1 point of damage every minute. The only way to protect yourself from this damage is to get out of direct sunlight or cover yourself completely with protective clothing. In space, you are also exposed to ambient radiation that can be harmful over time. For every hour of unprotected exposure to space, you take one dose of radiation (see below). Only specialized space and environmental suits can properly shield you from this radiation.

Your body will not instantaneously freeze if you're exposed to space—heat simply isn't radiated away that quickly. You take 1d6 points of damage each minute you are exposed to the extreme cold of space. There is no save and clothing is ineffective unless it is completely sealed and insulated against the cold.

Atmospheric Travel

On most habitable planets, the troposphere—the first layer of atmosphere in which weather occurs—is about 10 miles thick. As you ascend higher, the air gets thinner. Characters without adequate air supplies must make a Fortitude saving throw each hour (DC 15 + 1 per previous check), taking 1d6 points of subdual damage each time they fail.

After the troposphere, you reach the stratosphere, which extends from 10 miles to about 30 miles in altitude. In the stratosphere, unprotected characters suffer the effects of extreme cold (DMG 86). At these altitudes, characters without air supplies must make a Fortitude saving throw each minute (DC 15 +1 per previous check), taking 1d6 points of subdual damage each time they fail.

Above the stratosphere lies the mesosphere, which runs from 30 miles to 50 miles in altitude. Unprotected characters at this altitude suffer from extreme cold, but they take 2d6 points of subdual damage each time they fail the save. Fortitude saves against oxygen deprivation are required every round, and characters take 1d6 points of subdual damage each time they fail.

Beyond the stratosphere is the thermosphere, ranging between 50 miles and about 400 miles in altitude. It is much warmer at this level, though the air is so thin you couldn't feel the heat on your skin if you were somehow exposed. Exposure at this altitude can be treated in the same way as exposure to outer space.

Radiation

Exposure to radiation can make a living creature sick and can even cause a painful, lingering death. Radiation is measured in doses. A chest X-ray, for instance, is less than one dose and isn't a real hazard. A character exposed to direct sunlight in space might absorb one dose per minute. A character exposed to an unshielded or damaged reactor core might absorb 10 doses per minute.

Each time a creature takes a dose of radiation, he must make a Fortitude save (DC 10 for the first dose, +2 for each additional dose). There are two distinct effects of radiation exposure: hit point damage caused by burns and skin damage, and a chance to contract the group of related symptoms collectively known as radiation sickness.

A character who fails a Fort save to resist radiation exposure suffers 1d6 points of damage per dose of the exposure.

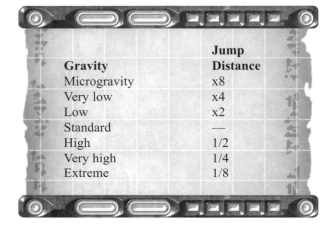

The character also has a 10% chance per dose of exposure to contract radiation sickness. A character who suffers from radiation sickness takes 1d4 Con initial damage and 1d4 Con secondary damage. Radiation sickness takes some time to manifest. The initial damage caused by a dose of radiation doesn't occur for 4d6 hours. The secondary damage caused by radiation poisoning is inflicted another 4d6 hours after the initial damage.

Ability damage from radiation sickness is permanent. In cases of extreme exposure, sickness is accompanied by symptoms such as hair loss and cancer, including leukemia, brain cancer, and skin cancer.

A character exposed to radiation is often unaware how sick the radiation is making him until it's too late. When a character takes a dose of radiation, the DM should make the Fortitude saves and timing rolls and hide the results from the player.

GRAVITY

In the course of your travels throughout the **Dragonstar** setting, you're bound to encounter planets with much different gravity. These range from the bone-crushing heavy Gs of a gas giant to the total weightlessness of deep space.

Extreme gravity levels can have a major impact on your ability to act effectively. Even slight variations can be problematic if you aren't prepared for them. The following table lists a range of gravities and the effects each has on your Strength and Dexterity scores. The gravity levels listed here correspond to those used in the section on world-building (see page 126).

GRAVITY CHECK MODIFIERS

Gravity	Dex Modifier	Str Modifier
Microgravity	–8	+8
Very low	–4	+4
Low	–2	+2
Standard	—	—
High	–2	–2
Very high	–4	–4
Extreme	–8	–8

If your Strength is reduced to 0 or less by the effects of gravity, you are pinned to the ground by your own weight and unable to move.

If your Dexterity is reduced to 0 or less by the effects of gravity, you are unable to move in any kind of coordinated fashion.

GRAVITY AND ARMOR

No matter what the gravity, your armor has the same effect on your speed and skill checks as it normally does. These effects are based more on the armor's bulk and the degree to which it restricts your range of motion rather than its weight.

JUMPING

Jumping is dramatically affected by variant gravity. You must adjust the distance you can jump in conditions of non-standard gravity. Use the standard rules to determine your distance, then modify the result according to the following table.

Gravity	Jump Distance
Microgravity	x8
Very low	x4
Low	x2
Standard	—
High	1/2
Very high	1/4
Extreme	1/8

CARRYING AND LIFTING LOADS

Your carrying capacity should also be adjusted for variant gravity. Modify your light, medium, and heavy loads according to the following table.

Gravity	Lifting Capacity
Microgravity	x8
Very low	x4
Low	x2
Standard	—
High	1/2
Very high	1/4
Extreme	1/8

For example, for a character with 10 Str, up to 33 lb. is a light load in standard gravity. The character can carry up to 66 lb. as a light load in low gravity but only 16 lb. in high gravity.

These modifiers are also applied to the weight a character can lift and drag. See the core rules for more information (PHB 142). Note, however, that gravity affects an object's weight but not its mass. This means that a moving object generates the same momentum in low gravity as it does in standard or high gravity. Once a massive object is in motion, it is just as hard to stop or control regardless of the level of gravity. As a result, where a moving object is concerned, you can often simply ignore the gravity modifier for the purposes of any attempt to stop or alter its motion.

EXAMPLE

Justica has Str 12, so her maximum load in microgravity is 1,040 lb. Working in the repair bay of an orbital station, she can push or pull a shuttle engine and manage to get it moving. Once moving, however, the engine's momentum is the same as it would be in standard gravity, and Justica had better stay out of its way.

CLIMBING

Variant gravity has a similar effect on climbing speed. A creature can climb up or down much more quickly in low gravity but must move much slower in high gravity.

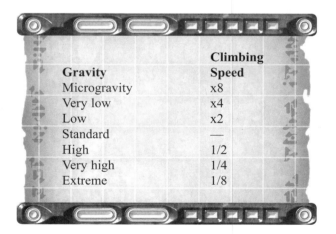

Gravity	Climbing Speed
Microgravity	x8
Very low	x4
Low	x2
Standard	—
High	1/2
Very high	1/4
Extreme	1/8

FALLING

Damage from falling, of course, is affected by variant gravity. Simply determine falling damage normally as if you were in standard gravity, then apply the following modifier.

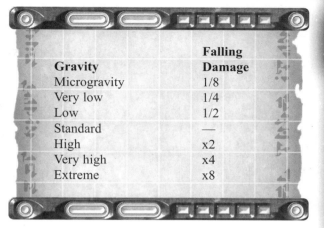

Gravity	Falling Damage
Microgravity	1/8
Very low	1/4
Low	1/2
Standard	—
High	x2
Very high	x4
Extreme	x8

FLYING

Variant gravity requires several special considerations for flying creatures. The basic game mechanics covering flying creatures are outlined in the core rules (DMG 69). The effects of variant gravity on base flying speed are listed in the following table.

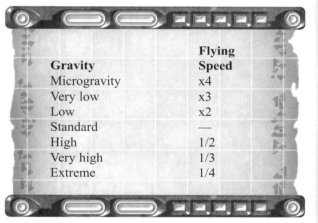

Gravity	Flying Speed
Microgravity	x4
Very low	x3
Low	x2
Standard	—
High	1/2
Very high	1/3
Extreme	1/4

To determine your maximum rate of ascent, modify your listed *up speed* according to the following table. The fastest you can ascend is still limited by your maneuverability class and flying speed, modified for gravity.

CHAPTER EIGHT: RUNNING DRAGONSTAR

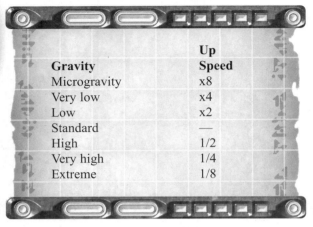

Gravity	Up Speed
Microgravity	x8
Very low	x4
Low	x2
Standard	—
High	1/2
Very high	1/4
Extreme	1/8

Gravity	Base Speed
Microgravity	x8
Very low	x4
Low	x2
Standard	—
High	1/2
Very high	1/4
Extreme	1/8

To determine your maximum rate of descent, modify your listed *down speed* according to the following table and add your modified flying speed.

Gravity	Down Speed
Microgravity	1/8
Very low	1/4
Low	1/2
Standard	—
High	x2
Very high	x4
Extreme	x8

For example, a gargoyle's base flying speed is 75 ft. Its up speed is 37.5 ft. and its down speed is 150 ft. In microgravity, the gargoyle's base flying speed and up speed are 300 ft., but its down speed is only 318 ft. In other words, because the effects of gravity are so negligible, the gargoyle can dive only slightly faster than it can fly laterally or climb.

MOVEMENT

Your movement rates are affected by variant gravity. You can move much more quickly in low gravity than you can in high gravity. Keep in mind, though, that the same rules that apply to moving objects apply to you as well. Momentum is based on mass and speed. Your mass doesn't change in variant gravity, so the faster you move, the more danger there is of mishaps.

RANGED WEAPONS

The range increments of thrown weapons and projectile weapons—including slug-throwers—should be modified according to the following table.

Gravity	Range Increments
Microgravity	x8
Very low	x4
Low	x2
Standard	—
High	1/2
Very high	1/4
Extreme	1/8

The maximum number of range increments at which a weapon can make an attack is unchanged. Thrown weapons are effective to five range increments and projectile weapons are effective to 10 range increments.

EXPLOSIVE DECOMPRESSION

When a spacecraft hull is holed, if there is pressurized air inside and hard vacuum outside, the air blasts out of the craft through the opening. If the breach is large enough, the air rushes out with such force that it's the equivalent of a hurricane inside the cabin that is decompressing. This is known as explosive decompression, and it lasts until the air in the room is entirely gone or the breach is sealed.

Roughly 1,000 cubic feet of air escape in the course of a single round through a Medium-size breach. This is the volume of air that fills a cube 10 feet on each side. Figure out the rough volume of the decompressing area, ignoring the furnishings and people inside. Divide the result by 1,000 to determine the number of rounds characters inside have before the air in the room is gone.

Once the air is completely gone, the hurricane-force winds subside, but anyone inside the decompressed area is exposed to hard vacuum. The intact bulkheads may shield the occupants from exposure to radiation.

As the air escapes, it pulls everything that's not secured toward the breach. When an object hits the outside edges of the breach—assuming it's large enough to do so—it takes damage as if it had fallen from its current position to the location of the breach. If the object survives the impact, it may actually block the breach. To do so, the object must have a hardness of at least 5 or be at least one size category larger than the breach. If the object is smaller than the breach or of insufficient hardness, it is sucked into space.

If a character cannot find something to hold onto or fails a Strength check (DC 15), he is sucked directly into the breach. If the breach is smaller than the character, this effectively seals the breach, but it can be extremely painful. First, the character takes the damage from the "fall" to the bulkhead. Then he takes an additional 1d6 points of bludgeoning damage per round from being buffeted against the bulkhead.

If the breach is up to one size category larger than the character, he must make a Reflex save (DC 15) to avoid being sucked out into space. If the character succeeds, he is wedged in the breach but is unable to block it entirely. He takes the buffeting damage listed above and also sustains damage from any loose item or person that is sucked onto him. While the character is partially blocking the breach, the DC of the Strength check for other characters in the decompressing area is reduced to 10.

If the breach is two size categories larger or more than the character, he must make a Reflex save (DC 20) to avoid being sucked out into space. If he succeeds, he must then make a Strength check (DC 20) every round to avoid being pulled through the breach. If the breach is much larger than the character, you can rule that he doesn't get near enough to an edge to have a chance to grab on and thus does not get a Reflex save.

SECURITY SYSTEMS

High-tech security systems around an aristocorp's research facility can be harder to penetrate than the traps infesting a lich's tomb. These systems are typically designed to alert security personnel and contain or incapacitate trespassers rather than to maim or kill. Nevertheless, in many parts of the Empire, lethal force

is justified in protecting one's property from trespassers. Lethal systems are therefore not unheard of in high-security facilities.

Most security systems incorporate electronics, and many feature mechanical systems as well. Unless otherwise stated, assume that all systems feature their own internal power supply or at least have a backup power source. This allows the systems to remain functional if the facility loses power for an extended period of time.

The same rules that apply to detecting and disabling traps in a traditional fantasy campaign also apply to high-tech security systems. In addition, a character must have the Technical Proficiency feat to identify and disarm a high-tech system. In some cases, the DM may allow a rogue who lacks the feat but has had thorough instruction on a specific system to make standard Search and Disable Device checks at the normal −4 penalty. A character with the Craft (trapmaking) skill can build a high-tech security system, but only if he has the Technical Proficiency feat.

The triggers of high-tech security systems are often more subtle and difficult to detect than the mechanical devices common in traditional fantasy settings. In some cases, though, the differences aren't all that pronounced—there may be little practical difference between an electronic and mechanical pressure trigger.

Other trigger mechanisms, however, are much more sophisticated than any non-magical devices found on technologically underdeveloped worlds. These include electric eyes, motion detectors, thermal sensors, and countless other devices. Systems can be designed to trigger when a trespasser fails to give the proper voice password or input an authorized identification code. Imaging triggers may even be capable of recognizing specific observable criteria, such as individuals who are not in the system's personnel files or those carrying weapons.

The following security systems are found throughout the Dragon Empire. Each description lists a Challenge Rating (CR), attack bonus (if necessary), damage (if applicable), DCs for saving throws to avoid or resist the system's effects, and DCs for Search and Disable Device checks.

Adhesive Spray Trap: CR 3; no attack roll necessary; Reflex save (DC 15) avoids; Search (DC 25); Disable Device (DC 25). *Note*: Hidden nozzle discharges adhesive liquid into area. Characters within 20 ft. of the nozzle who fail a Reflex save are entangled. Characters must make a new saving throw (+1 DC for each save after the first) each round they are in the affected area.

Alarm: CR 1; sounds an electronic alarm audible throughout the location; Search (DC 20); Disable Device (DC 20).

Automated Blaster: CR 4; +10 ranged (4d10/x2 crit); Search (DC 20); Disable Device (DC 25). *Note*: 300-ft. maximum range, target determined randomly from those in its path. The automated blaster can fire 20 shots before its ammunition is expended. It has hardness 10 and 25 hit points.

Automated Laser: CR 3; +10 ranged (3d10/x2 crit); Search (DC 20); Disable Device (DC 25). *Note*: 300-ft. maximum range, target determined randomly from those in its path. The automated laser can fire 20 shots before its ammunition is expended. It has hardness 10 and 25 hit points.

Automated Needler: CR 3; +10/+10/+10 ranged (1d10/x3 crit); Search (DC 20); Disable Device (DC 25). *Note*: 200-ft. maximum range, up to three targets per round determined randomly from those in its path. The automated needler can fire 18 shots before its ammunition is expended. It has hardness 10 and 25 hit points.

Automated Plasma Rifle: CR 5; +10 ranged (5d10/x2 crit); Search (DC 20); Disable Device (DC 25). *Note*: 500-ft. maximum range, target determined randomly from those in its path. The automated plasma rifle can fire 20 shots before its ammunition is expended. It has hardness 10 and 40 hit points.

Automated Screamer: CR 3; +10 ranged (4d6/x2 crit); Search (DC 20); Disable Device (DC 25). *Note*: 300-ft. maximum range, target determined randomly from those in its path. The automated screamer can fire 20 shots before its ammunition is expended. It has hardness 10 and 25 hit points.

Chainsaw Pit (20 ft. deep): CR 4; no attack roll necessary (2d6), +10 melee (1d4 chainsaw blades for 2d6 damage per successful hit); Reflex save (DC 20) avoids; Search (DC 20); Disable Device (DC 20). *Note*: Trap is a pit lined with chainsaw blades that activate when the trap is triggered. Each round the victim remains in the pit, he suffers attacks from 1d4 chainsaws.

Door Autolock: CR 1; locks all doors and windows in room; Search (DC 25); Disable Device (DC 21).

Flamethrower Trap: CR 3; +20 ranged (3d6); Search (DC 20); Disable Device (DC 25). *Note*: 100-ft. maximum range, target determined randomly from those in its path. The flamethrower can fire 10 shots before its ammunition is expended. It has hardness 10 and 25 hit points.

Flash-Bang Trap: CR 2; no attack roll necessary; Will save (DC 20) negates; Search (DC 25); Disable Device (DC 25). *Note*: Hidden emitter discharges blinding light and deafening noise. Characters within 20 ft. of the emitter who fail the saving throw are blinded, deafened, and stunned for 1d3 rounds.

Incendiary Trap: CR 5; no attack roll necessary; Reflex save (DC 20) for half damage; Search (DC 25); Disable Device (DC 25). *Note*: Hidden nozzle discharges burning liquid. Characters within 20 ft. of the nozzle are affected. The incendiary liquid may cause flammable materials to catch on fire.

Silent Alarm: CR 2; sounds an electronic alarm audible in another area, such as a security station; Search (DC 20); Disable Device (DC 25).

Stun Gas: CR 3; no attack roll necessary; Fortitude save (DC 15) negates; Search (DC 25); Disable Device (DC 25). *Note*: Hidden nozzle disharches noxious gas. Characters within 20 ft. of the nozzle who fail a Fortitude save are blinded and nauseated for 1d3 rounds after they have left the affected area. Characters must make a new saving throw (+1 DC for each save after the first) each round they are in the affected area.

Taser Trap: CR 3; no attack roll necessary (4d6 subdual damage); Reflex save (DC 20) avoids; Search (DC 20); Disable Device (DC 25). Note: Powerful taser discharge from metal gridwork in floor affects everyone in one 10-ft. square.

WORLD-BUILDING

Starfaring will be an important part of most **Dragonstar** campaigns. Most of your characters' early adventures may take place on a single planet or in a single star system, but eventually, they will yearn to reach out for the stars, visiting distant worlds and exploring new ones. Because the Empire is so vast—not to mention the expanse of the galaxy beyond it—there will always be a new system to explore and a new planet to discover.

As DM, you have the seemingly daunting task of keeping up with characters who can travel light years in an instant. To run a starfaring campaign in which the characters feel they can truly *explore*, you'll need to generate new star systems and new planets almost as quickly as you can generate random encounters. This chapter gives you the tools you'll need to do that.

STAR SYSTEMS

You already have a lot of information about the Dragon Empire: how big it is, how many stars it contains, where the major systems and planets are located relative to one another. But this book provides information on only a tiny fraction of the star systems in the Empire. Of those not detailed here, some may be systems completely devoid of planets, while others support worlds teeming with life and boasting great civilizations. These star systems are left for you to create and your characters to discover.

A vast ocean of interstellar space dominates the Dragon Empire. The particles of matter in this ocean are so scattered as to be almost non-existent for all practical purposes. Sprinkled throughout this ocean are tiny islands of light and life, and it is these islands that draw the sentient races to reach out across endless expanse of space. These islands are stars, and without them, the universe would be a black, empty place.

SYSTEM TYPE

A star system's most basic feature is the number of stars that comprise it. Many systems in the Dragon Empire—and throughout the galaxy—have two or three stars, and some have even more.

However, these multiple-star systems, called binaries and trinaries, only rarely support life-bearing worlds. As you will discover later in this chapter, the gods have created a universe in which most living things can only survive within very narrow environmental parameters. A little too hot or a little too cold, gravity a little to high or too low, an atmosphere a little too thick or too thin—all

of these conditions can prevent an otherwise suitable planet from developing or supporting life. Living things also require consistency, and too much variation—from one season to the next, or even from day to night—can be antithetical to life. Most planets in multiple-star systems—if they are not perpetually locked in bitter cold or infernal heat—have exotic orbits that entail radical changes in temperature and climate. A planet may be locked in ice for decades as its orbit takes it on a long journey far from its suns, only to be baked until its crust runs molten when it passes close between them.

When creating a new system, the first thing you should do is decide how many stars are present in the system. Systems with four or more stars are rare, though they may become more common the closer one travels toward the dense galactic core.

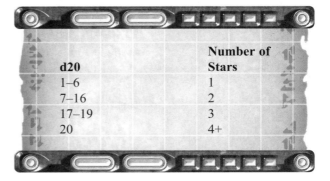

d20	Number of Stars
1–6	1
7–16	2
17–19	3
20	4+

STAR CLASSIFICATION

Stars have many different characteristics, and the scientists of the Dragon Empire have devised many different ways to categorize and classify them over the millennia. Currently, the only universally accepted system in the Empire is an amalgamation of different conventions pieced together and refined from the contributions of many different cultures. The oldest surviving written studies of astronomy are fragments from Elven texts on the planet Madara in the Halderon system. Many of the existing conventions are derived from this work and bear several unique traits common to elven cultures—namely terminology that treats stars as living things.

When creating a new star, you must first decide where it is in its life cycle. As stars age, they burn more and more of their nuclear fuel. When this process reaches a certain threshold, the star undergoes rapid, dramatic, and sometimes catastrophic changes. Stars that have not yet reached this threshold are called *juvenile* stars, while those that have are called *mature* stars. The vast majority of inhabited worlds are found in orbit around juvenile stars—the processes by which a star moves from the juvenile to mature stage of its life cycle are usually too destructive for life and civilization to survive.

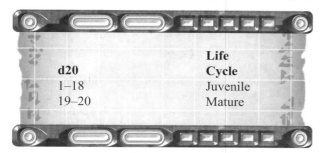

d20	Life Cycle
1–18	Juvenile
19–20	Mature

Juvenile Stars

Most stars in the galaxy are juvenile stars—those undergoing normal fusion processes and burning principally hydrogen fuel. These stars are classified by their color, which is in turn based on their surface temperature and mass. If you are generating a multiple-star system, simply roll on the table more than once—there is no need for each star to be of the same color and class. However, juvenile stars will very rarely be found in the same system as mature stars.

In the table below, temperature is listed as a multiple of the surface temperature of an average yellow sun, which ranges between 8,500° and 10,000° F. At the top of the scale, blue stars are the largest, hottest, and most short-lived. These stars often burn 10 times or more as hot as a standard yellow sun, and their juvenile life spans are only a tiny fraction as long. Habitable planets are extremely unlikely in systems with a blue or white star.

At the bottom of the scale are the dim, relatively cool red dwarfs. These stars, though plentiful in the galaxy, are also unlikely to support a life-bearing world. The planet would have to orbit so closely to the sun to gain sufficient light and warmth, it would become tidal locked: The star's gravity would halt the planet's rotation. The sun would bake the "day" side of the planet until it became an infernal, irradiated wasteland, while the "night" side would be locked in perpetual winter.

Only the yellow-white, yellow, and orange stars are truly suited to supporting life-bearing worlds, and the vast majority of inhabited planets in the Empire orbit yellow suns whose principal characteristics are almost identical to one another. Some believe this is evidence of the gods' design, while others believe it is the inescapable implication of physical processes. Most in the Empire believe they are one and the same.

d20	Star Color	Temperature	Life Span
1	Blue	5–10	1 million years
2	Blue-white	2–5	10 million years
3	White	1.5–2	400 million years
4–7	Yellow-white	1–1.5	4 billion years
8–11	Yellow	1	10 billion years
12–15	Orange	0.7–1	60 billion years
16–20	Red	0.7 or less	100 billion years

Mature Stars

When a juvenile star burns all of its hydrogen fuel, it changes and is henceforth classified as a mature star. Just how it changes depends on its mass.

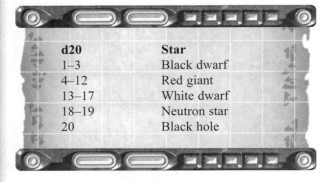

d20	Star
1–3	Black dwarf
4–12	Red giant
13–17	White dwarf
18–19	Neutron star
20	Black hole

A *black dwarf* star enjoys the most peaceful transition from its juvenile to mature stage. When a small star runs out of fusion fuel, it simply snuffs out—though the process is one of gradual dimming over millions of years. All that is left of the former star is the dark cinder of its cooling core. Planets may yet orbit this dead star, but only the most alien life could survive the total absence of light and warmth.

When an average-size star exhausts all of its hydrogen fuel, it begins to burn the helium produced during its juvenile phase. It cools and expands to several times its original dimensions, becoming a *red giant*. The star expands to so great a size that it engulfs any planets in its inner system—typically those most likely to have supported life. After a relatively short period of time, the red giant runs out of heavier elements to burn.

When an average red giant exhausts its fuel, it ejects its outer gaseous shell and becomes a *white dwarf*. These stars are very small and compact: A spoonful of the star's matter weighs between 10 and 100 tons. For a time, the surface of the star may burn extremely hot and bright, but it gradually dims and cools. Planets—or the remains of planets—may remain in the system, but the white dwarf star no longer emits enough light to sustain life.

When large stars have exhausted all their fusion fuel, their cores collapse in less than a second and a vast amount of energy is released—as much as 100 yellow suns produce over the entire course of their life spans. Within a couple days, the supernova is brighter than a billion suns. The star's gaseous shell, along with a titanic shockwave, expands into interstellar space. The remnants of the stellar core are very exotic stars.

A *neutron star* is the post-supernova remnant of a star no more than about three times the mass of an average yellow sun. These stars are very small, with diameters of around 12 miles. They are even denser than white dwarfs: A spoonful of their matter weighs more than a billion tons. Any planets that once existed in such a star system would have been destroyed during the supernova explosion. There may, however, be some planetary debris in the gaseous nebula surrounding the star.

When the largest stars collapse, the force of their gravity is so strong that they keep collapsing in on themselves until they form singularities. This is a superdense, supermassive body that is incredibly compact. The body's gravity is so strong that not even light can escape its maw, which is why it's called a *black hole*. Black holes are encircled by event horizons—boundaries that act as a point of no return, beyond which nothing can pass and escape the singularity's gravitational pull. As with neutron stars, no planetary systems exist in orbit around a black hole. However, a black hole may be ringed by an accretion disk of matter pulled into its immense gravity well.

Black holes are actually rents or tears in the space-time fabric of reality and are thought to be among the few natural portals between the planes. Archmages using powerful protective magic have actually passed through black holes and used their spells to return to the Material Plane. Others have never returned, and it seems that these portals are constantly in flux, brushing against one plane of existence for a few microseconds before blinking randomly to another. They are, as a result, rarely used as a voluntary method of planar travel.

PLANETS

Planets form as clumps of matter drawn together by gravity in a developing star system. Gravitational forces compress the matter, creating heat, and the newborn planet becomes molten. The heaviest elements, like iron, sink into the core of the molten clump, while lighter elements float on the top to form continental landmasses. As the planet cools, a rocky crust forms in cracked plates on the surface. These plates float on the planet's molten interior and can drift around and bump into each other.

Planets can form in just about any juvenile star system. However, they are somewhat less likely to form in systems dominated by very large, hot stars. On the following table, a result of 0 or less indicates that there are no planets present in the system.

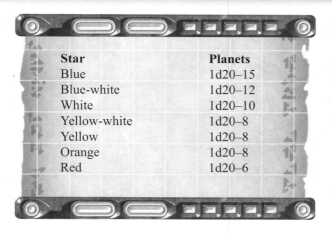

Star	Planets
Blue	1d20–15
Blue-white	1d20–12
White	1d20–10
Yellow-white	1d20–8
Yellow	1d20–8
Orange	1d20–8
Red	1d20–6

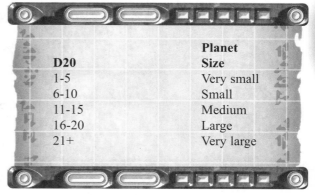

D20	Planet Size
1-5	Very small
6-10	Small
11-15	Medium
16-20	Large
21+	Very large

Once you know the number of planets in your star system, the next step is to determine their type.

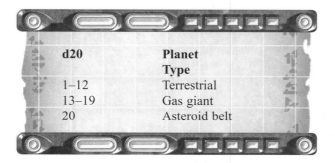

d20	Planet Type
1–12	Terrestrial
13–19	Gas giant
20	Asteroid belt

A *terrestrial* planet is a relatively small, rocky world with an iron core. These planets are by far the most likely to support life.

A *gas giant* is typically a very large planet dominated by an incredibly thick, dense atmosphere of light gasses such as hydrogen, helium, methane, and ammonia. Most gas giants are cold, inhospitable worlds in the outer orbits of a star system, though gas giants may occasionally form close to the system's star.

An *asteroid belt* is a formation of variably sized planetoids of ice, rock, and metals. Some asteroid belts are the debris of planets that have been destroyed, while others are comprised of matter that simply never formed into planets. Asteroids range in size from tiny pebbles to rocks as large as mountains, but they are never large enough to hold an atmosphere. Asteroid belts are usually rich in minerals and are frequently home to expansive mining operations in settled systems.

SIZE

The next step in the creation of a planet is to determine its size. Add 15 to your roll if the planet is a gas giant.

Very small planets may be only a few hundred to a couple thousand miles in diameter. These planets are little more than large asteroids and are much too small to retain an atmosphere. These planets have very low gravity.

Small planets are only a few thousand miles in diameter. Many have thin atmospheres, and some may be habitable for relatively brief periods shortly after their formation. Most of these planets' atmospheric gasses will escape into space, however, preventing the emergence of indigenous life.

Medium planets are the most likely to support life. They are large enough to retain breathable atmospheres, but not so big that gravity and atmospheric density become intolerable for living things. While medium planets are the right size to support life, most of them don't: Many other variables have to be just right for the gods to grant a world the gift of life.

Large planets occasionally support life, though their higher gravity makes things difficult. Large planets may enjoy a period of habitability that ends when the gradual accumulation of gasses renders the planet too hot or the atmosphere too dense (or both).

Very large planets are always gas giants and are hostile to most lifeforms in the galaxy. Their atmospheres are incredibly dense and their surface pressures can be many times those of the deepest ocean trenches on terrestrial worlds. Simple ecosystems of very strange creatures may survive in a gas giant's upper atmosphere.

GRAVITY

Your planet's gravity is related to its size and is extremely important in determining whether or not the planet is habitable.

Planet Size	Microgravity	Very Low	Low	Standard	High	Very High	Extreme
Very small	1–6	7–14	15–20	—	—	—	—
Small	1–2	3–10	11–18	19–20	—	—	—
Medium	—	1–2	3–7	8–5	16–20	—	—
Large	—	—	1–2	3–5	6–12	13–18	19–20
Very large	—	—	—	1–2	3–10	11–16	17–20

Microgravity is typical of asteroids and small plane-toids and is 0.1g or less. Planets with microgravity cannot retain an atmosphere.

Very low gravity is typical of large asteroids or plane-toids and very small planets. It ranges between 0.1g and 0.5g. Planets with low gravity cannot retain breathable atmospheres long enough to develop life.

Low gravity is typical of small planets and those whose cores are composed of lighter, less dense elements. Low gravity ranges between 0.5g and 0.8g. Planets with low gravity can retain breathable atmospheres, though may be rather thin. Iron and other heavy metals will be very rare on low-density worlds and are therefore very unlikely to develop technological civilizations.

Standard gravity is common to most habitable worlds in the Dragon Empire. It ranges between 0.8g and 1.2g. Planets with standard gravity are most likely to retain breathable atmospheres of the proper density and are therefore most likely to support life.

High gravity is common to large or dense planets and ranges between 1.2g and 2.0g. Planets with high gravity often retain atmospheres, but they may be much denser than those on worlds with standard gravity. Worlds with dense metallic cores may be very rich in heavy metals.

Very high gravity is common to very large or very dense planets, including most gas giants, and ranges between 2.0g and 4.0g. These worlds often retain very dense atmospheres with sufficient pressure to make unaided respiration impossible. Most of the races and species found in the Empire can survive on a very high gravity world for extended periods, though even minimal physical activity can be exhausting. Life on these worlds may seem stunted and strange to visitors from more hospitable planets. Humanoids, if they are present, may be short and squat, with oversized hearts to pump blood that is many times heavier than it is on a standard world, and powerful lungs to inhale and exhale the heavy air. Tall trees may be nonexistent, as plant life favors sprawling vines that can more easily draw moisture from the earth. Large animals may be entirely confined to the oceans, where the effects of high gravity are minimized.

Extreme gravity is common only to the largest, densest planets, such as the most titanic gas giants. Gravity of more than 4.0g is intolerable for most of the races and species found in the Empire, and many creatures will be completely unable to move. Planets with extreme gravity are likely to retain very dense atmospheres, but they are almost never inhabited.

ATMOSPHERE

Your planet's atmosphere is the single most important factor in determining whether or not it can support life. The vast majority of living species in the Empire require oxygen, extracting it either from air or water. There are

Atmospheric Density						
Gravity	Vacuum	Very Thin	Thin	Standard	Dense	Very Dense
Microgravity	1–19	20	—	—	—	—
Very low	1–9	10–18	19–20	—	—	—
Low	1–5	6–10	11–15	16–20	—	—
Standard	1–2	3–6	7–10	11–15	16–19	20
High	—	1–3	4–7	8–11	12–16	17–20
Very high	—	—	1–2	3–6	7–13	14–20
Extreme	—	—	—	1–2	3–10	11–20

two major components of your planet's atmosphere: density and composition.

Density

The first thing to determine about your atmosphere is simply how much of it there is. Even if they are composed of breathable elements, atmospheres that are either too thick or too thin can pose serious challenges to living creatures. An atmosphere's density is related to the planet's gravity.

Planets with no atmosphere are exposed to the *vacuum* of space. A true vacuum is typically only possible in an artificial environment, but these planets are close enough to vacuum to make no practical difference. On a vacuum world, there is no air to breathe and no medium to conserve or dissipate heat. Objects or creatures in a vacuum exposed to direct sunlight quickly become superheated, while those in shadow are frozen solid. Characters must wear vacuum suits to survive in an airless environment for more than a few seconds.

Composition

For most **Dragonstar** campaigns, the important thing to know about your atmosphere is whether it is breathable, breathable with technological assistance, or not breathable at all.

D20	Atmospheric Composition
1–5	Breathable
6–10	Tainted
11–15	Hostile

A *breathable* atmosphere is composed of the right mix of oxygen, nitrogen, carbon dioxide, water vapor and other elements to support life without technological assistance. The vast majority of life-bearing worlds have breathable atmospheres.

A *tainted* atmosphere is one composed of breathable elements, but with significant levels of toxic or corrosive compounds. Characters exposed to atmospheres tainted with toxic elements must wear filter masks for normal respiration. Some toxic atmospheres may require hostile environment suits to prevent exposure to poisonous chemicals. In atmospheres tainted with corrosive elements, characters must always wear vacuum suits or hostile environment suits.

A *hostile* atmosphere is one with insufficient levels of breathable elements or excessive levels of toxic or corrosive elements. Characters exposed to a hostile atmosphere must wear a vacuum suit to survive.

Soulmechs are not affected by toxic atmospheres, but they too must be protected to survive a tainted or hostile corrosive atmosphere.

GEOLOGY

This entry describes how active and varied your planet's topology is. Your planet's geology is somewhat dependent on its gravity and atmosphere and plays an important role in determining what kinds of environments can exist there.

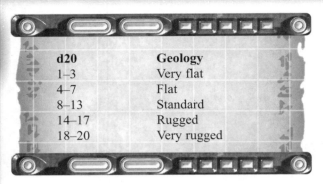

d20	Geology
1–3	Very flat
4–7	Flat
8–13	Standard
14–17	Rugged
18–20	Very rugged

A *very flat* planet is one that is tectonically inactive. It has smooth landforms, and mountains and trenches are very rare, if not nonexistent. Its seas, if it has any, are uniformly shallow. Most of a very flat planet's topography may be caused by meteor craters and other impacts. A planet with a very thin or no atmosphere may be especially cratered, as meteors do not burn up on approach and there is little or no wind and water erosion to wear the craters down over time. These planets typically have no volcanic activity at all.

A *flat* planet may be inactive, but it has had a long enough period of tectonic activity to form low mountains, trenches, and shallow seas. These features are rare, however, and most of the planet's surface is smooth and uniform. These planets have little or no volcanic activity.

A *standard* planet is one with normal tectonic activity and varied topology. There are flat plains and tall mountain ranges, shallow seas and deep-ocean trenches. The planet has active plate tectonics and moderate instances of earthquakes and volcanic activity.

Rugged planets are those with extremely varied landforms. The planet has many high mountains, and deep trenches and canyons. This kind of geology is most common on low gravity worlds with a history of significant tectonic activity. If there is little or no atmosphere to erode land formations, the planet may currently be inactive. Otherwise, there may be a high level of tectonic activity, with frequent earthquakes and volcanic activity.

Very rugged planets feature the most extreme geology. The planet's crust may be torn and buckled by high levels of tectonic activity or tidal forces. The planet may feature jagged mountains that tower many miles above relatively smooth plains, and abyssal trenches or canyons that fracture the planet's crust and expose the molten interior. The extreme level of tectonic activity, with titanic earthquakes and volcanoes, may make the planet's surface very dangerous for habitation.

HYDROSPHERE

This entry describes the amount of water present on your planet. Water is a necessary component of life throughout the known galaxy. Along with its atmosphere, a planet's hydrosphere determines whether or not it is capable of supporting life.

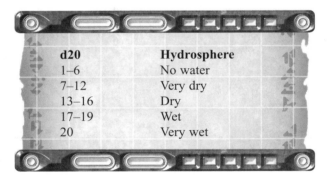

d20	Hydrosphere
1–6	No water
7–12	Very dry
13–16	Dry
17–19	Wet
20	Very wet

A planet with *no water* is incapable of supporting life as it is understood in the known galaxy. Scientists speculate that substitute liquid compounds may support the development of alien lifeforms unknown in the Empire.

On a *very dry* planet, most or all of the water is locked in ice at the poles, at the bottoms of impact craters, or deep underground. On some of these worlds, there may be small amounts of water vapor in the atmosphere, but there are no liquid oceans. Life is unlikely on such a planet, and where it exists it will only congregate where liquid water is available, such as thermal oases in the polar regions or in vast, underground cavern systems.

A *dry* planet is one where less than 50% of the surface is covered by oceans. The planet may support only a few shallow seas, as most of its water is locked in the polar ice caps. A dry planet may be habitable, but with large areas that are too arid to support life. Barrens, deserts, and dust plains may dominate much of the world's surface, with little or no life found in these inhospitable regions. Temperature extremes may be more pronounced, as there are insufficient oceans to serve as a thermal reservoir.

A *wet* planet is one where 50% to 75% of the surface is covered by oceans. Oceans are extensive enough to separate clearly defined continental landmasses. These worlds have hydrospheres sufficient to support life, and the oceans help to regulate climate. Very dry areas, such as deserts, may still be common on the planet, but they are usually exceptions based on geography and climate, rather than the norm.

A *very wet* planet is one where more than 75% of the surface is covered by oceans. On the most extreme of these planets, no continental landmasses may be exposed at all. Scattered islands, most of them volcanic in origin, are the only landforms that extend above the surface. The vast oceans regulate temperature, and climate may be largely uniform across the globe.

BIOSPHERE

This entry describes the frequency and complexity of organic life on a planet. A planet's biosphere is intricately connected to several other characteristics. For example, a planet with no hydrosphere is very unlikely to ever develop organic life, and even less likely to support it over a significant period of time. Oxygen-producing plants are necessary to create a breathable atmosphere, and a breathable atmosphere is necessary to support most forms of animal life. Add 3 to your roll on the following table if your planet has a wet or very wet hydrosphere.

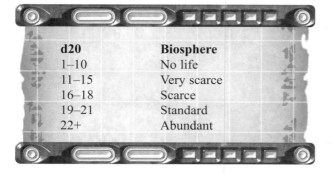

d20	Biosphere
1–10	No life
11–15	Very scarce
16–18	Scarce
19–21	Standard
22+	Abundant

A planet with *no life* is a barren and empty ball of rock. The planet may have an atmosphere, but its composition will be tainted or hostile.

A planet with a *very scarce* biosphere typically supports a relatively small number of very simple species. The planet may support algae, fungi, sponges, or a variety of single-celled animal life forms, but it boasts no higher-order plant or animal life. The oceans of such a world may be rich organic soups, but the landmasses are usually barren rock occasionally covered with patches of tough mosses, lichens, or other growths.

A planet with a *scarce* biosphere supports higher-order plants and animals but suffers from a substandard level of species diversity. Species common throughout the known galaxy may be absent on the planet. There is often little interspecies competition for specific ecological niches, and some niches may be entirely vacant. There are planets in the Empire that gave birth to only a single sentient humanoid species, planets where there are no living oozes or motile plant life forms, and even worlds where there are no magical beasts or aberrations.

A planet with a *standard* biosphere supports higher-order life forms and enjoys an average level of species diversity. Some species found elsewhere in the known galaxy may be absent on the planet, but most ecological niches are filled and there is usually significant competition between species.

Planets with *abundant* biospheres are comparatively rare in the known galaxy. These worlds are teeming with life of all varieties, from the simplest plantlike organisms to the rarest magical beasts. The wilderness areas of such planets are often extremely dangerous, as hyper-competition between species creates a savage ecology ruled by tooth and claw. Planets with standard biospheres may even experience relatively brief periods of abundant speciation followed by mass die-offs and extinctions.

POPULATION

This entry describes the population levels of existing civilizations on the planet. For these purposes, "civilized" beings are those who band together in some form of social organization, from tribes to cities to nation-states. Sentient creatures who live solitary lives in the wilderness are not accounted for in a planet's population listing. Planetary characteristics such as atmosphere, hydrosphere, and biosphere must usually be capable of sustaining life to support a large population. Small outposts and bases on inhospitable planets are possible using advanced technology such as pressure domes and other self-contained environments, but they are not likely to support large populations. You do not need to roll for this characteristic if your planet is uninhabited.

d20	Population
1–5	Very low
6–9	Low
10–15	Moderate
16–19	High
20	Very high

A planet with *very low* population has less than one million civilized inhabitants. Two types of worlds typically fall into this category. The first are planets that are technologically very primitive. The scattered populations of these planets live in small tribes or clans, and dense population centers are either very rare or nonexistent. The second category includes planets that are home to small imperial outposts or bases, from military garrisons to mining complexes. These planets typically have no indigenous sentient life of their own, and may have no biospheres whatsoever.

A planet with *low* population has less than one billion civilized inhabitants. Most of the technologically underdeveloped planets in the Outlands fall into this category. Dense population centers are relatively few and those

that exist are typically much smaller than modern metropolises. The largest cities on these worlds rarely support more than 100,000 people. Most worlds colonized by the Empire remain at this level of population for several decades before immigration and local development spur rapid population growth.

A planet with *moderate* population has one to five billion civilized inhabitants. Dense population centers are relatively common on these worlds, and most of the population lives in urban areas. Most of the developed planets of the imperial core fall into this category. Outlands worlds colonized by the Empire usually reach this population level within one century. Most throneworlds fall into this category as well, because their populations are carefully controlled and regulated.

A planet with *high* population supports five to 10 billion civilized inhabitants. Dense and sprawling population centers dot the surface of these planets, and inhabitants who live in the few remaining rural or wilderness areas are extremely rare. The oldest and most developed planets of the Empire fall into this population category.

A planet with *very high* population supports more than 10 billion inhabitants. These planets are very rare, and most of their surface areas are covered with massive, super-dense urban centers. Wilderness areas on these planets are usually nonexistent, having given way

to the vast agricultural and industrial infrastructure necessary to support the teeming populations.

TECHNOLOGY

This entry summarizes the most advanced technological level achieved by civilizations on the planet. Many planets are home to several distinct civilizations, each with a different level of technological development. As a result, this classification simply identifies the highest level of technological development achieved on the planet. These categories are necessarily gross generalizations and allow for a great deal of practical variation from one civilization to another. Planets with an established imperial presence almost always enjoy an imperial technology base. Beyond the borders of an imperial enclave, however, any technology level may be the rule.

d20	Technology
1–5	Primitive
6–9	Pre-industrial
10–15	Industrial
16–19	Post-industrial
20	Imperial

A planetary civilization with *primitive* technology has access to only the simplest tools, weapons, and productive techniques. Tools and weapons are commonly fashioned from stone, wood, or bone, and metallurgy is either nonexistent or extremely simplistic and very rare. Peoples dependent on this level of technology are usually hunter-gatherers or herders, though some civilizations may have developed rudimentary agriculture. Most people, even the leaders, live at a subsistence level, spending most of their daylight hours producing the food, water, and shelter necessary for survival.

A *pre-industrial* technology base is the most common on the pre-contact Outlands worlds. These civilizations have made significant progress in the arts, sciences, and trades. Tools and weapons are typically fashioned of iron and some simple alloys, such as bronze and steel. Simple mechanical devices are constructed, though even the most complex must usually be powered by the labor of people or beasts. Agricultural production and basic manufacturing both remain extremely labor-intensive, with expansive peasant and artisan classes responsible for most production. Most people live at or near subsistence level, though the ruling and merchant classes enjoy lives of relative leisure.

An *industrial* technology level is characterized by mechanization and the development of mass production. Labor-intensive production methods are replaced by large-scale factories in which improved efficiency is possible with machines and assembly lines. Tools and weapons are commonly constructed of heavy but durable metal alloys, and relatively sophisticated machines driven by steam, wind, or other natural power sources become commonplace. Global transportation and communication become possible with inventions such as steamships, railroads, and telegraphs. The peasant and artisan classes are largely transformed into a growing underclass of urban laborers and factory workers. The fortunes of the landowning and ruling classes begin to decline, and the middle class of skilled professionals, merchants, and capitalists becomes increasingly prosperous.

On a planet with a *post-industrial* technology base, heavy manufacturing is in decline and the economy is increasingly driven by the service and technology sectors. On most worlds, this technological era sees the development of space travel, information technologies, and nuclear power. A global civilization develops as aircraft, superhighways, telecommunications networks, and computers connect even the most isolated regions. Social conditions are highly variable, with some civilizations virtually eliminating poverty while others are marked by increasingly severe rifts between rich and poor. Medical technology has usually improved sufficiently for at least a segment of the population to enjoy significantly extended lifespans. Skilled scientists and technicians prosper in these civilizations, creating an exclusive upper middle class with opportunities that often exceed those of the traditional merchants, capitalists, and industrialists.

A planet with an *imperial* level of technological development is capable of supporting a starfaring civilization. Robotics, advanced computers, fusion power, and advances in materials technology has revolutionized manufacturing, allowing for the cheap, efficient, and usually pollution-free production of a dizzying variety of goods. Continents, planets, and even different star systems are assimilated into coherent civilizations by advances in space travel and information networks. Medical technology has advanced to the point where many common diseases and genetic defects can be easily eliminated, at least for those who can afford the best health care. As with post-industrial civilizations, social conditions can be extremely variable and are usually the result of political decisions rather than technological and economic limitations. This is the base technological level of the imperial core worlds, and most colonized Outlands worlds have at least a single outpost or enclave built on imperial technology as well.

MAGIC

This entry describes the frequency and sophistication of magic use and knowledge on the planet. As with technology, this almost always varies from one civilization to another, and this classification simply identifies the highest prevailing level of achievement in the magical arts. Note that the potential for magic is actually extremely consistent throughout the known galaxy: There are very few "dead magic" or "high magic" zones where magic either doesn't function at all or functions at an unusually high or low level. Instead, this classification describes the level of understanding and application achieved by civilizations on different planets.

d20	Magic
1–5	Primitive
6–9	Low
10–15	Moderate
16–19	High
20	Advanced

Magic is extremely rare on planets with *primitive* levels of magical achievement. On some of these worlds, magic may even be considered a superstition, myth, or long-lost relic of ancient times. Sorcerers, wizards, bards, and others who can wield arcane magic are virtually nonexistent. Divine spellcasters are extremely rare and typically limited to adepts, tribal shamans, or freak prodigies who appear once a generation. On some planets, magical knowledge was lost in the aftermath of wars, natural disasters, or magical cataclysms that left great civilizations in ruins. On others, the understanding and craft of magic were simply never discovered or developed. Magic items are either extremely rare or nonexistent. On some primitive magic worlds, magical beasts and supernatural creatures are similarly rare and nonexistent. On others, it is only the practice of magic that is unknown.

On a planet with *low* magic, arcane magic is extremely rare or unheard of, divine magic is very uncommon. Adepts, witches, hedge wizards, and shamans usually represent the height of magical craft on these worlds. Charms, potions, and other items of modest power may be relatively common on these worlds, but few more sophisticated magic items exist. Artifacts are objects of legend and myth. Magical creatures such as fey folk and dragons are often the most powerful practitioners of magic on these worlds.

On planets with *moderate* magic, divine magic is relatively common but arcane magic remains rare. The natives of these planets are familiar enough with magic that it is rarely considered a superstition, but most people nevertheless live their whole lives without ever encountering a spellcaster. Magic items of moderate power can be found in the hands of the wealthy and powerful or in the hidden places of the world, but they are rarely if ever found on store shelves or offered for sale. Secretive cults and cabals of wizards, clerics, and other spellcasters may have achieved a significant level of magical knowledge and craft, but this lore is jealously guarded and rarely offered to would-be students and acolytes.

High magic is the standard level for the developed worlds of the Dragon Empire. On these planets, powerful spells up to 9th level are possible, though spellcasters nevertheless remain relatively uncommon. Magic items and practical applications of magic are fairly abundant and can often be purchased or commissioned in the major cities. Artifacts are rare and the secret of their creation has been lost to modern practitioners of the magical arts. Accomplished spellcasters, while uncommon, often rise to positions of considerable political power and influence.

Civilizations that have achieved *advanced* magic remain the subjects of legend in the Dragon Empire. On these worlds, spellcasters are commonplace and mighty nations are often ruled by powerful archmages and priests. Magic may be so routine on some worlds that most common folk are even capable of casting a few cantrips or low-level spells. The most accomplished practitioners create artifacts and relics of incredible power and use them to build awe-inspiring empires and monuments to their craft. It is believed that these legendary wizards and clerics could cast spells greater than 9th level and work magics undreamed of in the Dragon Empire.

BUILDING A BETTER WORLD

As noted at the beginning of this section, a starfaring campaign can present the DM with a seemingly daunting task. It's hard enough to create an exciting campaign world with sufficient depth and detail to really come to life for the players—creating dozens of such worlds for your **Dragonstar** characters to explore may seem impossible.

Fortunately, a satisfying starfaring campaign doesn't require that every world the characters visit be fully detailed down to the last item on the menu of the smallest tavern in the smallest hamlet. As DM, you will often create star systems and planets in which a single adven-

ture is set, and the characters will rarely have the opportunity to explore all of their nooks and crannies. You need to develop the knack of creating locations that are intriguing and memorable at a glance, even if they would appear a bit sketchy to a more careful inspection.

The preceding section on world-building gives you the tools you need to create star systems and planets quickly and easily. The characteristics produced by this system really just form the bare bones of your adventure locations, however. To create interesting, truly memorable locations, you'll have to add a little detail. For star systems and planets your characters will often visit once and never return to again, you don't have to add a lot.

When you create a new star system or planet, you should try to include three things: an interesting feature, an interesting place, and an interesting NPC. It's not much, but you'll find that these three details will make otherwise nameless, forgettable systems and planets unique and memorable for your players.

FEATURES

Players tend to identify locations with specific features that are unusual or interesting. In a traditional fantasy campaign, they may remember a particular town because of the old stone wall around it that was built by dwarves. Maybe they remember the town because it was illegal to use arcane magic within the city limits, or because of the fantastic wine available at their favorite inn. The same goes for star systems and planets in your **Dragonstar** campaign. It doesn't really matter what it is—a single interesting feature will lodge itself in your players memories more securely than whole books full of history, geography, and other mundane details. A few possible examples include:

- A star system with only a single planet orbiting the sun
- A star system littered with the ruins of some unknown, alien, starfaring civilization
- A star system contested by rival imperial domains
- A star system whose primary is becoming increasingly unstable
- A star system with several inhabited planets on which dwarves are the only sentient race
- A planet with no clerics where organized religion is outlawed
- A planet completely covered by water and dominated by a great merfolk civilization
- A planet covered by jungles and dominated by dinosaurs and lizardfolk
- A planet whose continent-spanning primeval forests are rich with darkwood
- A planet where a rare magical herb grows once every hundred years

PLACES

Each star system you create may have dozens of planets and moons, multiple civilizations, countless nations, cities, and cultures, and hundreds of potential adventure locations. Of course, you'll never detail them all, and even if you did, they would soon be forgotten when the characters climbed back in their ship and set course for the next star. However, if you make sure that every star system you create boasts a single interesting place for the characters to encounter or explore, it will make them far more memorable for the players. Examples include:

- A dwarven mining outpost in the asteroid belt
- A space station orbiting the moon of a gas giant where starships stop to refuel
- A high-security prison on an otherwise uninhabited world
- A secret imperial research base
- A city renowned for its cutting-edge spellware clinics
- A fabulous seaside resort built by a decadent aristocrat
- An orbital shipyard
- A great temple dedicated to one of the Twelve
- The ruins of a planetary civilization completely destroyed by war
- The royal palace where an Outlands king is being corrupted by the ISPD

NPCs

Finally, your players will remember the star systems and planets you create if you populate each one with a single unique and interesting non-player character. This character could be a contact, an ally, a patron, an enemy, a villain, or an innocent bystander. The character's precise nature and role are not as important as whether his interactions with the party are enjoyable and memorable. Even when the players have forgotten everything else about your system or planet, they'll remember it as the home of this NPC: "Oh yeah, that's the planet where we first ran into Perrywinkle the Mad Gnome and he tried to kill us!" NPCs will always be unique to your own campaign, but some examples that might provide inspiration include:

- An Outlands peasant with the imagination and intelligence to grasp advanced technology
- A customs agent who always insists on a thorough inspection of the characters' ship
- A smuggler who can always get whatever the characters' need
- A deranged beggar who thinks he's related to one of the characters
- A kindly cleric who offers healing and other spells to those who heed his spiritual guidance
- A freighter captain who knows the local system better than anyone else alive
- A soulmech who mourns for his lost life as an organic being
- A kobold trader who claims to be a distant relative of Mezzenbone
- An undercover ISPD agent who poses as the characters' ally
- A rogue paladin obsessed with vengeance who left his order and is looking for new allies

CHAPTER NINE

DRAGONSTAR CAMPAIGNS

Dragonstar was designed from the ground up to provide both a detailed framework for your campaign and plenty of flexibility to allow you to customize the setting to your preferences and style of play. The Dragon Empire represents an enormous volume of space, and just about any fantasy campaign setting can find a home among the imperial worlds or the limitless frontiers of the Outlands. With a little bit of thought and preparation, just about any world you've every played in—or wanted to—can be seamlessly integrated into the **Dragonstar** universe.

For details on how to introduce existing d20 System characters into a **Dragonstar** campaign, consult the *Starfarer's Handbook*. This book provides rules for character races and classes, new feats and skills, equipment, magic and more.

THE DRAGONSTAR CAMPAIGN

Dragonstar's flexibility means there's many different ways to approach it. Once you've decided to use the setting, you need to decide how best to approach it. Will you start a brand new campaign or will you incorporate your favorite campaign setting into the Dragonstar universe? This section explores the many options available to you.

A FRESH START

Your first option is to start a new campaign set in the **Dragonstar** universe. The players, of course, will need to create new characters, and you'll need to consider how best to prepare for the new campaign. Starting with the setting information provided in this book, you should choose a starting point for the campaign, develop sufficient detail of the location for your style of play, create prominent NPCs and adventure hooks—in short, do the same work you'd do to prepare for any other new campaign.

This option has a number of advantages. First, you don't have to worry about integrating all of your old plot lines and villains into a larger galaxy. In some cases, stories, themes, and characters that were larger than life in a traditional setting may appear diminished and even inconsequential in the context of the epic scope of the Dragon Empire. While it can be interesting and enjoyable to consider how the great heroes and villains of your world would react to contact with the Empire, it might also undermine the struggles, triumphs, and tragedies that made your campaign memorable and unique.

Your existing campaign setting may also prove difficult to incorporate into the Dragon Empire due to its cosmology, mythology, or other features. If you've told the characters that "space" is a crystal sphere with celestial lights imbedded in its interior surface, you'll have a difficult time making the transition to the more conventional **Dragonstar** cosmology. If the gods take an active part in your world, walking the earth and fighting its battles personally, your players may have a hard time accepting an abrupt shift to Unification Church theology.

Starting fresh also gives the players an opportunity to create characters specifically tailored to the **Dragonstar** setting. While it's a strength of the setting that it can integrate existing characters from a wide variety of campaigns, players may prefer to begin the campaign with characters from the imperial worlds. A player who

wants to try out a mechanist, pilot, or soulmech character—or even a gun-toting orc—won't be able to if you begin the campaign with traditional Outlands characters.

KIDNAPPED!

If you choose this option, the player's characters from your existing campaign are somehow abducted from their homeworld and thrust unceremoniously onto the vast stage of the Dragon Empire. Perhaps they were taken against their will by agents of the ISPD or Adamantine Order for some nefarious purposes. This can be an exciting way to kick off a **Dragonstar** campaign, but keep in mind that mid- to high-level characters can be extremely hard to abduct. Chances are, at least some of them will find a way to escape your trap and at best you'll have a split party to contend with.

If you'd like to bring the existing characters into your new **Dragonstar** campaign, but want to leave your campaign world relatively untouched, this is an attractive option. The characters are forced to leave their homeworld and find their place among the stars, but perhaps they will return years later—to retire from their life of adventure, or maybe to warn of an impending invasion

from an empire ruled by dragons.

If you want the introduction of **Dragonstar** into your campaign to be a surprise to the players, this is a pretty safe option. If the players are less enthusiastic about the campaign's new direction than you'd hoped, you can allow the characters to return to their homeworld and resume the original campaign. The experience will inevitably affect their worldviews, but they'll be able to pick up where they left off with little additional disruption. Indeed, this option can be used as a predetermined, short-term twist on the campaign. A brief voyage to the stars will give the characters a new perspective and force the players to reexamine some of their preconceptions about your campaign world. With this kind of scenario, you can leave the ultimate decision of whether to remain in the Dragon Empire or return to their homeworld up to the characters and their players.

The only real drawback to this approach is that the players aren't given the option to create imperial characters. As Outlands heroes, they will be complete strangers in an unfamiliar, almost incomprehensible world. They suddenly discover that they're considerably less powerful—at least in combat—than imperial characters of equal levels. They'll have difficulty understanding even the simplest technological devices, and they'll find that many of their own skills, feats, and equipment have become archaic or downright primitive. Some players may relish this challenge, but others may resent their characters' loss of power and status. As DM, you know your players and their characters almost as well as they do, and you should be able judge their reaction ahead of time. If you're unsure, don't surprise them. Surprise twists in a campaign can be a lot of fun for all involved, when they work. But if you're unsure, it's always wisest to ask your players for their input before making radical changes to an ongoing campaign.

FIRST CONTACT

A better option for experienced PCs might be to have them contacted by a more benevolent organization, such as a Royal Exploratory Society Contact Team. Perhaps the RES team needs the PCs help with some local task necessary to accomplish their mission, or maybe the PCs have information about their homeworld the team needs. The team may be gathering intelligence prior to contacting the rulers and influential leaders of the planet's major nations. This scenario may be particularly appropriate to introduce high-level heroes to the **Dragonstar** universe. Using this approach, the characters' early adventures might take place entirely on their homeworld and their contact with imperial characters may be very limited. The characters' actions and decisions may affect not only their own futures but also the fate of their world.

There are many different approaches you can take with this "first contact" scenario. Maybe the campaign world has never been visited by the Royal Exploratory Service. Perhaps the characters first encounters with imperial characters are with freelancers, mercenaries, or independent traders. Or maybe they stumble upon a deadly conspiracy in which ISPD agents are working with local villains to destabilize or overthrow the government or leadership of a just nation.

IMPERIAL OUTLANDERS

Many worlds have been colonized by the Empire but are still deep in the Outlands frontier. These worlds have one or more imperial enclaves, usually centered in the largest cities. These enclaves are like islands of advanced technology and imperial culture in an otherwise conventional fantasy world.

Given the level of technology common on these worlds, it's entirely possible for a world to have been contacted and colonized for months or even years before native characters learn of the newcomers. Once they do, it will be up to them to decide how to react to the news. Do they begin organizing a resistance effort intent on

forcing the colonists off of their world? Or do they travel to the imperial enclave to learn more about the newcomers?

Even if the characters try to ignore the imperial presence on their planet, they won't be able to for long. Eventually, the enclave will begin to spread, beginning in the heart of a capital city and gradually expanding to encompass a kingdom, a continent, and eventually, an entire world. On most Outlands worlds, this process takes years or even centuries. In some cases, though, depending on how attractive the planet is to colonists, corporations, and government agencies, the process of urbanization, industrialization, and technological development seemingly occurs overnight.

INVASION

Perhaps the most dramatic way to incorporate your existing campaign world into the Dragon Empire is with a small fleet of imperial cruisers. A full-scale invasion of the characters' homeworld could serve as the basis for an entire campaign. The characters may be caught up in the events surrounding the evasion, struggling merely to survive and protect their friends and families. Or they may get involved in the fighting themselves, joining with an organized resistance to repel the invaders.

An investigation and reconnaissance of the planet by agents of the ISPD or Adamantine Order usually precedes an invasion. You can even merge the first contact and invasion scenarios, beginning an epic campaign arc with the characters' discovery of the ISPD's presence and activities on their world and culminating with their efforts to stop the invasion or salvage as much as possible in its aftermath.

You can get even more drama out of an invasion if you surprise the players with it. As noted in the "kidnapped!" discussion, however, you should be cautious using this approach. There is even more risk inherent in the invasion scenario—it affects the entire campaign world, not just the PCs, and there's no going back once the cruisers are in orbit, the dropships are screaming through the atmosphere, and the shock troops in powered armor are ravaging your campaign world.

If you decide on an imperial invasion of your campaign world, you have a couple different options. First, the Dragon Empire can sweep in and take control, virtually overnight. If your campaign world enjoys neither advanced technology nor very high-level magic, this is the most likely outcome of an invasion. This is perhaps the simplest option, as it gets the invasion out of the way and lets you focus on the characters' reaction to it. In this scenario, the invasion itself isn't as important as what the characters do next. It is essentially used as a plot hook and serves as a starting point for your

Dragonstar campaign.

Of course, your PCs may not take the invasion lying down, no matter what the odds. Powerful heroes are especially likely to get involved. If your players have been playing high-level characters for an extended period of time, they're probably used to being able to influence and even control events on a global scale. It's even likely that they've saved their world from disaster at least once in the recent past. Your players may well feel cheated and railroaded if their powerful heroes have no chance to stop or affect the invasion.

If you choose this option, you need to know something about the procedures the Empire follows when it invades an Outlands world. As you might recall from the setting details provided earlier in this book, your campaign world is most likely to be invaded by one or more of the houses of Asamet. Qesemet very rarely uses such tactics, and even then only if the planet is deemed a real threat to its domains. The kingdom might invade an Outlands world that had been overrun by outsiders, for example, or a planet on which metallic dragons were being exterminated. Otherwise, your campaign world is likely to be the victim of one of the chromatic clans.

On most Outlands worlds, the only real threat to an imperial invasion is magic. Powerful spellcasters, magical creatures, and mighty artifacts can make an assault extremely costly, even if they fail to stop it. Even the most powerful technological weapon is predictable. With adequate intelligence, the generals and admirals planning an invasion will know how it works, what it can do, and how it's likely to be used. Magic is inherently unpredictable. High-level wizards, clerics, and magical beings working together can be a real concern, especially because it's effectively impossible to anticipate what they'll do. Mezzenbone typically dispatches agents of the Adamantine Order or ISPD to identify these threats prior to the invasion, and neutralize or turn them if possible. When the invasion is launched, these threats are among the first targets. Arcane guilds, known wizards' strongholds, and prominent temples are hit with orbital strikes. Individual spellcasters and creatures are targeted by assassins, strike teams, and imperial spellcasters. Dangerous artifacts are located and either recovered or destroyed.

After these initial attacks, troops are deployed in dropships to take control of the major population centers. This typically enables the invaders to neutralize any concentrated military opposition. The civilian populations can also be used as political hostages to discourage any further resistance. Reports of mass executions of civilians by the ISPD are relatively common on Outlands worlds where armed opposition continues for an extended period of time after the initial invasion. Qesemet, the Elven Nation, and other good-aligned political groups protest these atrocities in the Imperial Council and other forums, but there is little they can do to either prove or put an end to them. Control of the cities also gives the invaders control of the local political leadership. The ISPD always tries to keep at least one member of the ruling government alive so that power can be transferred to the Empire in an orderly fashion.

On most Outlands worlds, only a fraction of the population lives in cities. Most of these cultures are based on agrarian, pastoral, or hunter-gatherer economies, and most people live and work in rural or wilderness areas. After the cities have been secured, troops are deployed to these regions to crush any resistance efforts and round up the scattered civilian populations. Sprawling interment camps are constructed around the cities, and the civilians are relocated to them. These "clean up" operations can take months or even years and are often the most dangerous assignments for Imperial Legionnaires. Clearing farmers and shepherds out of the fields and hills is one thing. Rooting out dwarves who have retreated deep into subterranean holdfasts, or cleaning goblinoids out of seemingly endless cave networks that riddle impassable mountains is an entirely different proposition. In many of these operations, the terrain and the opponent neutralize the Empire's technological advantage, and the Legionnaires must contend with both enemy soldiers and hostile civilians on their own turf and their own terms.

Conditions in the interment camps are generally atrocious. Overcrowding and poor sanitation inevitably breed disease. Civilians are interred together with no regard for race, culture, or alignment and violence is the inevitable result. The strong prey on the weak and violence based on differences of race, religion, politics, and alignment is an everyday occurrence. Because there is strength in numbers, gangs inevitably form around these cultural traits and the violence escalates and spreads.

Once the cities are firmly under martial law, the former rulers have capitulated to the Empire, and the relocation of the civilian populations to the interment camps is well underway, the viceroy and his entourage arrive. The viceroy is usually a lesser noble of one of the royal houses whose job is to make the planet a productive colony. His initial tasks are to coordinate with the ISPD on security issues, conduct a census of the local populations and issue identification numbers to them, and establish an administrative plan for the colony.

The PCs may play a variety of roles in these events, from the most modest to the most heroic. Perhaps they will try to protect their village, tribe, or kingdom from the invaders. Or maybe they'll try to unite all the villages, tribes, and kingdoms in their region to stand as one. The characters may try to protect friends and family in an interment camp, or they may have to survive the camps themselves. Perhaps they will seek to learn more about the invaders and eventually try to make contact with friendly parties in the Empire who might be able to help them.

Whether or not the characters have any chance at all to repel the invaders—or even hold them off for a significant period of time—is up to you as the DM. If you want the campaign to focus on the PCs' introduction to and exploration of the Dragon Empire, the invasion and colonization of their homeworld should be relatively quick and complete. On the other hand, if you want the campaign to focus on the invasion itself and the characters' response to it, you should give them more opportunities to win a few battles along the way. Ultimately, few Outlands worlds will be able to hold off the Empire for long. Even if the outcome is inevitable, though, victories on a smaller scale may be possible for the PCs. They protect their families in the camps until they're allowed to return to their homes. They help the master wizard escape to another plane where help might be found. They escort the princess and heir to the throne out of the city and help her establish a government-in-exile in some hidden location—or even on another planet.

ADVENTURES

Once you've decided on the kind of **Dragonstar** campaign you want to run, you need to give some consideration to the adventures that together will make up the campaign. This section discusses the kinds of adventures you can run in a **Dragonstar** campaign and how to get the characters involved in them.

GETTING STARTED

There are three basic methods you can use to get an adventure underway. You can tailor the adventure to the characters, you can tailor the characters to the adventures, or you can design an adventure that is suitable for a wide variety of different characters. One of the great maxims of entertainment of any kind is "Give them what they want." This is as true in a roleplaying game as it is in any other form of entertainment. The goal of your game is for everyone to have fun. The best way to reach that goal is to create adventures that will engage and motivate your players.

TAILORED ADVENTURES

If you don't have a specific adventure in mind when you start a new **Dragonstar** campaign, there is no better resource to turn to than your players. Before you start planning the campaign, have the players create their characters, complete with at least a rough background.

By examining the characters the players create, you can get an idea of what kinds of adventures they're anticipating. Most players want two basic things out of an adventure: They want interesting and enjoyable role-playing opportunities, and they want opportunities to exercise their characters skills and abilities to overcome challenges.

If a player creates a character that focuses on raw firepower and combat ability, you'll keep him happy if you create adventures that feature lots of monsters and opponents to defeat in combat. A player who creates a ranger character will be looking forward to adventures based in wilderness areas. A rogue may be best suited for adventures that reward stealth, while a mechanist is in his element when adventures feature technological devices to be operated, repaired, or sabotaged.

These considerations will be old hat to veteran DMs, but giving special attention to them is always worth the effort. The opportunity for the characters to use their unique abilities in exciting situations is probably the most important component of an adventure. Even if you don't think your background story is a masterpiece and your NPCs aren't as well realized as you'd like, you'll find that most players are pretty forgiving if you give them interesting and exciting things for their characters to do.

It may seem that you'll run into problems with this approach when the characters in your party are suited to many different activities and styles of play. If half of the group wants combat-heavy adventures and the other half is interested in social intrigue, how can you design adventures that will satisfy everyone? This variety of characters and abilities is actually one of the game's real strengths. Because everyone has something different and unique to contribute, adventures you tailor to the party will feature many different kinds of encounters and events, and this variety will help to keep the game fresh and exciting.

Create adventures that give each character a chance to shine. To continue the above example, maybe the PCs have to locate and infiltrate a high-tech imperial base hidden in the wilds of an Outlands world. The rangers and fighters will have to fight their way through the monster-infested wilderness. The rogue will have to figure out a way to enter the base without sounding alarms or alerting the guards. And it will be up to the mechanist to sabotage the base's primary weapon, hack into the computer and download the secret data, or accomplish some other objective that got the characters involved in the adventure.

Even if your group has several characters with the same area of focus, it can be fun to put them into unfamiliar situations on occasion. This may encourage the players to develop skills and abilities for their characters that they might otherwise ignore. Further, one of the best ways to really challenge a player is to put his character in an unfamiliar situation where his skills and abilities are less than optimal. Some of these situations may entail only modest departures from the norm. For example, a fighter optimized for ranged combat might be forced into a series of close-quarters battles in which melee combat is called for. Others may involve more radical changes that will really test the player's ability to think on his feet and roleplay his character. The fighter may find himself responsible for negotiating a vital agreement with a pacifist tribe that is religiously opposed to fighting and violence.

Tailored Characters

Another option is to discuss with the players ahead of time the kind of campaign you want to run and the adventures that are best suited to the campaign. If you go this route, be sure to give your players plenty of input. Ideally, you should settle on a campaign style that everyone, including you, will enjoy. The biggest pitfall of this approach is that you'll inadvertently force the players into roles they aren't comfortable with or won't enjoy.

For example, you might decide you want to run adventures set in the courts of the Dragon Empire's royal houses. Ideas for court intrigues, treachery, and diplomatic gambits have inspired you to create a truly sinister plot the characters will spend several game sessions untangling before they even begin to figure out what's really going on. However, if your players are more interested in hunting fell monsters in the Outlands, the adventures you have planned might entirely fail to engage or interest them. It's probably the most basic advice for DMs, but always remember that the players are not mere spectators in the game watching your carefully crafted plot unfolding around their characters. They are active participants in the events surrounding them, and in the most enjoyable campaigns, those events—however modest in scope or scale—will hinge on their decisions and actions.

A discussion of the players' preferences before the campaign begins will go a long way toward navigating around this pitfall. Your players will also really appreciate that you've asked for their input, and you'll find they're much more likely to become active and cooperative partners in your campaign as a result.

One of the big advantages of this approach is that you can work to set the proper tone from the very beginning and create adventures that reinforce the theme and flavor of your campaign. It also gives the players a fixed point to hang their character concepts around, with built-in traits and features that give them a reason to work together. In a campaign that follows the adventures of a group of disparate and disconnected characters, it's often the DM who does the following. When the characters are tailored to the adventures, the DM can create the sense that the characters are part of something larger than themselves, giving them the opportunity to carve out their own place in the known galaxy.

Fixed Adventures

You will probably create many adventures that have neither a specific connection to the characters nor a crucial role to play in the overarching backstory of your campaign. These adventures are often based on interesting locations that remain the same whether the characters investigate them or not. A derelict starship with no life signs aboard, a dwarven asteroid mine infested by alien aberrations, an evil temple in an active volcano on an Outlands world—all are examples of premises for fixed adventures. Nor do fixed adventures have to be location based. They can also be based on events that are not directly connected to the characters and that would occur whether or not they become involved.

Fixed adventures can cultivate the sense that the world is bigger than the characters, that not everything hinges on their actions and decisions. This can go a long way toward making the world seem more real to both you and your players. The other advantage of fixed adventures, of course, is that you're not limited in what you can do. If you have a cool idea for the plot of an event-based adventure or for the location of a site-based adventure, you can just run with it. Even if all you have is a great idea for an NPC villain, you can build an adventure around it. You'll have to figure out a way to introduce the PCs to the adventure, but you'll find that the players will cooperate—they want their characters to have adventures just as much as you want them to. Be careful, however, that the fixed adventure or the motivations you provide the characters aren't in conflict with their personalities or backgrounds. You don't want a player to have to choose between breaking character and passing on the adventure you've lovingly detailed.

TYPES OF ADVENTURES

The following is a list and brief discussion of several types of adventures that work well in **Dragonstar**. Each entry also provides a number of plot hooks that may serve as a starting point to help you develop your own adventures.

DELIVERY

The characters must transport an item or creature from one place to another. The cargo may be contraband, such as weapons, drugs, or slaves the PCs are required to smuggle past the authorities in the Domains of Qesemet. Alternatively, the cargo may be perfectly legal but valuable enough—at least to someone—that an effort will be made to intercept it.

- The characters must smuggle high-tech weapons to resistance fighters on an Outlands world.
- The characters must escort a dangerous convict to a remote prison planet.
- The characters must deliver a message from a mysterious employer to another party on the other side of the Empire.
- The characters must deliver an ancient, sacred tome from the Outlands world where it was discovered to the holy city of Aani.
- The characters must deliver exotic creatures to a zoo in the Domain of Esmer. One of the creatures is a pixie.

DESTRUCTION

The characters must destroy an item or creature. Perhaps a monster is ravaging the underbelly of a city, or terrorists are using a bioweapon to threaten an entire planet. Alternatively, the target may be an innocent who appears to be a threat. The characters may not know the target's true nature when they undertake the quest. Once they discover what's really happening, they'll have to decide whether or not to complete their task or attempt to help the misunderstood innocent instead. In some cases, this might put the characters at odds with an employer or others who still want to be rid of the target. The adventure might shift to a protection scenario, as described below.

- The characters must assault a military research base conducting illegal arcane genetic research. The test subjects are innocent civilians abducted from isolated colonies, but they've been engineered into lethal killing machines.
- An evil wizard is attempting to open a permanent gate to the Abyss on a recently colonized Outlands world. The characters must locate and defeat him

before the planet is overrun by fiends.
- The characters must track down and destroy a homicidal soulmech. But what will they do when they discover what drove it to madness?
- A tribe of kobolds on an Outlands world has discovered a cache of high-tech weapons, armor, and other equipment, and are causing all manner of mischief as a result. The characters must locate the cache and destroy it before the kobolds become a serious threat to the neighboring kingdom.
- A pirate crew in a well-armed corvette has been attacking merchant shipping in a remote planetary system. The characters must set an ambush for the pirates and destroy the corvette.

EXPLORATION

In this kind of adventure, the PCs must enter an unknown area and fulfill some objective. This may be a simple matter of survival, or they may need to gather some specific information about the location. Perhaps they are doing a reconnaissance of the area to identify threats, or maybe they're trying to create a detailed map of an uncharted region.

- The characters are sent to an uncharted Outlands world. The ruins of ancient elven cities are scattered across the major landmasses...but what happened to the elves?
- The characters are sent to investigate a derelict starship found drifting in space. The previous team sent to the ship never returned, but garbled radio communications indicate that it is haunted.
- The characters' ship crashes on an unknown Outlands world. They need parts to fix the ship, and they might be able to find them in the ruins of an ancient civilization they discover on the planet.
- The characters' ship suffers a starcaster malfunction and they find themselves deep in the Dark Zone. They must figure out where they are so they can return to imperial space while avoiding the local denizens.
- The characters are assigned to map an abyssal trench that plunges miles below the ocean surface of a recently colonized world. In addition to the lethal environment, they must deal with the things that dwell in the oldest and deepest parts of the planet.

LOCATION AND RECOVERY

The characters must find and retrieve a specific item or creature. The quarry could be something that was stolen from its rightful owner, a kidnap victim, or just something that an employer or patron desires. These adventures can be challenging for the characters,

because people in the Dragon Empire can travel great distances in practically no time at all. A location and recovery adventure might require the characters to track their quarry to the other side of the known galaxy.

- The characters must travel to a pre-contact Outlands world to find and recover an exotic—and dangerous—spell component.
- The characters must track and down a missing aristocrat and return her to her family. But what will they do with the rebellious, juvenile dragon when she doesn't want to go home?
- Explorers have reported sightings of a new dragon subspecies on a remote Outlands world. The characters must travel to the planet and return with a living specimen.
- Agents of a rival corporation have stolen a prototype space fighter. The characters must find the prototype and steal it back.
- The characters return from the wilderness to discover that their ship's starcaster is missing. Hopefully whoever took it is still on the planet.

PROTECTION

The characters must guard, protect, or escort something or someone. Perhaps it is a valuable item that must be guarded from thieves or a powerful artifact that must be kept from those who would use it for evil. Maybe the characters have to protect an aristocrat who is in danger or help a fugitive escape from the law.

- The characters must escort a diplomatic envoy from the Kingdom of Qesemet to an Outlands world whose elven population is rebelling against the colonization of the planet.
- The deposed king of an Outlands realm has been placed in the general population of an imperial interment camp. The characters must protect him from the orc veterans whose warlord the king defeated in battle years ago.
- The characters are assigned to guard a storage facility at a remote mining outpost. The facility is filled with priceless mithral ore and the outpost is being overrun by xorns.
- The characters are charged with protecting an evil NPC, such as a vampire, from the rogue paladins who are trying to murder him or her.
- Druids entreat the characters to protect an ancient and magical grove of trees from an encroaching logging corporation. The company is a subsidiary of a powerful aristocorp.

ALL THESE WORLDS

Dragonstar takes the traditional fantasy setting as its starting point and asks, "What if there were a whole galaxy, or universe, of such worlds out there?" In all respects, it stays true to the unique brand of swords-and-sorcery fantasy presented in the core rulebooks. The **Dragonstar** universe is populated by metallic and chromatic dragons, elves, dwarves, halflings, orcs, mind flayers, beholders, and displacer beasts. Its clerics are divine instruments of the gods with the power to heal, raise the dead, and shake the earth. Its arcane spellcasters are divided between those who were born with an innate ability to wield the power and those who gained their mastery through long hours of study.

Many d20 System games and campaign settings depart from this traditional genre. While published **Dragonstar** products will stay true to the settings classical roots, there's no reason you can't incorporate non-traditional worlds and settings into your campaign as well. It's impossible to cover in detail every possible genre or setting you might want to include, but the following offers a brief discussion of the most common and popular options.

GUNPOWDER AND STEAM

Few worlds in the Outlands have achieved star travel, but many have advanced beyond the level of technology at which wars are fought with swords and bows and motive power is supplied by horses and oxen. These worlds might feature primitive firearms, printing presses, steam engines, and other pre-industrial or early-industrial technologies that will have a profound effect on the setting. Most of these civilizations are still confined to a single planet, so they're just as easy to integrate with **Dragonstar** as a traditional fantasy setting.

Characters from these worlds may have a much easier time adjusting to the technology of the Dragon Empire. Depending on the details of the setting's technology base—how broad it is, how accessible it is to non-specialists, etc.—the DM may reduce the circumstance penalty for technical non-proficiency to –2. Characters from these worlds also gain a +2 circumstance bonus on Intelligence checks to figure out a technological device. These characters must still gain a level of experience with high technology to receive the Technical Proficiency feat, however.

Space Fantasy

In the Dragon Empire, spacecraft use advanced technology and teleportation magic to travel between the stars. While technology is relatively inexpensive and mass producible, it is not the only method of reaching the heavens in the known galaxy. Some civilizations never develop advanced technology but advance the art of magic to such a high level that space travel is possible. The spacecraft of these civilizations may look very similar to archaic sailing vessels or they may be fanciful designs built of magic and imagination. Characters from such a civilization may already be accustomed to the notion of star travel, though the experience would be very different from that common in the Empire.

A magical spacefaring civilization can be easily integrated into the **Dragonstar** universe. Perhaps the civilization encompasses several star systems on the edge of the Outlands. Perhaps it lies along the border of the Dark Zone and is locked in a war of survival with the technologically advanced mind flayer empire. Even if your PCs hail from the imperial worlds, this kind of pocket empire might make an excellent setting for an extended campaign that focuses on exploration and contact with exotic civilizations.

Characters from a magical spacefaring civilization will often be no more familiar with advanced technology than those from more mundane Outlands worlds. They may find it easier to adjust to the interstellar civilization of the Dragon Empire, but they'll have to learn to use technology just like other Outlanders.

Modern Fantasy

There are a number of d20 settings already available that are set in the modern world—or a reasonable facsimile of it. The level of technology might range from that of the Old West to that of a near, dark future. Magic in most of these settings is much less prevalent than in a traditional fantasy campaign setting, or even nonexistent. It's a relatively simple matter to incorporate these worlds into **Dragonstar**.

Depending on the level of technology available, you might consider allowing the characters to begin with the Technical Proficiency feat. For example, in a setting based on early 21st century Earth, characters would no doubt adjust quickly to the differences between the technology they're used to and the standard of the Dragon Empire. In a less advanced setting, such as one based on the Old West or a Steam Age milieu, you might reduce the penalty for not having the feat to –2.

The biggest challenge of this approach is always incorporating the "real world" into a fictional setting. Players may easily buy into their favorite fantasy setting becoming part of the Dragon Empire, but you may meet more resistance to doing the same with Earth. The premise of **Dragonstar** is that the universe is filled with traditional fantasy worlds—how does our planet fit into that universe? To the people of Earth, it would look as if the universe had been populated with the creatures of our fairy tales and myths.

If you're ready to provide a justification for this that will seem plausible to players and their characters, you'll be able to pull it off. Otherwise, you're probably best advised to keep the focus of the campaign on your fantasy Earth and introduce only a few elements of the **Dragonstar** universe. The players may well be able to accept that the legendary dragons are real and that they rule a star-spanning empire, but they'll quickly lose their suspension of disbelief if they discover that the universe is populated with all the creatures from the core rulebooks.

Of course, worlds that have developed industrial or post-industrial levels of technology have a much better chance of resisting an invasion by the Dragon Empire. A planet with massive stockpiles of nuclear weapons, chemical weapons, and bioweapons is going to force the empire to move slowly and cautiously. Even Mezzenbone's most aggressive commanders will demand extensive preliminary intelligence gathering and covert operations from the Adamantine Order, ISPD, or blackguard orders before committing to a full-scale assault. Even then, a campaign of destabilization and infiltration might well be chosen in favor of a military invasion. Specifically, the invaders might seek to seize control of the weapons of mass destruction before bringing in the fleet.

Science Fiction

You can also integrate **Dragonstar** with a traditional science fiction game. You have a number of options depending on the scope of interstellar expansion in your sci-fi setting. If the interstellar civilization is relatively small, as is the Dragon Empire, there's plenty of room for both in the galaxy. If your interstellar civilization is

much larger, it may require a galaxy (or galaxies) of its own. Now you just have to decide how to introduce the two civilizations.

If the two galaxies are relatively close neighbors, you could have explorers from one travel to the other. Perhaps a massive generation ship filled with the descendants of those who set out from the neighboring galaxy centuries ago shows up in the Dragon Empire. Or maybe a small explorer ship from the Dragon Empire with an astral drive manages to make the long, perilous voyage to a nearby galaxy. Either of these options could serve as the basis for an extended campaign.

If truly vast reaches of space separate the two galaxies, perhaps a wormhole or portal is discovered in some remote system that connects the two. Such a gateway could even link two parallel universes or alternate dimensions. This could become a major commercial hub if the two empires establish trading relations or a deadly battlezone if they go to war. The two civilizations may be completely different. You could introduce a civilization in which humans are the only sentient race and there is no knowledge of magic. Or perhaps it's a civilization of aliens completely unlike anything found in the Dragon Empire. Maybe their technology is much more advanced, and the Imperial Legions find the tables turned as they must fight against a superior foe. Contact between the two civilizations might even reveal that physical laws are not uniform throughout the universe: Perhaps there are places where magic does not exist, or where technology more advanced than simple tools cannot function, or where things impossible to achieve with technology in the Dragon Empire are commonplace.

If you explore these options, you'll be moving into unknown territory further and further away from the "official canon" of the **Dragonstar** universe. The game is yours, though, and you should use it in whatever way gives you and your players the most enjoyment. The setting was designed to be inclusive, to accommodate many worlds, genres, and play styles, and these explorations are perfectly suited to the spirit of **Dragonstar**.

USING TECHNOLOGY

The biggest difference between Outlands characters and those native to the imperial worlds is the latter's basic familiarity with and understanding of technology. In game terms, characters who were born or have lived in the Empire for a significant period of time gain Technical Proficiency as a bonus feat. This means they are able to identify and use a vast array of technological devices without penalty. They recognize a credit chip when they see one and know how to use it to transfer funds between accounts. They know how to operate a computer and use it to perform a variety of basic tasks. They understand the basic functions and mechanisms of modern firearms and can figure out how to toggle the safety on and off, load a new minicell, and fire the weapon—even if they aren't accomplished marksmen.

Characters from less technologically advanced worlds typically won't have any idea how to use any of these devices. An insightful Outlands character who sees a blaster rifle in action might be able to make sense of it in terms of weapons he's familiar with—a crossbow, for example. Devices like starships, however, are so far beyond such a character's experience and understanding he likely can't even conceive of them before he first sets eyes on one. The Outlander's view of the universe might not even allow for starships, even if he were to imagine them in the abstract. If a visitor from the Dragon Empire were to tell this character that he was born on a different world under a different sun, the Outlander would probably consider him a madman—or perhaps an outsider from another plane of existence.

When confronted with a technological device, an Outlands character is normally at a complete loss. However, most non-specialized devices are designed to be relatively easy to use. With a bit of instruction, it's possible for the character to determine what a device's purpose is and how to use it.

Complexity	Example	DC
Simple	Flashlight	12
Tricky	Personal comm	15
Difficult	Firearm	18
Wicked	Datapad	20

To figure out how to use a device, the character must make an Intelligence check. The DC of the check depends on the complexity of the device, as shown in the above table.

If sufficient time is available, the player may take 10 or take 20 on this check. If the DM permits, you may attempt to figure out a complicated device one component at a time. For example, if you're trying to teach yourself how to drive a hovercraft, you might start by figuring out how to turn it on (DC 12). Next, you can work on how to make the vehicle move (DC 15), and then how to control it (DC 12).

Trial-and-error experimentation with unfamiliar technology can have unpredictable results. If you roll a 1 on your check, make the check again. If the second check also fails, you've made a horrible mistake. It's up to the

DM to determine the exact results, depending on the kind of device you're experimenting with. Harmless devices such as flashlights and datapads shouldn't mysteriously explode just because an Outlander rolled poorly. Instead, the character might remove the battery and be unable to put it back in, or he may erase the memory on the computer. Experimentation with firearms, explosives, and other dangerous devices, of course, may have more severe consequences.

These checks can be avoided altogether if the Outlander receives instruction from a technically proficient character. The Outlander must receive instruction on each device he wishes to use, even if a new item is very similar to another one he is already familiar with. This instruction usually requires 10 minutes per complexity category of the device. After receiving the instruction, the Outlander can use the device subject to the standard –4 circumstance penalty on skill checks for non-proficiency.

An Outlands character exposed to technological civilization can eventually gain the Technical Proficiency feat. If the character spends an entire level studying, working with, or surrounded by high technology, he gains the feat for free. In most campaigns, this need not be strictly realistic. It can be fun for players to encounter high technology in a fantasy game for the first time.

Roleplaying these experiences can add a great deal of enjoyment to the game. However, for most players, the fun won't last once the novelty wears off. Eventually, they'll want their characters to stop looking like primitive clowns and finally learn how to use the many new tools at their disposal. This opportunity, of course, is one of the most unique elements of **Dragonstar**.

COMBAT

If you've read through the *Starfarer's Handbook*, you've probably noticed that combat with high-tech firearms is extremely dangerous, especially for low-level characters. The blaster rifle—a simple weapon—will do enough damage (22 points) on an average hit to kill all but the toughest 1st-level characters. This section discusses the options you have for accommodating this increased level of lethality in your **Dragonstar** campaign.

The first thing you should do is put the discussion in context. While high-tech firearms are both common and deadly, you as DM should always be in control of the level of lethality in your campaign. Just because weapons are available does not mean that you should be equipping every goblin, orc, or kobold with laser and blaster rifles. A CR 2 ogre with a greatclub inflicts an average of 14 points of damage on a successful hit—

about the same as a blaster pistol. Just as you wouldn't expect your 1st-level PCs in a traditional fantasy campaign to be tackling ogres in every encounter, you shouldn't have them under constant blaster fire, either.

Because modern weapons and armor can greatly increase offensive and defensive capabilities, you need to be able to adjust the Challenge Rating of opponents to reflect their high-tech equipment. The following adjustments are presented as general rules, but you should feel free to modify them to account for extreme cases or unusual situations. Keep in mind that the CR system is quite "grainy," and that incremental increases in the CR often represent significant increases in ability. Also remember that high-tech weapons and armor increase damage potential and Armor Class, but they don't increase Hit Dice, attack bonuses, saves, and other characteristics that are important in determining a creature's CR.

For creatures with base CRs of less than 1, simply increase the CR by a number of steps equal to the modifier. For example, an orc (CR ½) with an assault rifle and armor vest would be CR 1. If he had an assault laser and combat armor, he'd be CR 2.

Using these guidelines, you should be able to design encounters and adventures that are appropriate challenges for your PCs.

Of course, there may also be situations in which the PCs' technology gives them a major advantage over their opponents. For example, if a party armed with energy weapons catches a monster in the open at a range of several hundred feet, they'll often be able to gun it down before it can ever reach them. In situations like this, use the guidelines for modifying encounter levels and XP awards in the core rules (DMG 167). Be careful when doing so, however. Just because a monster lacks advanced technology doesn't mean it's helpless. The same monster that would be gunned down if caught in the open could be a challenging encounter if the PCs must face it in close quarters where their ranged weapons are less useful. In a situation like this, you will often not need to adjust the encounter level at all.

For 1st-level characters, you'll clearly need to limit the number and difficulty of firefights you throw at them. How do you do this? If everyone can get their hands on guns, how do you limit the number of gun-toting opponents you throw at the PCs without breaking the setting's assumptions?

Fortunately, the Dragon Empire is a big place, and as we've already discussed, there are lots of different kinds of adventures you can create for a **Dragonstar** campaign. Adventures set on Outlands worlds may not feature any high-tech equipment at all, especially if the PCs are trying to blend in with the locals. Likewise, local laws may restrict the kinds of weapons civilians can carry or the armor they can wear. These restrictions may apply to whole cities on imperial worlds, or they may apply only to specific locations that figure prominently in your adventure—a royal court, a hospital, a spaceport, an orbital station, etc. By setting the characters' early adventures in locations where the legality or frequency of firearms would reasonably be limited, you can tone down the lethality level and stay true to the setting.

Keeping the characters alive isn't *entirely* your responsibility—the players have to be smart, too. You should emphasize the lethality of high-tech firearms and stress the importance of caution and good tactics. The best way to survive combat in **Dragonstar** is to avoid it. In most adventures, there will be opponents the PCs must defeat, but the party should attempt to avoid gunfights whenever possible. In many cases, this simply involves getting the drop on the opponent and taking him out before he can react. An enemy with a gun is only dangerous when he has a chance to return fire. In **Dragonstar**, the time that would typically be used to trade blows with an opponent might be well spent developing a plan that will secure victory without an exchange of fire.

EQUIPMENT CR MODIFIERS

Equipment	CR Modifier
Slug-throwers, high-tech melee weapons, high-tech light armor	+1
Energy weapons, high-tech medium or heavy armor	+2
Heavy weapons, powered armor	+3
Vehicle weapons, combat vehicles	+4

As DM, don't worry about your PCs gunning down the opposition before they have a chance to react. In many cases this is perfectly appropriate, and if the enemy has guns, the characters will constantly feel threatened. In a traditional fantasy game, suspense in melee combat is created through the exchange of blows: Will the PCs be able to reduce the monster's hit points to 0 before all of them go down? In **Dragonstar**, suspense is created by the constant threat of a single, potentially lethal attack. In this respect, the experience is closest to fighting a spellcaster in a traditional fantasy game—the PCs know they have to defeat the enemy wizard or cleric before he gets off the spell that takes them all down.

Because it emphasizes ranged combat, **Dragonstar** typically rewards tactical maneuvers more than a traditional fantasy campaign. The PCs can strike their foes at a distance, and this gives them a lot more options—they don't have to charge up to within five feet of the opponent and start attacking.

They can strike from ambush, hit and run, and most importantly, use concealment and cover. Concealment provides a flat miss chance for all attacks over and above any bonuses to Armor Class the character receives. Natural conditions sometimes provide concealment, but devices such as smoke grenades can also be extremely useful. Cover is the PCs' best friend. If

they can't avoid a firefight, their best chance of survival is to avoid being hit—even once. Cover bonuses to AC stack with Dex bonuses, dodge bonuses, armor bonuses, natural armor bonuses, and deflection bonuses.

Magic also provides a wide range of protection, even at low levels. The *shield* spell offers a +7 cover bonus to AC. Spells like *entropic shield*, *blur*, *blink*, and *displacement* offer miss chances similar to natural concealment. The elemental resistance spells—*endure elements*, *protection from elements*, *resist elements*, etc.—provide varying degrees of protection from energy weapons such as blasters and lasers. *Protection from arrows* provides the target with damage reduction against all projectile weapons, including slug-throwers. Spells like *expeditious retreat*, *fly*, and *invisibility* can significantly enhance a character's tactical maneuvers, making him much more effective in a firefight. All of these spells are 3rd level or lower and all will greatly improve your party's chances of surviving combat with high-tech weapons.

The impact of high-tech firearms on the game means you'll have to change your philosophy somewhat when creating encounters to fill out your adventures. The standard from the core rules is that a good encounter should deplete the party's resources by 20%. On this level, the game becomes one of strategic resource management: The player's try to navigate a series of encounters expending as few of their resources as possible. The DM tries to create challenging encounters that force the PCs to expend their resources at a predictable rate. It never works with mathematical precision, of course, but it's a sound and workable approach to balance and pacing.

In **Dragonstar**, it's very difficult to fall back on the "20% rule." An orc with a blaster rifle may be an acceptable 1st-level encounter (CR 2). However, the encounter will almost never result in the depletion of 20% of a 1st-level party's resources. Frequently, a single shot will drop the orc before it has a chance to act. If the orc does get to act and manages to hit, he'll do an average of 22 points of damage with the blaster rifle. You won't be able to spread that around between multiple characters, either—it'll all be on one and it will probably be enough to kill the character. Obviously, that's not a good outcome and the "20% rule" doesn't really apply.

Over the course of an adventure, you won't be able to rely on this rule to slowly whittle away the characters' hit points and spells, eventually forcing them to rest and recover before continuing on. The damage dealt by high-tech firearms is simply too prone to "spikes" to allow for this kind of gradual, predictable process. As DM, you should instead be concerned with devising encounters that represent an appropriate level of risk.

At this level, the strategic resource management model of the core rules is replaced with strategic risk management: The player's try to navigate a series of encounters safely by minimizing the risk inherent in each encounter. The players' focus changes from managing their available resources—though that element is still present—to identifying and minimizing the risks presented by each encounter. Good intelligence and preparation become extremely important. In a traditional fantasy game, it's usually of no import what weapons the dungeon denizens are using. Whether the orcs are using scimitars, spears, or axes is of little consequence for the PCs. In **Dragonstar**, this information can often spell the difference between surviving an encounter unscathed or losing a companion or two. Knowing where the opponent is and what technological resources are at his disposal allows the party to plan successful assaults, choose effective spells, and avoid unnecessary encounters and complications.

CHAPTER TEN

THE HOSTAGE

INTRODUCTION

The Hostage is an introductory **Dragonstar** adventure for four 1st-level characters. It features combat, conspiracy and intrigue, roleplaying and interaction, and elements of horror and dark fantasy. Both high technology and the supernatural will present challenges to the characters in the adventure. It is suitable for characters of any race and class. It can be played by imperial characters and Outlanders, and the adventure will test the strengths and weaknesses of both. Undead play a prominent role in the adventure, so a cleric will be especially helpful. The adventure can be easily scaled to challenge higher-level characters, as described below.

The adventure takes place in Praxilus, the divided colonial city on Primogen II described in Chapter 4. With some modification of the backstory, the adventure can be placed in just about any colonial city anywhere along the Outlands frontier. By modifying the adventure hook, it could even be placed in a developed metropolis in the Dragon Empire.

You should read the adventure carefully before running it for your players. A firm grasp of the motivations and personalities of the key NPCs is essential, and you should also familiarize yourself with the combat tactics of the characters' opponents.

The Hostage has been designed to serve as a good introduction to **Dragonstar** in general and the city of Praxilus in specific. The adventure may give the players some experience with firearms combats, offering the opportunity for them to discover how to win them and how to survive them. The anarchic streets of the city controlled by gun-toting gangs gives the adventure a gritty, sci-fi feel. The conspiracies, intrigues, and twisted alliances that serve as the backdrop and motivation for the adventure illustrate that, in **Dragonstar**, things aren't always neatly separated into black and white, even in a city that is literally divided along lines of race and alignment. The encounter with the ghouls will teach the PCs that opponents don't need high-tech weapons and armor to be dangerous. It also reinforces the supernatural and high-fantasy elements that set **Dragonstar** apart from traditional science fiction settings.

The adventure should also serve as a useful introduction for you, the DM. It should provide concrete examples of how to create encounters that are challenging, but not too deadly. It illustrates how you can weave many different organizations and plotlines from the **Dragonstar** setting into even the most straightforward adventure premise. It shows you how to create events and outcomes surrounding your adventures that will give the players the sense that things are really happening in the campaign, and their characters can play an important role in them. And finally, the adventure provides an example of how to incorporate both the sci-fi and fantasy elements that are so important to **Dragonstar** into an adventure.

The game statistics of NPCs and creatures, as well as rules and mechanics derived from the d20 SRD, are designated as **Open Game Content**.

ADVENTURE SUMMARY

The PCs encounter a Royal Marshal Service paladin working undercover as a journalist at the Hotel Praxilus. The "journalist" is doing a story on illegal ISPD activities on Primogen II and was supposed to meet with a half-orc insurgent who has information for her. The insurgent was unable or unwilling to deliver this information electronically. Because he lives in the eastern section of the city controlled by the Army of the Faceless Man, the undercover paladin could not safely go to him without jeopardizing her cover. As a result, she used her media connections to get him a pass into the imperial enclave and arranged a meeting with him at the Hotel Praxilus. Unfortunately, he never arrived.

The paladin has since learned that the insurgent was abducted by Free Nations militia soldiers during a raid into AFM-controlled territory. She has also learned that the soldiers never made it back across the Green Line to the section of the city controlled by the Free Nations militias. Chances are, they're already dead. But they could be holed up somewhere, and the paladin wants to make sure.

For the same reason she couldn't meet the half-orc in AFM territory, the paladin can't go there herself and try to rescue him. First, journalists almost never venture outside the imperial enclave unless they have the personal protection of one of the militia leaders. Second, if she did go and there was a confrontation with militia thugs, her cover as a journalist would quickly be blown.

The paladin is operating alone in Praxilus, so she's decided to seek the aid of adventurers. If the PCs agree to help her, they'll have to enter AFM territory, find out what happened to the Free Nations soldiers and their hostage, and discover where they're holed up. Then they'll have to penetrate the AFM siege of the place, deal with the ghouls that infest the old bombed-out tenement, find the surviving members of the Free Nations raid, and convince them to give up their hostage—or defeat them and convince the half-orc to accompany them. All that accomplished, the PCs just have to make it back out of AFM territory to the imperial enclave.

ADVENTURE BACKGROUND

When the archmages of the desert realms defeated the Faceless Man and his armies, they nearly destroyed their planet as well. Ironically, while this destruction put an end to the epic clashes of mighty armies, it did nothing to end the ancient war between the peoples of the desert realms and the goblinoid tribes. Clashes continued as the descendants of both groups slowly migrated north to escape the expanding deserts that encircled the planet. There was a brief lull in the nearly perpetual fighting when the Empire arrived on Primogen II, but it wasn't to last.

The imperials did nothing to resolve the ancient enmity between the two groups, and in fact, their arrival merely served to draw them together in close proximity.

When the imperial enclave was established in Praxilus, thousands of people from both groups rushed in to occupy the town. When these desperate people began to organize into militias and arm themselves, the imperials did nothing. When the fighting inevitably resumed with renewed ferocity, the imperials simply tightened security on the walls and checkpoints around their enclave.

The viceroy of the city has decided that the local garrison of Imperial Legionnaires is too small to keep peace in the Old City. Emperor Mezzenbone, who needs his Legionnaires to fight his ongoing campaign across the frontier, has decided that the garrison in Praxilus will not be reinforced. Why send more troops to a planet whose natives are mostly concerned with killing each other and seem to be leaving the imperials alone? Instead, Mezzenbone directed the small ISPD contingent in Praxilus to ensure that fighting between the militias continued and even escalated. The ISPD has followed this directive by arming both militias with high-tech firearms and explosives. The streets of the Old City have therefore become a killing field, but the imperial enclave remains secure with no new troop deployments.

The ISPD has maintained tight security on this operation. Even the militia leaders themselves don't know who is supplying their weapons, though rumors are rampant in the city that it's a smuggling ring with connections to the Black Hole Syndicate (see page 40). The imperial laws—those that all houses must abide by—are pretty limited, but using imperial tax revenues to arm violent insurgents and create a state of anarchy in a colonial city certainly violates several of them. At the very least, public disclosure of the operation would earn the ISPD and the Emperor the scrutiny of powerful dragon lords in the Imperial Council.

Unfortunately for the ISPD, the security around their gun-running operation has been penetrated. At least one person in Praxilus knows what they're up to, and he has the evidence to back his claim. Korig Freeman is a half-orc who lives in the AFM-controlled, eastern section of Praxilus—his race leaves him no other option. Korig is the offspring of the violence that AFM thugs have long visited upon innocent civilians living in the Free Nations-controlled part of the city. His human mother died early in his childhood—whether of sickness or resentment of him, Korig has never known—and he has been forced to survive by his own wits on the streets of the city for more than 20 years. While he's lived most of those 20 years in AFM territory, Korig has no loyalty for either of the militias.

Instead, his sympathy is reserved for the innocents who are killed, kidnapped, beaten, or robbed every day on the streets of the city. And while he despises the militias and their leaders who perpetuate the violence, his true hatred is reserved for those who have the power to stop it but choose to cultivate it for their own purposes: the imperials.

Over the course of the last several years, Korig has gradually become a radical and idealistic anti-imperial dissident and insurgent. He knows the Empire isn't responsible for all his people's problems, but he believes that it is the tyranny and injustice of the Empire that denies his people the freedom to solve their problems on their own. He has quietly and thus far privately dedicated his life to overthrowing this regime, or at least winning his own people's freedom from it. Surrounded by civilians who live in constant fear and militia thugs who care for little besides killing their enemies and grabbing what personal power and wealth they can, Korig has so far been forced to act alone. He hopes to eventually make contact with others who share his beliefs.

The journalist Korig was to meet, Rebecca Stone, is a paladin of the Judge in the Royal Marshal Service. She has extensive experience in undercover operations, and was assigned to Praxilus to investigate suspected ISPD violations of imperial law. The city creates a constant stream of sensational news events, and the Hotel Praxilus is filled to overcapacity with journalists and investigative reporters from all over the Dragon Empire. Posing as one of them provided an excellent cover for Stone, as it explained her presence in Praxilus, gave her access to people and places that she otherwise wouldn't have, and provided a reason for her poking around and asking questions. She wasn't having much success in penetrating the ISPD's operational security before she was contacted by Korig. The half-orc, calling from an undisclosed location, told her in brief who he was and that he had information that would blow the lid off the ISPD's activities in Praxilus and give her a career-making story.

Stone immediately arranged to meet with Korig. She couldn't risk entering AFM territory, so she pulled some strings and got Korig a visitor's pass that would gain him entry into the imperial enclave for a day. They agreed to meet in the bar at the Hotel Praxilus.

Korig, of course, never made it to the meeting. His taxi was stopped at a roadblock set up by Free Nations militia raiding into AFM territory. The taxi drivers of Praxilus—a courageous lot—are usually given a free pass by the militias, because everybody uses them to get around the city and they provide healthy protection kickbacks to both groups. This particular militia, however, broke that unwritten rule and abducted Korig from the cab. The hobgoblin driver's angry protests earned him a sound beating from the human, elven, and dwarven soldiers, but they allowed him to go with both his taxi and his life.

Usually, taxi patrons are among the wealthy or important people of Praxilus—everyone else is generally far too poor to afford such luxuries. The militia leader assumed the half-orc was some kind of local boss, wealthy merchant, or other VIP that they could either ransom or obtain valuable information from. They ignored his protestations that he had neither money nor power.

After abducting Korig, the militia abandoned their roadblock and set out to return to Free Nations territory. On their way, they encountered a large AFM patrol, and a running battle through the war-torn streets of Praxilus ensued. After more than an hour of fighting, the Free Nations militia realized they were cut off, had no chance to return their own territory, and were losing a war of attrition that would be over before long. In desperation, they decided to hole up in a burned-out, abandoned tenement. The militia simply hoped they could defend the building long enough for reinforcements to arrive.

Almost immediately after they entered the building, they were attacked by inhuman monsters whose claws rent their flesh and whose bites paralyzed their bodies with cold numbness. Most of the militia force was wiped out by the ghouls, and the survivors retreated further into the decrepit building, up the stairs to the second floor, and eventually to the small, dark attic. Temporarily satiated, the ghouls elected to rest before assaulting this final refuge of their prey. Over the last couple days, however, the militia soldiers slain by the ghouls have risen as ghouls themselves, and they are ravenously hungry.

Meanwhile, the AFM thugs are still outside the tenement. They've heard rumors of the things that live in the building, and they're content to maintain their siege until they're sure everyone inside is dead. They would just burn the building down, except that the blaze would likely claim most of the neighborhood, and perhaps those bordering it as well.

SCALING THE ADVENTURE

The Hostage was specifically designed to scale easily to higher power levels. As DM, you have a number of options available to you, depending on the character levels of your party.

First, the orc soldiers of the AFM militia who are besieging the tenement where Korig is being held are armed with slug-throwers and light armor. As noted in Chapter 9, this high-tech equipment modifies them to CR 1. Therefore, each CR 1 orc you add to each encounter with the soldiers increases the EL by 1. If you do not want to increase the orcs' numbers, you have a couple options. You can give the orcs energy weapons and even medium armor to increase them to CR 2. If you choose this option, keep in mind that the Challenge Rating system is pretty grainy, and there's a significant difference between orcs in battle suits (+7 armor bonus) armed with laser pistols (2d10 damage) and orcs in combat armor (+9 armor bonus) armed with blaster rifles (4d10 damage). Either option might be appropriate for your game, depending on the characters' levels, equipment, and spellware (*trauma symbiotes*, etc.). The other option you have is to give the orc soldiers class levels. If you make them 1st-level fighters, that will also increase them to CR 2. Point Blank Shot and Improved Initiative would be their most effective choices for feats.

By using different combinations of these options, you should easily be able to modify the encounters with the orcs to be challenging to characters as high as 7th level or so. Much beyond that, and the orcs would have to be so high level or so numerous as to strain plausibility.

The characters' other major opponents in this adventure are the ghouls that infest the tenement where Korig is being held. Once again, the ghouls are CR 1 creatures, so you can increase the EL of encounters with them by 1 for each additional ghoul you add. Be careful not to add too many, however. If the characters are greatly outnumbered, this will significantly neutralize the advantage given them by their high-tech ranged weapons. Simply put, the more ghouls there are, the easier it will be for some of them to engage the characters in melee. Once in melee, the ghouls can be a serious problem for firearms-wielding characters, as discussed in the Ghoul Tactics section (see page 170).

If you want to be especially devious, you can give the ghouls class levels. While they don't ordinarily advance by character class, there's no real reason why they couldn't. A single level in fighter will increase a ghoul's CR by 1 and enhance its combat effectiveness considerably. Consider choosing Combat Reflexes and Pressing Attack as the ghouls' feats, as this will make them deadly terrors in melee combat against gun-wielding PCs. Combat Reflexes will allow them to make multiple attacks of opportunity against PCs who try to make ranged attacks in a threatened area, and Pressing Attack will prevent the PCs from taking a 5-foot step back to get out of a ghoul's threatened area. Consider giving the pack leader levels in cleric. This will allow it to cast protective spells on itself, such as *endure elements* and *entropic shield*, which will greatly increase its ability to withstand fire from energy weapons. It will also give the pack leader a chance to dispel turning effects against its ghoul minions.

If increasing the numbers of the ghouls and giving them class levels isn't enough to challenge your higher-level party, you can also substitute other types of undead. Substitute wights (CR 3) for the ghouls if the characters are 4th to 6th level. The pack leader can be replaced with a wraith (CR 5). Again, you can tweak the ELs up a bit further by increasing their numbers or giving them class levels.

If that still isn't enough, you can give 7th level or higher PCs all they can handle by replacing the pack leader with a vampire (CR equal to previous race and class +2) and the ghouls with vampire spawn (CR 4). Once again, these are intelligent undead, and there's no reason you can't add class levels to increase the ELs of these encounters even higher.

BEGINNING THE ADVENTURE

The way you introduce the PCs to this adventure will vary greatly depending on your campaign. If you're staring a new **Dragonstar** campaign from scratch, you have lots of options. If the characters are Outlanders, they could be natives of Primogen II. If they are imperials, perhaps they have been lured to the planet by the promise of riches hidden in the great desert. If you're running a legacy campaign, Primogen II might be the closest planet to their homeworld with an established imperial presence. Alternatively, of course, you could create a reason for the characters to visit Primogen II that is tied in to the background or previous events of your campaign. Maybe one of the characters has a relative on the planet. Perhaps the party's paladin was assigned to the planet by his order. If the characters are freelancers or mercenaries, maybe they've simply learned that Primogen II is a world in turmoil and it's a likely to place to earn fame and fortune. If the characters have a starship of their own, perhaps they had to stop over on Primogen II for fuel, recharging, repairs, spare parts, or other supplies.

Regardless of how you decide to introduce the adventure, the PCs should find themselves in the imperial enclave in Praxilus. They've managed to secure a room or two at the Hotel Praxilus, despite the fact that it's usually filled beyond capacity. The Northern Hemisphere is locked in a weeks-long night, and many imperials have taken the opportunity to get away from the depressing place until the sun returns.

This introduction assumes that the characters have been in Praxilus for a couple days. The paladin, Rebecca Stone (Pal5/Rog3, Bluff +10, Diplomacy +12, Sense Motive +8), needs some time to observe the characters and determine their alignment and capabilities. Based on what she learns, she'll decide whether to confide in them or maintain her cover when she enlists their aid.

As with all of the boxed text in this adventure, you can read or paraphrase it to your players.

You've been in the city of Praxilus for a couple days and had a chance to settle in and get to know the place. You're staying at the Hotel Praxilus, a noisy, crowded place in the imperial enclave that buzzes with activity around the clock. Based on your observations in the bar, the lobby, and the restaurant, you think most of the hotel's patrons are journalists and reporters. All of the Dragon Empire's major media outlets seem to be represented in the war-torn city, as it provides a constant stream of sensational and dramatic stories.

Still, you're sure that not everyone staying in the hotel is a reporter. There are business executives in expensive suits with even more expensive companions. Many of these are affiliated with Noros Interplanetary, the aristocorp that is the dominant economic player in the Primogen system. There are other patrons you suspsect work for the imperial government—the Hotel Praxilus provides a home-away-from home for bureaucrats and civil servants on temporary assignment in the city. It's also widely regarded as a den of spies, agents, and operatives, but they rarely call attention to themselves.

Stone will make every effort to make contact with the characters privately. If the characters have datapads with wireless communications, she'll call them or leave them an electronic message. Otherwise, she'll visit them in their rooms or approach them in the bar or restaurant. Initially, she tells them only that she is a journalist and wishes to speak to them about a job opportunity. She suggests that they meet somewhere they can have a reasonably private conversation—preferably in her room or the characters' rooms, though the bar will do if the characters are reluctant to be alone with her.

At this meeting, Stone's approach depends on what she's been able to learn about the characters. If she has determined that the characters are good-aligned or politically loyal to Qesemet, she reveals her identity as a paladin in the Royal Marshal Service. If she believes that the characters are freelancers or mercenaries, she tells them that she is an investigative reporter with the Imperial News Network, a major media conglomerate with offices throughout the Dragon Empire. Once the introductions are out of the way, she makes her proposal.

Rebecca Stone is tall, slender, and possessed of a somewhat cold, unapproachable beauty. Her skin is fair, her eyes are pale blue, her features are sculpted and angular, and her long straight hair is so blond it's almost white. She watches you closely, apparently studying your reactions, as she begins to explain why she approached you.

"I am in Praxilus investigating activities of the ISPD that may be in violation of imperial law. It's no secret to anyone who keeps up with current events that the ISPD are involved in all sorts of illegal activities, all across the Empire—it's just that no one can ever prove it. A few days ago, I caught a lead that might have given me uncontestable evidence of the ISPD's crimes in Praxilus. I was contacted by a man named Korig Freeman, a half-orc living in the AFM-controlled part of the city. He claimed to have definitive proof that the ISPD has been supplying modern weapons to both the AFM and Free Nations militias, thereby not only perpetuating the violence in Praxilus but contributing to its escalation. I did a little digging into his background, and I learned enough about Freeman that I'm buying his story. In the interests of his privacy, I won't go into detail—as I'm sure you understand.

"Freeman was unwilling or unable to deliver his information electronically. I suspect he believes the ISPD has him under surveillance. Instead, he insisted we meet in person. It was impossible for me to go into AFM territory, so I got him a one-day visitor's pass to the imperial enclave. We agreed to meet here, at the hotel, almost three standard days ago.

"As you can probably guess, Freeman never made it. At first, I had no idea what had happened. I figured he probably just got scared away at the last moment—for someone in his position, that would be understandable and it happens all the time with my sources. I checked into it, though, and I'm afraid the situation is rather more unfortunate than that.

"From what I have been able to determine, Freeman got into a taxi outside his apartment almost 60 hours ago. Somewhere on the way to the eastern gate of the enclave, the taxi was stopped at a roadblock set up by Free Nations militia raiding into AFM territory. Freeman was abducted from the cab by the militia. The taxi driver was beaten by the militia but eventually allowed to leave. He drove away and never looked back. I've spoken with him, and he has no idea what became of Freeman.

"From other sources, I've learned that the Free Nations militia ran into an AFM patrol on their way back to their own territory. There was a running battle in the streets, during which as many as a dozen militia soldiers and at least two civilians were killed. The Free Nations militia got cut off and never made it back across the Green Line. They may all be dead—along with Freeman—but it's possible that they were able to hole up or hide somewhere inside AFM territory.

"I need to know if Freeman is alive or dead. If he's alive, I need someone to rescue him and deliver him—and his information—to me. This isn't something I can do myself, but I suspect you might be capable. I'm operating on a limited budget, but I can offer you each 1,000 cr in return for your assistance. If you're in, I'd be happy to answer any further questions you have, though I should warn you that I don't know much beyond what I've already told you."

Having made her proposal, Stone pauses and waits for the characters' response. She's been pretty true to her word—she knows little else about the situation that she hasn't already shared with the characters, though she answers questions as well as she is able. Of course, if she has chosen not to confide in the characters, she attempts to deflect any questions about her background. If one or more of the characters attempt to make Sense Motive checks on Stone, she should oppose them with a Bluff check. She makes every effort to protect her cover and abandons her attempt to enlist their aid if she feels the characters will jeopardize it.

Stone really is working on a limited budget, and she won't be able to negotiate much on the payment she is offering. If a character wins an opposed Diplomacy check against her, she agrees to pay 500 cr in advance and the other 500 cr on completion of the assignment. She also offers this advance if the characters demonstrate a real need for additional equipment, supplies, or other resources. She wants the characters to succeed as much as they do, and she makes any reasonable effort to give them the best chance possible.

If the characters agree to help Stone, she thanks them warmly for their assistance and tells them that she will remain at the hotel for at least three days. She also gives them a private number and network address where they can call her or leave her an electronic message if necessary. If the characters are equipped with datapads or other communications devices, they'll have wireless access from anywhere in the city.

Before they part company, Stone makes one final plea to the characters.

"There's one more thing. Praxilus is a violent city, and the eastern part of the city controlled by the AFM militias is probably more violent than most. You'll need to be armed and prepared to defend yourselves if you hope to succeed. However, I ask you personally to take care in your use of force. Know who is, and is not, your enemy before you fire. The innocent people of this city have suffered far more than their fair share of violence and bloodshed, and I'd rather not be responsible for giving them even more, even indirectly."

At this point, Stone leaves and the characters are on their own. They may want to purchase additional supplies or equipment, and any mundane items they need are readily available in the imperial enclave. If they want weapons, ammunition, or explosives, they'll have to acquire them from black market sources outside the enclave. An Urban Lore check (DC 10) provides them with a contact who can get them slug throwers, simple energy weapons, and ammunition for just about anything. An Urban Lore check (DC 20) gives the characters access to martial energy weapons, explosives, and just about anything else they can afford to buy.

Make sure you emphasize that the city is currently shrouded in perpetual night, the sky lightening almost imperceptibly during the daytime hours to a state of dim twilight. The characters shouldn't undertake this adventure unless they are well equipped with light sources.

The characters may also want to seek additional information from the hotel patrons. A Gather Information check (DC 10) turns up a few reporters who have met Stone and know of her work with the Imperial News Network. A Gather Information check (DC 15) allows the characters to speak with a journalist who was assigned to cover the same story as Stone several years ago, on another planet on the other side of the Empire. Both encounters should only strengthen Stone's cover, if she did not reveal her true identity to the PCs. No one in the hotel knows that she is a paladin or a royal marshal.

If the characters spend enough time at it, they can gather a great deal of information from the many journalists in the hotel. They can learn pretty much all of the basic information about the planet's history, the AFM and Free Nations, and the political situation on the planet. A Gather Information check (DC 10) allows the PCs to meet a journalist who heard about the recent abduction and subsequent clash between AFM and Free Nations militias. He checked into it, but it offered little to distinguish it from other, almost identical incidents that occur almost every day in Praxilus. No one knows about Korig, his significance, or what happened to the Free Nations militia after they were attacked by the

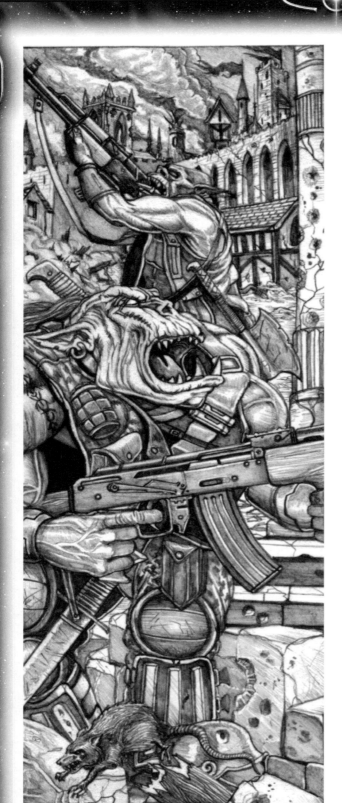

AFM patrol. If the PCs seem unsure about how to proceed after running into this wall, the reporter points out that "the only way to find the real new in Praxilus is to get out in the streets of the Old City and talk to the people who live there."

THE OLD CITY

Eventually, the characters will have to leave the imperial enclave and venture into the eastern part of the Old City of Praxilus controlled by the AFM militias. The guards manning the security checkpoints allow the characters to leave the imperial enclave with few questions. They'll be under more scrutiny getting back in, but shouldn't have any real problems as long as they have proof of their registration at the hotel. If they are detained for any reason, Stone quietly pulls some strings to secure their release. She will not intervene on their behalf, of course, if they do something both immoral and illegal, like gunning down a guard who stops them for routine questioning.

As written the adventure assumes the characters proceed directly to the eastern part of the city to begin their investigation. If, instead, they go to Free Nations territory first, they quickly learn that no one knows what happened to the missing militia. Most assume they are dead, and there are no plans to send a force into AFM territory to search for or resuce them.

The PCs first task will be to find out what happened to the militia and where they are—if they survived. The route the taxi took after it picked up Korig, the location of the roadblock, and the path of the militia's retreat as they tried to win their way back across the Green Line are all marked on the city map on page 166.

The only way for the characters to gain this information is persistent legwork. They must walk the streets, visit several different neighborhoods, and ask the humanoids they meet if they saw or heard anything about it. Given the amount of walking they must do, this requires the better part of a day. Before the players begin their investigation, have one of them make a Gather Information check. What they learn over the course of the day's legwork depends on the check result.

5+ A grizzled, goblin shopkeeper squints at you suspiciously and speaks in heavily accented Common.

"Yes, one of the bedamned Free Nations militias attacked us a few days ago." The shopkeeper pauses to spit on the muddy ground, narrowly missing a PC's boot. "Most of them's dead, but I guess a few lived. Don't know what happened to them. But there's a bunch a AFM camped out in a lot over on Guild Street. I guess I'd look for 'em over that way."

10+ A pathetic and clearly diseased kobold beggar grovels in the mud outside the ruins of an old temple.

"Yes, yes, I know all about it, and I'd be happy to tell, I would, if you could just spare a few coins for a poor old kobold?" The beggar ends the sentence as a question and peers hopefully at the PCs. If they give him a few credits, he thanks them profusely and bows awkwardly without getting up from the mud.

"Oh, thank you, thank you, kind people. Say, you wouldn't happen to have a bit of spirits on you? It's so terribly cold and dark out here, and a poor beggar could use something to warm him up."

Whether or not the characters give him alcohol, the kobold will eventually tell them what he knows.

"Yes, you see, I was over on Guild Street a couple days ago...eh, looking for a job, so I could feed my hungry children, you know...and then I heard a sound like hail against a wood roof. Then a bunch of humans, and elfs, and dwarfs, and I don't know what else came running down the street, and they were stopping and looking back, firing their guns back the way they came, and then running down the street again. Then I saw the militia soldiers...the AFM ones, you know, who protect us from the elfs, and dwarfs, and their ilk...coming up behind them, firing their guns. And then there were more coming from the other direction, and the westsiders were trapped! They fired their guns some more but then they ran into an old building to hide. I don't know what happened next...cause I had to go, you know...but I don't think the militia soldiers...the AFM ones, you know...followed them into the building. Could still be there, you know—I haven't been back that way."

15+ A hulking bugbear taxi driver leans out the window of his cab and snarls at you. "I'm workin' here," he growls in rough Common. "'Less you wanna pay my fare, make it worth my time...?"

If the PCs give the driver 10 cr or so, he continues.

"Yeah, Domin—the hobgoblin driver what got stopped—told me about what happened, and I went over there to Guild Street to check it out. Just like them westsider thugs to break their agreement and

bust one of us up after all the damned money we pay them every week. Anyway, I went over there, and there's AFM militia crawling all around this old tenement building. They got rifles, even some of the fancy ones what shoot real fast, but they ain't doin' much with 'em. Mostly just sittin' around, watchin' that building. Makin' sure nothin' comes back out, is what I figure. That's all I know, and now I gotta get back to work. And just between you and me, I know old Korig. He's an okay sort. I hope you find him. I get his newsdisk."

The bugbear makes a frightening attempt at a wink and hands them a datadisk. If the PCs load it onto a datapad, they're treated to an amateur video recording of the half-orc Korig Freeman presenting his views on the current state of the city and the injustice of imperial rule. He doesn't specifically mention the ISPD in the broadcast, though he alludes to their presence and activities as just one representative of a tyrannical government on their planet. There is certainly nothing in the broadcast that would constitute proof of any illegal ISPD activities in Praxilus.

20+ A wizened old orc woman pulls a small cart full of groceries on her way back home from the market. She begins nodding when the characters ask their questions and seems eager to share the news.

"I live on Guild Street, just down the way from where it happened! A small group of Free Nations goons had kidnapped a fellow with a fair amount of orc blood, by the look of him. They were dragging the poor man into the old building at the end of the lot, and the AFM were moving in on 'em from all directions. Once they got inside the building, though, the AFM soldiers left off the chase. No reason goin' in there. The last couple nights, I've heard them screamin' in there, but I figure they got what was comin' to 'em. I just hope that poor orc fellow is okay, though I don't think anyone ever came out of that building alive."

If the PCs press the woman about what makes the building so dangerous, she makes some kind of gesture they're unfamiliar with—almost certainly a ward against dark spirits.

"That building is haunted, and everyone who lives 'round here knows it. No one ever goes in it, and those who are smart don't even go near it at night. Those that do, we never hear from again. Sometimes the dogs bring home bones from there, probably them that went missing. And the dogs weren't the only things been gnawin' on them bones."

AFM PATROLS (EL 4)

As the characters walk around the Old City, they attract their share of stares and hurled insults from the civilians on the street. The intensity and frequency of these insults increase in proportion to the number of elves and dwarves in the party. Humans, halflings, and other races are looked on unfavorably in AFM territory, but elves and dwarves are truly despised. A large group may even earn a few thrown rocks from goblinoid children.

The characters won't be in any real danger from the civilians, however. Most of them have too much violence in their everyday lives to go looking for more, and many assume the characters are Free Nations militia. All but the most aggressive will be too afraid of the PCs to challenge them or pick a fight.

Spending a day or more walking the streets of Praxilus's east side, the PCs will inevitably encounter one or more AFM patrols. Because it is dark outside, spotting distance is determined by range of sight. Make Spot checks as normal as described in the core rules (DMG 60).

The AFM thugs do not immediately attack the characters when they spot them. Their primary motivation is always greed, and they would much rather extort the PCs' money than fight them for it. The patrol detains any characters they spot and asks them their business in AFM territory. If the PCs offer a non-threatening response and show the proper respect, the leader of the thugs (Ftr2, Diplomacy –1) informs them that their presence in Praxilus requires them to pay a visitor's tax of 100 cr each. They are willing to accept barter (especially weapons) instead of cash. The patrol leader will drop the tax to a minimum of 50 cr each if one of the characters negotiates and beats him at an opposed Diplomacy check. If the characters are openly carrying energy weapons, the patrol allows them to pass even if they refuse to pay the tax. The patrol—reinforced to double strength—will then attempt to ambush the characters later that day. Otherwise, the thugs attack if the characters refuse to pay. The rubble and debris that lines the street, as well as a burned-out car or two, provide ample cover for both sides in any firefight that develops.

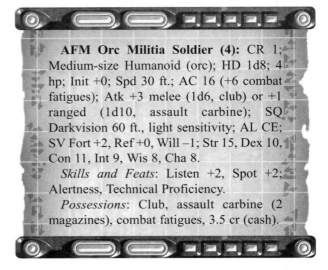

AFM Orc Militia Soldier (4): CR 1; Medium-size Humanoid (orc); HD 1d8; 4 hp; Init +0; Spd 30 ft.; AC 16 (+6 combat fatigues); Atk +3 melee (1d6, club) or +1 ranged (1d10, assault carbine); SQ Darkvision 60 ft., light sensitivity; AL CE; SV Fort +2, Ref +0, Will –1; Str 15, Dex 10, Con 11, Int 9, Wis 8, Cha 8.

Skills and Feats: Listen +2, Spot +2; Alertness, Technical Proficiency.

Possessions: Club, assault carbine (2 magazines), combat fatigues, 3.5 cr (cash).

Patrol Tactics: Initially, the orcs leave their rifles slung over their shoulders and try to beat the PCs with their clubs. If the characters draw firearms, the AFM thugs respond in kind.

Once the shooting starts, the orcs immediately try to take cover and then return fire. Each round, there is a 50% chance that an orc fires a three-round burst rather than a single shot, even if he has no chance to hit his target with multiple shots.

If half of their number are killed or subdued, the rest attempt to flee.

If the PCs take out one of the patrols, they'll earn some respect from the AFM militias. They'll be shadowed for the rest of their stay in AFM territory, but they won't be detained or attacked again unless a patrol has an opportunity to ambush them. If the characters give in to the patrol's demands and pay their "tax," they get the same treatment (probably from a different patrol) the following day, assuming they are still in AFM territory. This time, however, the tax starts at 150 cr each. The patrols will try to squeeze as much money from the characters as possible—as petty extortionists, that's what they do.

THE SIEGE

Eventually, the PCs should gather enough information to make their way to the old tenement building on Guild Street. There is no light on the streets outside the building, so read the following only if the PCs approach closely enough or have sufficient visibility to see these details. If they cannot see well enough to make out details of the building, they may still be able to hear the orcs talking, laughing, and cursing.

The tenement is a two-story brick building that sits at the end of a vacant lot choked with weeds and filled with piles of rubble and garbage. Despite its decrepit condition, the building appears to have been built fairly recently. It once boasted glass windows, though you don't spot a single one that is intact. Most have been boarded up. Brightly colored graffiti is scrawled across the walls. A six-foot-high chainlink fence surrounds the building, and there is an opening in the fence at the front.

Large groups of armed orcs are camped at both the front and back of the building. They are perched on debris, the hoods of derelict vehicles, overturned trash cans, or anything else they've been able to scavange to make their surveillance more comfortable. Most are talking or playing dice, but a few seem to be keeping an eye on the tenement building. Others are patroling the perimeter of the lot. The orcs are equipped like the patrols you've encountered, with assault rifles, clubs, and combat fatigues.

ORC GUARDS (EL 9)

There are seven orc soldiers camped at the front of the building and five more at the back. Three more are always on patrol duty, making a slow circuit around the perimeter of the building, outside the fence.

The orcs have been ordered to stop anyone from going in or out of the tenement. If the characters approach, the orcs attack. Make Spot checks and determine surprise normally, keeping in mind the visibility conditions.

All of the orcs have the same statistics as the AFM patrol soldiers listed previously. If they are attacked at range, the orcs take cover behind whatever debris or derelict vehicle is closest and return fire with their assault rifles. They try to spread out in case the attackers have spells or explosive weapons. If they are attacked in melee, they defend themselves with their clubs. However, the orcs always take any opportunity to withdraw from melee and use their firearms to attack their opponents. If one group is attacked, the other group joins the fight the following round.

Keep in mind that it is not the orcs' job to defeat the characters—they just have to prevent them from getting in the building. If the PCs attack and then retreat, the orcs let them go and take the opportunity to regroup and send for reinforcements.

UNDERGROUND

Given how seriously they are outnumbered by the AFM thugs, the characters should seek another way into the building.

Fortunately for the characters, there is another way into the tenement, one the orcs don't know about. The building shares the lot with mounds of rubble and debris that used to be a similar tenement before it was destroyed by a car bomb. The rubble conceals an entrance to the ruined building's basement. When the building was destroyed, the explosion blew out a wall that separated the basement from the one adjacent to it—the one below the surviving tenement that Korig Freeman is in.

If the characters search the debris, they eventually find the entrance.

THE BASEMENT

1. STAIRS

You find a set of scarred and blackened concrete stairs hidden in the debris. The stairs descend about 10 feet into a cellar or basement. The way is choked with rubble and dust, but there seems to be a clear path below. The basement is even darker than the night outside and looks like it has partially flooded, as brackish water conceals the floor from view.

It is completely dark in the basement. It has indeed flooded, with about a foot of standing water throughout. The footing is also treacherous, as shattered concrete, rocks, the remnants of wooden furniture, and broken glass are strewn across the floor. Moss covers the concrete walls and the sounds of dripping water and crawling vermin greet the characters' ears as they descend.

2. ENTRY ROOM (EL 1)

When you reach the bottom of the stairs, you find yourself in a small room with bare, moss-covered concrete walls. Standing water conceals the floor from view, but piles of debris and garbage that have fallen or been thrown down from above emerge from the surface. The sound of vermin moving in the darkness is louder here.

PRAXILUS

ADVENTURE MAP

Green Line

Tent Town

Tent Town

Tent Town

Tent Town

Old City

Korig's Route

Point of Abduction

Imperial Enclave

The Tenement

Tent Town

Old City

Tent Town

Green Line

Tent Town

N

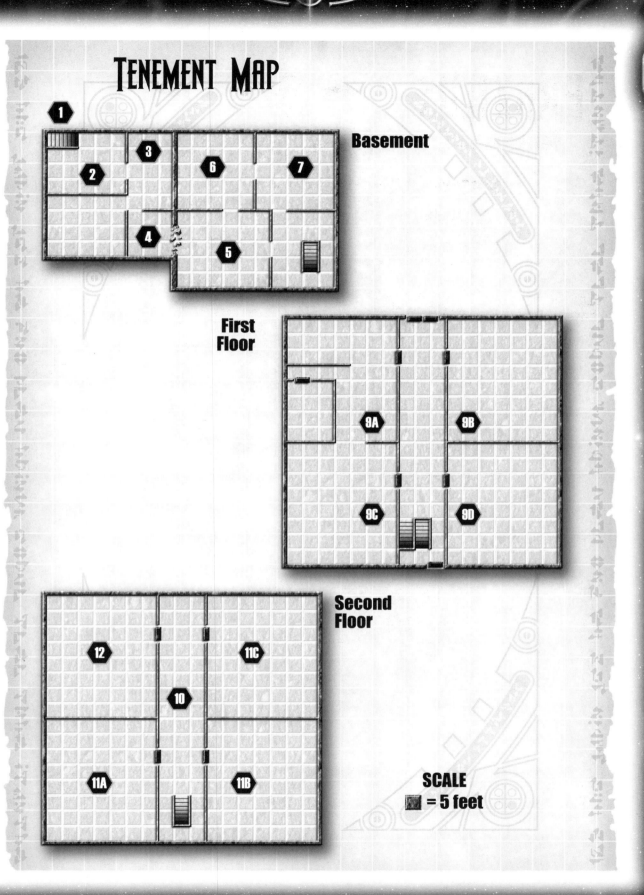

TENEMENT MAP

Basement

First Floor

Second Floor

SCALE
= 5 feet

A small family of dire rats has built a nest amidst the garbage in this room. The rats are extremely territorial and attack the characters as soon as they enter. If half of them are killed, the others attempt to flee. The rats have no possessions, but 8 sp and 19 cp of ancient mint are hidden in their nest.

A narrow opening in the concrete walls leads out of the room and further into the basement.

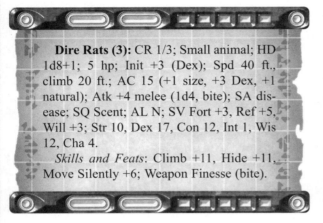

Dire Rats (3): CR 1/3; Small animal; HD 1d8+1; 5 hp; Init +3 (Dex); Spd 40 ft., climb 20 ft.; AC 15 (+1 size, +3 Dex, +1 natural); Atk +4 melee (1d4, bite); SA disease; SQ Scent; AL N; SV Fort +3, Ref +5, Will +3; Str 10, Dex 17, Con 12, Int 1, Wis 12, Cha 4.
Skills and Feats: Climb +11, Hide +11, Move Silently +6; Weapon Finesse (bite).

3. MAIN ROOMS

Passing through the doorway, you enter another small room similar to the last. There is less debris here, though the remnants of wooden shelves and furniture float on the surface of the water. A doorway to the west opens into another empty, ruined chamber, and one to the south opens into a smaller room.

There is nothing of value in these two adjoining rooms. If the characters spend some time searching, they can find scraps of wood, shards of glass, broken ceramics, a humanoid bone or two, and perhaps a few scraps of tattered and rotting fabric, but little else.

4. COLLAPSED WALL (EL 1)

You look through the doorway into a small room, no more than 15 feet on a side. There is a lot of concrete rubble in the room, and it looks like part of the eastern wall has crumbled away, leaving a narrow opening into another basement. You're pretty sure that this adjoining basement must lie under the old tenement building you're trying to get in to.

The ghouls who lair in the tenement building constructed a crude trap to protect this opening. They tore out the concrete and dug a small pit, only about five feet deep, in front of the opening in the collapsed wall. A fall into the water-filled pit won't actually hurt a character. However, the ghouls set several sharpened stakes into the floor of the pit. A character who steps into the hole may impale himself on one or more of these crude spikes. The wooden stakes are also filthy, and a character injured by one or more of them is at risk of infection. The player must make a Fortitude save (DC 12) to avoid contracting filth fever (DMG 75).

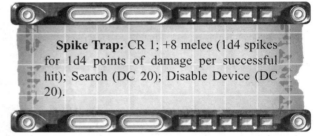

Spike Trap: CR 1; +8 melee (1d4 spikes for 1d4 points of damage per successful hit); Search (DC 20); Disable Device (DC 20).

5. BONE ROOM (EL 1)

As you play your light around this room, you see several small piles of bones emerging from the surface of the water. Many of the bones appear humanoid, but there are small animal bones as well.

When the PCs arrive, a ghoul is in this chamber gnawing on a leg bone. If they are approaching stealthily, the ghoul should make a Listen check opposed by the characters' Move Silently checks. The ghoul automatically hears any character who falls into the spike trap. If the ghoul hears the characters' approach, it attacks them in the opening to this room. Otherwise, they enter and see the ghoul crouching in a corner, chewing on its grisly prize. Allow them a surprise round before the ghoul can react. For the ghoul's game statistics and combat tactics, see page 170.

The other ghouls in the basement area ordinarily won't react to sounds of a struggle. They're used to them—the ghouls frequently emerge from their den to grab passersby—and their pack leader doesn't allow them to fight each other over food. The ghouls are usually content to let each other satiate themselves when they make a kill and then move in to claim their share of the leftovers. If the sounds of fighting go on for more than three rounds, however, the ghouls from areas 6 and 7 come to investigate.

6. PANTRY

As soon as you enter this room, you're met with a horrifying sight. The half-eaten remains of three humanoids are suspended over the water from rusted chains bolted into the concrete ceiling.

This is where the ghouls store the food they haven't yet finished. One of the corpses is an orc, one is a goblin, and the other is an elf. The latter was a member of the Free Nations militia killed by the ghouls. The other victims were either completely eaten or spawned as ghouls. The orc is missing one foot, but his remaining boot conceals a small gem worth 100 cr.

7. GHOUL ARTIST

The concrete walls of this room are covered with dried blood, gouges, and scratches that form distinct patterns and images.

A ghoul who was a painter in its former life uses this room to continue its work. The scenes adorning the walls are predictably horrifying, filled with violence, suffering, and death.

You should make a Listen check for the ghoul opposed by the characters' Move Silently checks. If the PCs' approach quietly, they find the ghoul crouched in front of the far wall, scratching at the concrete wall with a bone that has been chewed to a sharp point.

8. STAIRWAY

This small room holds a rickety wooden stairway that ascends to the ground floor.

These stairs lead to the first floor of the old tenement building. There is nothing else of interest in the room.

9. FIRST FLOOR

You climb the stairs and find yourselves in a long, wide hallway. A pair of doors, one to either side of the hall, are just ahead of you and two more flank the hallway further down toward the front entrance. All of the doors stand ajar and two of them hang halfway off their hinges. Another stairway to your left leads up to the second floor of the tenement.

If the characters make a Spot check (DC 15), they find several signs of the struggle that took place here two nights before. The plaster walls are scarred in places by laser and blaster fire and shell casings are scattered across the floor. There is also recently dried blood on the floors and walls in several places.

If the characters check room 9d, they find the corpse of a human the ghouls have left to spawn as one of them. A character with the Track feat can make a Wilderness Lore or Urban Lore check (DC 10), to identify the bloody trail left on the dusty floor where the ghouls dragged their comrade-to-be in from the hallway where he died.

If the characters investigate room 9a, a Search check (DC 15) allows them to discover the blaster pistol and laser carbine that were once the property of the two Free Nations victims (the elf in the pantry and the human in 9d).

10. SECOND FLOOR

The stairs lead up to a small landing, and then another short stairway continues up to the second floor. The layout of this floor looks identical to the first, with four small apartments flanking the wide hallway.

If the characters have managed to approach stealthily, have them make Move Silently checks opposed by the Listen checks of the ghouls in 11a, 11b, 11c. Any ghoul that hears the characters immediately moves into the hallway and attacks. Those who do not hear the characters join the attack the following round. The pack leader waits in room 12 for the characters to approach.

One of the benefits of living in a neighborhood controlled by evil humanoids is that it's always possible to find those willing to deal with you, even if you're an undead monster. The pack leader can afford to be patient with the characters because it paid a local wizard years ago to construct a magic trap to protect the ghoul's lair.

The trap is marked on the map and is particularly devious. The ghoul pack leader has become extremely familiar with modern technology and the danger it poses to it and its minions. Working with the wizard, it devised a magic trap based on the *power down* spell (SHB 147). When the trap is triggered, it suppresses any device relying on electrical power within 30 feet for 2d6 rounds. This includes flashlights, personal communicators, datapads, and of course, energy weapons. The internal power supplies of soulmechs are even affected, though they are only powered down for 1d3 rounds. Normal equipment and devices do not receive a saving throw, but magic items and soulmechs can make a Fortitude save (DC 13) to resist the effect.

The pack leader generally knows the instant the trap is triggered when all the flashlights and electric lanterns shut off, and it seizes the advantage to attack immediately. The PCs will certainly know that their flashlights, personal communicators, and other active devices have shut down, but they won't know that their energy weapons are suppressed until they try to fire them.

This is a pretty simple magic trap, but it can be lethal in this situation. The ghouls have darkvision and very effective melee attacks, while most **Dragonstar** PCs will have had their biggest advantage—high-tech weapons—completely neutralized, at least temporarily. If the characters have had a tough time with the adventure to this point, you might consider giving them a break and eliminating the trap.

> **Power Down Trap:** CR 2; no attack roll necessary; Search (DC 27); Disable Device (DC 27). Note: Trap suppresses electrically powered devices for 2d6 rounds and soulmechs for 1d3 rounds. Magic items and soulmechs can make a Fort save (DC 13) to resist the effect.

11. APARTMENTS (EL 3)

There is a ghoul in each apartment when the characters reach the second floor. As noted previously, the ghouls attack the characters as soon as they become aware of them.

As with the first floor, the apartments themselves have long since been ransacked and looted. The PCs find nothing in them but ruined furniture, crumbling plaster, and gnawed bones.

Ghoul Tactics: Ghouls are not mindless undead—they are possessed of a cunning intelligence. They are familiar with advanced weapons and know how lethal they are. The ghouls always attack intelligently, seeking to neutralize their opponents' advantages and maximize their own. If possible, the ghouls use stealth to attack the characters with surprise and quickly engage in melee. Once in combat, the ghouls use their multiple attacks to their advantage. Against characters wielding firearms, a ghoul usually attempts to paralyze its victim with a bite, then follows up with one or more disarm attempts with its claw attacks. These attempts do not provoke an attack of opportunity unless the target has a bayonet, and the ghoul gets a +4 bonus on every disarm attempt.

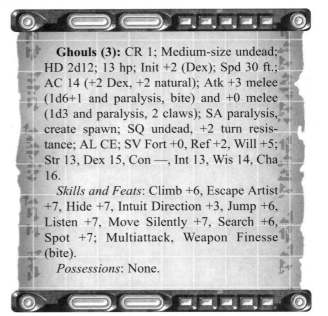

> **Ghouls (3):** CR 1; Medium-size undead; HD 2d12; 13 hp; Init +2 (Dex); Spd 30 ft.; AC 14 (+2 Dex, +2 natural); Atk +3 melee (1d6+1 and paralysis, bite) and +0 melee (1d3 and paralysis, 2 claws); SA paralysis, create spawn; SQ undead, +2 turn resistance; AL CE; SV Fort +0, Ref +2, Will +5; Str 13, Dex 15, Con —, Int 13, Wis 14, Cha 16.
>
> *Skills and Feats*: Climb +6, Escape Artist +7, Hide +7, Intuit Direction +3, Jump +6, Listen +7, Move Silently +7, Search +6, Spot +7; Multiattack, Weapon Finesse (bite).
>
> *Possessions*: None.

12. PACK LEADER (EL 1)

The ghoul pack leader attacks if its trap is triggered or if the characters reach the doorway to its lair. However, it will be significantly more deadly if the characters triggered the trap and must fight the pack leader in the dark with no energy weapons. The pack leader fights until it is destroyed.

> **Ghoul Pack Leader:** CR 1; Medium-size undead; HD 3d12; 20 hp; Init +2 (Dex); Spd 30 ft.; AC 14 (+2 Dex, +2 natural); Atk +4 melee (1d6+1 and paralysis, bite) and +1 melee (1d3 and paralysis, 2 claws); SA paralysis, create spawn; SQ undead, +2 turn resistance; AL CE; SV Fort +1, Ref +3, Will +5; Str 13, Dex 15, Con —, Int 13, Wis 14, Cha 16.
>
> *Skills and Feats*: Climb +6, Escape Artist +7, Hide +8, Intuit Direction +3, Jump +6, Listen +7, Move Silently +8, Search +6, Spot +7; Multiattack, Weapon Finesse (bite).
>
> *Possessions*: None.

The pack leader's lair isn't in any better shape than the other apartments. It is littered with broken furniture, crumbling plaster, scraps of rotting curtains, and other debris.

Treasure: The pack leader hid a few valuables in a pile of old bones in one corner of its lair. Carefully wrapped in a tattered and stained scrap of cloth is a masterwork laser pistol. A chipped ceramic jar contains 3 silver pearls, each worth 100 cr.

RESCUING KORIG

A careful investigation (Search DC 20) of the second floor of the tenement reveals a trapdoor in the ceiling behind the stairway. The door pulls down and a foldout ladder leads up into an attic.

Two humans, the surviving Free Nations militia soldiers (War1, 6 hp, heavy autopistol, Diplomacy +0), are huddled in the attic with their half-orc captive, Korig Freeman.

The humans will be delighted that the ghouls are dead, but they won't be particularly eager to give up the hostage that got them into this mess to begin with. They don't really want to return home with nothing but a body count to show for their troubles.

Have the party's spokesperson make opposed Diplomacy checks with one of the Free Nations soldiers. If the character gets a better result, the militia let Korig go with no argument. If the soldier wins, he asks the characters to "ransom" Korig. He starts at 1,000 cr and negotiates down all the way to zero. Unless they actually outnumber the surviving (and unparalyzed) PCs, the soldiers are in no position to make any demands. If the characters are tough with them, they give Korig up and follow the PCs out of the building.

Assuming the characters leave the way they came in, they should easily be able to get away without encountering the orc militia. If they do encounter the orcs for whatever reason, they'll either have to fight or give up the Free Nations soldiers. The orcs insist on taking the humans back to their lieutenant for just punishment. Once Korig explains that the characters rescued him, however, the orcs give the PCs safe passage to the gates of the imperial enclave.

CONCLUSION

After his ordeal, Korig is at first a bit suspicious of the characters and their motives for rescuing him. Once he realizes they mean him no harm, he warms up and thanks them repeatedly for their efforts. As the group returns to the imperial enclave, Korig speaks animatedly about the Empire's injustices and how he plans to make a difference. If the characters seem sympathetic to his cause, Korig asks them to join him in his resistance efforts. This can serve as a campaign hook giving the characters an opportunity to create a new insurgent cell

in the city of Praxilus.

Stone has again arranged a pass for Korig, and the group has no trouble entering the enclave. When they return to the Hotel Praxilus, the undercover marshal meets them and thanks them warmly for their excellent work. If she has confided in them and some of the characters are wounded, she offers to take them to her room and heal them. She gladly gives them their agreed-upon reward and wishes them luck in their future endeavors. She also makes sure they can contact her if they need anything while they are in the city.

Stone interviews Korig privately. Sewn into the half-orc's jacket is a simple datachip. The chip contains grainy video footage of a drow meeting with a large orc in a dimly lit warehouse. A cargo hovercraft is parked behind them, and several goblinoids are unloading crates with the seal of Asamet stamped on the sides. A bugbear in the background has opened one of the crates and is admiring an assault laser.

The orc in the video is the AFM militia leader, Yaruk. The drow, predictably, is an ISPD officer. Despite Korig's protests, the video footage does not give the royal marshal all the evidence she could have hoped for. The drow is not in uniform, and she doesn't recognize him. Unless she can positively identify him as an ISPD operative, the footage won't prove anything.

Nevertheless, Korig's video represents the first hole in the ISPD's security around their operation in Praxilus. It could lead to further developments in your campaign—possibly involving both Korig and Stone—at your discretion.

If the characters succeeded in rescuing Korig, they'll have made solid allies in both the half-orc and royal marshal. Both could aid the PCs in the future or be used

to introduce new adventure hooks. Depending on their interactions with the AFM and Free Nations, they may have made enemies or allies—or both—in the city.

The Hostage could lead to many further adventures on Primogen II. Perhaps the characters will get involved in the war for the streets of Praxilus, joining one of the militias. They may sympathize with one side or the other based on their race or alignment, or one of the militias may hire them as mercenaries or freelance operatives. Given the characters' capabilities, they would be valuable assets to either side.

Alternatively, the PCs may choose to join forces with Korig. Perhaps they will continue his attempts to investigate the ISPD and other imperials in the city while distributing the half-orc's dissident video broadcasts to the citizens of Praxilus. On the other hand, they may decide to take more direct action, organizing an insurgent cell with the eventual goal of liberating Praxilus or perhaps all of Primogen II. If the characters choose this course, they'll have to avoid arrest by the ISPD, make peace between the AFM and Free Nations, and perhaps make contact with insurgent cells on other planets.

Of course, Primogen II offers many opportunities for adventure beyond the city limits of Praxilus. The ruins of an ancient civilization lie hidden below the shifting sands of the great deserts. The characters may decide to brave the dangers of these ruins in search of powerful magic, hidden lore, and perhaps some clue to the identity and purpose of the Faceless Man, the desert realms' ancient nemesis.

If the characters successfully completed the adventure, you should give the players a story award of 300 XP and reward good ideas and roleplaying as you see fit.

INDEX

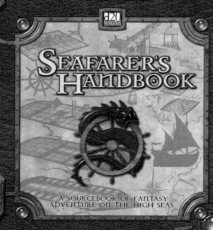